In The Psychology of Public Relations, Michal Chmiel reframes PR as applied social psychology, placing the individual at the center of communication analysis. Bridging theory and practice, he offers a compelling case for evidence-based, goal-oriented PR grounded in contemporary psychological science. A timely and essential read for anyone serious about the future of the profession.

Prof. Dr. Dejan Verčič, *Head of Centre for Marketing and Public Relations, Faculty of Social Sciences, University of Ljubljana, Slovenia*

Chmiel's examination of the historical and conceptual intersections between psychology and public relations enhances our understanding of public relations as the building of relationships between organizations and their publics. After all, these meso-level connections are always executed by individuals operating in and from their own micro-levels of psychological development, trauma, and adjustment.

Prof. Bey-Ling Sha, *Dean, College of Media and Communication, Texas Tech University and Co-author: Cutlip & Center's Effective Public Relations (11th edition)*

The Psychology of Public Relations is a detailed exploration of the connections between psychology and PR. Through explorations of the history of psychology and its utilization in PR, a compelling argument is made for a transdisciplinary approach to PR that addresses the needs of an issue-abundant society.

Dr. W. Timothy Coombs, *Centre for Crisis and Risk Communications*

This book reasserts the central role of psychology in public relations, offering a timely perspective on navigating publics polarized around divisive societal challenges. Emphasizing a functionalist approach, it is a must-read for anyone who values the evidence-based, transformative power of public relations in society.

Dr Ganga S Dhanesh, *Associate Professor in Public Relations, University of Maryland*

Michal's book 'The Psychology of Public Relations: From Industry Practice to Societal Challenges of the Profession' brings a new angle to apply concepts in social psychology and personal agency to making social impact. It enlightens public relations practitioners in their daily decisions in brand communication and content co-creation.

Professor Kara Chan, *Associate Dean, School of Communication, Hong Kong Baptist University*

THE PSYCHOLOGY OF PUBLIC RELATIONS

Although the origins of public relations can be firmly traced back to an approach integrating psychology, sociology, politics, and journalism, the psychological component has not been well developed in current PR theorising and education. This book is the first to offer a comprehensive understanding of the role of psychology in public relations practice and scholarship.

The book presents the original, goal-centred approach that comprises psychological evidence, level of analysis, and methodology to address everyday and societal challenges facing PR practitioners. The author develops a micro-level, psychological perspective in public relations and provides an argument for integrating the psychological scholarly acumen with the existing body of PR knowledge, proposing an integrative framework for blending psychological insight with existing PR practice. *The Psychology of Public Relations* offers definitions of audience and publics members developed around the topical subject of content. The abundance of content is considered a constituent characteristic of the current communication and media landscape, leading to the formation of divided publics.

This novel approach will appeal to postgraduate students and scholars across public relations and communication studies in particular, as well as organisational and applied psychology.

Dr Michał Chmiel is Senior Lecturer (Associate Professor) in Psychology and Director of External Engagement and Partnerships of the School of Life Sciences and the Environment at Royal Holloway, University of London, UK.

THE PSYCHOLOGY OF PUBLIC RELATIONS

From Industry Practice to Societal Challenges of the Profession

Michał Chmiel

Routledge
Taylor & Francis Group
LONDON AND NEW YORK

Designed cover image: smartboy10 via Getty Images

First published 2026
by Routledge
4 Park Square, Milton Park, Abingdon, Oxon OX14 4RN

and by Routledge
605 Third Avenue, New York, NY 10158

Routledge is an imprint of the Taylor & Francis Group, an informa business

British Library Cataloguing-in-Publication Data
A catalogue record for this book is available from the British Library

ISBN: 978-1-041-00547-6 (hbk)
ISBN: 978-1-041-00546-9 (pbk)
ISBN: 978-1-003-61040-3 (ebk)

DOI: 10.4324/9781003610403

Typeset in Sabon
by SPi Technologies India Pvt Ltd (Straive)

For Agnieszka

CONTENTS

ILLUSTRATIONS

Figures

Tables

ABOUT THE AUTHOR

Michał Chmiel (PhD, SFHEA, MCIPR) is Senior Lecturer (Associate Professor) in Psychology and Director of External Engagement and Partnerships of the School of Life Sciences and the Environment at Royal Holloway, University of London. Michal's academic experience spans over the period of 19 years and includes various teaching and research roles at the London College of Communication (UAL), New York University Stern School of Business, University of Kent, and the Jagiellonian University in Kraków.

As a former Public Relations practitioner, he has successfully incorporated social psychological evidence into PR and communications projects for multinational companies, NGOs, governmental bodies, and public figures.

ACKNOWLEDGEMENTS

This monograph is my first attempt to comprehensively put forward the psychology of Public Relations. I have had this idea in mind for many years since my first days in the world of corporate and brand PR. It was during that time, when in one business meeting, I was told that whatever I had learnt studying for a university degree in psychology, I should forget it. I remember this conversation vividly and the impact it had on me, which instigated the motivation to demonstrate the applicability of psychological evidence and theory to the practice of PR.

Over the years, the idea for the book has moulded and the scope has changed several times. Each choice, what to include and accentuate, and what to omit, was difficult and even painful. The book I finally wrote is a monograph, and not a textbook, so it is not an exhaustive source of all theories that can be applied to Public Relations. Writing it would not be possible without practical experiences and many people who have inspired and taught me.

Firstly, I would like to thank Malcolm Hurlston (CBE) for teaching me about the societal responsibilities of organisations during my internship at the Employee Share Ownership (Esop) Centre in London and to the supervisor of my MSc and PhD projects, Małgorzata Kossowska from the Jagiellonian University in Kraków. Also, I will always be thankful to all my students, who over the last 19 years have been the source of inspiration and motivation.

I would like to express my gratitude to Adrian Crookes, Karen Douglas, Robbie Sutton, and Polly Dalton – I would like to thank you for offering me job and for trusting the newcomer. To my work colleagues: Victoria Bourne, Katie Willis, David Simon, and Laurie Parsons, for accepting me into the community of academics at Royal Holloway, University of London, and allowing me to co-create the BSc (Hons) Environment and Social Change, a unique interdisciplinary undergraduate programme built on insights from Geography, Psychology and Public Relations.

To all esteemed colleagues from Education and Women in PR networks of the European Association for Public Relations Education and Research: Martina Topić-Rutherford, Raluca Moise, Anca Anton, Monique Abbenbroek, and Maria João Cunha. Without our monthly meetings, my understanding of PR would be limited.

To the welcoming communities of scholars, who meet annually to discuss the practical and pedagogical challenges of Public Relations at the International Public Relations Research Symposium Bledcom in Slovenia, organised by Dejan Verčič, Krishnamurthy Sriramesh, and Ana Tkalac Verčič. It was during one of Bledcoms that I had the distinct pleasure of meeting Jacek Barlik, a prolific scholar, who, as a practitioner, trailblazed the introduction of modern PR in Poland.

Thank you to my close colleagues and collaborators for insights, trust, and willingness to share your knowledge. First, I would like to thank Lynsey Mahmood, who is my longest colleague in the UK, for her openness and advice. Lynsey also read the first version of the manuscript of the book and gave me important comments. To Raluca Moise, with whom I managed an undergraduate programme in Public Relations at the London College of Communication and wrote several papers. To Martina Topić-Rutherford who is the champion of interdisciplinarity in PR. To Gareth Thompson, with whom I share the passion for researching the history of PR and understanding the roots of spreading fake news.

Anna Sajkowska, Grzegorz Przęczek, and Piotr Szymski, thank you for your friendship.

Most importantly, I would like to thank my wife, Agnieszka Chmiel, who happens to be an expert marketing communicator. I am not only privileged to have you by my side, but also lucky to have a partner with whom we can comment on the practice of public relations and marketing communication daily.

Any mistakes and misreadings committed in this volume are entirely mine.

Egham Hill, 15th of May 2025

1

THE CONTEXT

Introduction

The Context of the Development of PR

Public Relations (PR) is an inherently transdisciplinary field of practice. This transdisciplinarity is fundamentally linked to the multifaceted nature of the context in which the discipline was born. PR can be seen as a field of practice that emerged at a critical juncture in history, driven by economic and political factors and the need to build relationships with publics that were growing in power and importance. As demonstrated by scholarly explorations of the roots of PR in the US during the 19th century (Cutlip, 1994) and in Britain after the First World War (L'Etang, 2004), this context is well evidenced. I argue that the three specific contextual elements that played a pivotal role in the development of the modern practice of PR were the democratic constitution of the state, the free-market economy, and the existence of an individual member of the public whose decisions are not predetermined and can be influenced. These factors led to the development of a system of information exchange whereby the state, businesses, and other organisations, as well as individuals, need to build relationships based on an understanding of respective needs and goals. It is only when the following three conditions: (1) democracy, (2) free-market economy, and (3) the free-willed, thinking individual as a member of the public are present that PR can develop fully. Obviously, tools used by contemporary PR are all not entirely new. Propaganda instruments aimed at influencing the masses through systematic communication have been employed by monarchs, political leaders, military leaders, and religious leaders for centuries (Lasswell, 1979). However, PR is not simply persuasive communication.

DOI: 10.4324/9781003610403-1

Although similarities can be drawn between different mass communication, propaganda techniques, and PR, the modern practice of the discipline is characterised by the critical aspect of relationship building. That is why, unlike a few other authors (e.g. Brown, 2014; Gras, 1945), the view I advance here does not see PR as having a long history, which can be traced back to the birth of human civilisation. Relationships require longitudinal effort, have a temporal dynamic, and involve the exchange of information as well as emotions. These characteristics require different effort, skill sets, and goal orientations than propaganda and mass communication. Although political and economic layers have already been recognised in PR scholarship, the final element – individual members of the public has not. The present volume explores the implications of the perspective and aims to provide science-informed guidance for practitioners (Figure 1.1).

The first constituting contextual layer of the practice of PR is a *political one*. Cutlip (1994), who locates the beginning of the industry of US PR in the mid-1900s in Boston, considers PR a 'vital cog in the nation's public information system'. For Cutlip, PR has been tied to democracy and citizens' decisions of different types for which they need information: political, economic, social, etc. In a democracy, citizens are given the power to explicitly and legitimately influence the decisions of governments and – in a reciprocal manner – governments and politicians are interested and depend on the support of individual members of society. Even though the political context of the discipline of PR has been acknowledged by many authors (Bernays, 1928, 1940; Cutlip, 1994; Grunig, 1997), perspectives on the role of the state and

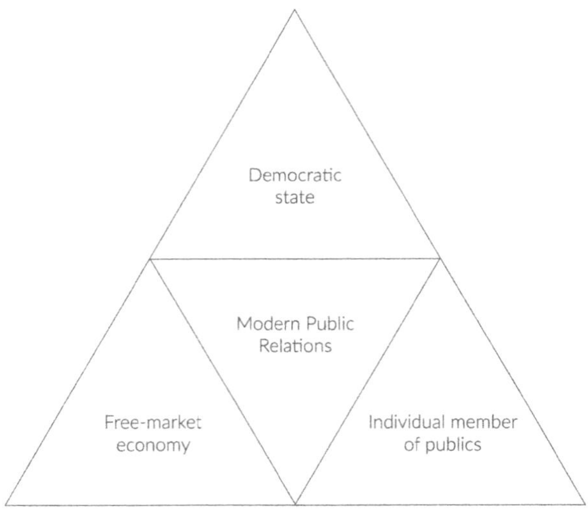

FIGURE 1.1 The context triangle of the fully developed practice of PR.

politics in shaping and influencing decisions of members of society have been different, partly mirroring the discussion on the legitimacy of influences one group of people can have over another. Despite somewhat limited attention given to the political aspect of conducting PR, this context, especially today, requires attention. For Verčič (2005), 'public relations provides an essential component of contemporary free society', and countries that are hostile towards democracy are, in fact, not democracies.

The second contextual layer is *economic*. This element of context is related to the movement of capital. In a free-market economy, the prices of goods are determined by the interaction between sellers and buyers. In other words, a single decision of an individual is only as valuable as it can legitimately influence the course of political action or the financial success of an enterprise. Although connections between the economy and PR exist (Ławniczak, 2009), this scholarly area is also considered underexplored, as proper links between economic theory and PR are said not to have been thoroughly investigated (Verčič & Grunig, 2000). Examples from non-Western European countries suggest that historically, fragmented PR-resembling mechanisms can develop when democratic freedoms are restricted, but free-market economic ideas are – to some extent – allowed. For example, in the former Yugoslavia, which experienced greater democratic freedoms than other countries of the former Soviet bloc, PR instruments were found to develop to some extent, but only to the extent that it was in the government's interest and only as far as the state granted the freedom for such development. In comparison, for example, in Poland, propaganda techniques were exploited during the Cold War period and Soviet Union dependence until 1989, but the arrival of PR can only be attributed to the regaining of democracy and the introduction of the free-market economy. This intricate relationship between PR, democracy, and free-market economy can be seen when examining the concept of transition PR introduced by Ławniczak (2001, 2004, 2005).

The *individual-psychological* element of the PR context more broadly represents the evolution of the concept and importance of an individual in society. Bernays succinctly explained it in 1986, when he defined PR as 'a field of activity which has to do with the interaction between an individual, a group, an idea, or other unit with the publics on which it depends' (Bernays, 1986, p. 1). Although the role of the public, understood as the mass population, as well as publics, defined by Grunig as 'groups of for which public relations programmes are planned' (Gruning, 2013, p. 778), is acknowledged in PR scholarship, the implied direction of analysis suggests the top-down, group-to-individual process of examination. In the majority of cases, the roots of PR are contextualised against the evolution of the concept of public opinion (e.g. Grunig, 1997). I argue that for PR to develop fully, that is, for relationships built between members of the publics and (political, business, or state) organisations to be based on mutual understanding involving a two-way process of exchange of information that results in establishing trust, one additional contextual element seems necessary: the human factor, which involves the appreciation of individual-level psychological processes. Although the optics of the concept of public opinion vary across disciplines, it could be argued that in political, media, and sociological studies, the voices of individuals are seen through the perspective of a public – a mass of citizens or even a crowd, as in the early formulation of the PR theory of Edward Bernays (e.g. Bernays, 1923, 1928). Although differences in power or importance assigned to the public have existed throughout history, it was not uncommon to view the public as a singular force. This is why, in my view, the last element of the contextual background of PR proposed in this monograph – individuals as members of publics – has not earned adequate attention in PR scholarship.[1]

Historically, in PR, the opinion of the masses was considered to understand how information should be transmitted for a desired effect. As Bernays said, 'the successors of the rulers, those whose position or ability gives them power, can no longer do what they want without the approval of the masses' (Bernays, 1928). However, the crowd and the individual were juxtaposed with each other, as guided by different needs. Early applications of psychology to PR conducted by Bernays (explained in detail in Chapter 3) differentiated between a reasonable individual and an emotional crowd and resulted in different ontological and epistemological traditions of analysis performed on the publics. How humans make their decisions and what influences them, or more generally, how to explain human behaviour, has been – for long – the subject of psychology. Unlike Mead's sociological approach (discussed in Chapter 2), psychology considers the individual as the starting point of analysis and seeks to identify the influence coming from other people and the external environment as a moderator or mediator of behaviour. Psychologists examine how information is processed, considering the goals and needs that are satisfied. Unlike in the writings of Edward Bernays and Ivy Lee, psychology today does not see a crowd or mass as a new animalistic entity that acts against reason and is emotion-driven only. It could be argued that although the direction of analysis, the sociological top-to-bottom versus psychological bottom-up could be seen as subtle. However, for the theory, methods, and practice of PR, it could lead to different outcomes and limit the much-needed understanding of contemporary audience members.

The progress psychology has made in the last 100 years seems more impactful than between Descartes asked his questions about human nature and the early 20th-century ideas of Freud and behaviourists. The first-order psychological question, about how the apparatus responsible for thinking is connected to the body, was most prominently asked by René Descartes. In 1641, in Meditationes, he boldly proposed that the body may perform actions without the steer from the soul. Three hundred years later, Bernays also appreciated the automatic character of some of the behaviours of audience members. However, to some extent, the Cartesian impasse – the impossibility of determining the relationship between the body and the mind and what behaviours are learned versus what is the biological equipment bestowed by nature – could manifest in the contemporary practice of PR. Especially as long as practitioners refuse to acknowledge the extent to which PR involves behavioural science, understood here as the analysis and modification of behaviour, the doors for psychology to demonstrate its value in PR will remain closed.

When it comes to individual-level analyses, whether PR discusses audiences, publics, or the general public, ultimately, these groups of people consist of individuals – independent thinkers whose psychological characteristics should be explored and the theoretical knowledge behind them – updated.

Interdisciplinary Nature of PR

The need for a broad skillset drawing from different disciplines is especially noticeable from the ground. In the field of PR, junior professionals typically assume responsibility for tasks such as collecting data through secondary research on clients or competitors, contributing to evaluation and monitoring processes, and assisting in event organisation (e.g. venue comparison). Additional responsibilities may include analysing information related to target audiences, creating social media content, and designing visual materials. As one progresses in their career, the role evolves towards a more strategic aspect. First, by directly building relationships with opinion leaders, journalists, and experts, they take responsibility for PR strategy. Finally, in those few instances when they are invited to the table, they co-create the business strategy of an organisation. While some may perceive this role as glamorous and relatively knowledge-lite (Bowen, 2003), it, in fact, demands a broad set of skills from multiple disciplines. The ability to communicate and write effectively remains paramount, along with fundamental journalism and psychology of communication skills.

Additionally, a firm grasp of marketing principles, encompassing market and audience research, consumer segmentation, media landscape analysis, branding, product development management, and fundamental campaign evaluation techniques, is crucial. Furthermore, a working knowledge of management, strategy development, and the macro- and microeconomy is essential. A substantial repertoire of managerial competencies, encompassing project and time management, people management, leadership, and soft skills such as problem-solving, creative thinking, negotiations, and public speaking, is likely to resonate well with individuals with experience in PR. The subfield of public affairs adds a layer of expectations associated with the knowledge of the political environment. This list, however, does not seem even remotely exhaustive. With every new client or project, a whole new set of knowledge needs to be studied. Are you launching a brand of paper diapers? Studying the psychology of child development, as well as physiological needs and the technologies used in diaper production, will be crucial. Researching the characteristics of local and national sewage systems will be essential. Understanding the needs and expectations of parents and learning how to communicate with them using parent-friendly and appreciative language – yet another piece of the puzzle. (In my view, the nature of the practice of PR attracts individuals who embrace complexity and tolerate ambiguity well.)

Public Relations is not unique in its neglect of incorporating different disciplines. In fact, the opposite could be true, and the discipline has firmly acknowledged the role of several disciplines, for example, management, media studies, journalism, and sociology. At the same time, tensions between the disciplines that are major sources of evidence and inspiration have existed for a long time. This is expected when different levels of analysis are expected to be incorporated in solving relevant practical problems. Hambrick and Mason (1984) put it quite well when reviewing organisational theory research:

> One reason may be that inquiry into the linkages among individuals, organisations, and their competitive environments necessarily requires a multidisciplinary approach. A gulf, however, continues to separate psychologists, sociologists, and researchers with a strategy or economic orientation. It would be the rare researcher who could draw equally on all camps.
>
> *(p. 194)*

Inevitably, when a higher-level field – PR – subsumes all the main actors of the potential conflict, tensions, competitions, and even power games transpire. In addition, the internal environment of a discipline is defined not only by the discipline itself but also by other disciplines that discuss its theory and methods. According to Stichweh (2015), it is quite common for a discipline to be commented on by other scientific disciplines that compete with it. What arises from the competition, conflicts, and provocations is a 'parallel level of interdisciplinary science', and often disciplines are motivated to attack and 'take over parts of the domain of other disciplines' (Stichweh, 2015, p. 13730). Although Nothhaft and Zerfass are hopeful about the future of PR and expect that 'one day the discipline will become beautiful and find its true home', they immediately add that 'where the home lies is not entirely clear', and 'public relations' modest wish boils down to acceptance as a proper academic discipline by insiders and outsiders alike' (Nothhaft & Zerfass, 2023, p. 249). Perhaps what PR needs is not a home but an understanding of the foundations of the discipline and its history. As Terry Pratchett said, if you don't know where you are coming from, you might end up going in the wrong direction.

The interdisciplinary character of the knowledge and skillset necessary to practice PR was acknowledged early by Bernays, who recognised the need to integrate knowledge from several fields as well as appreciate the value of theory (Bernays, 1986). In the practice of PR, the requirement of interdisciplinarity is challenging to achieve, too. The curricula of university PR degrees are not built on an interdisciplinary philosophy. In the context of higher education, the need for better integration of interdisciplinary findings has not been fully addressed. More than 50% of PR lecturers disagree about which paradigm is best for teaching the practice of PR (Chmiel & Moise, 2024). It is somewhat understandable. There are very few interdisciplinary scholars in the field of PR who would be able to confidently teach foundational knowledge of more than one field of science. In addition, communication between disciplines is not an easy task, especially when each discipline (and sometimes subdiscipline) is adamant about adhering to its own epistemological and methodological traditions. Gaps between the practice of PR and scholarship exist, too, and the relationship between academia and practitioners is even more complex and nuanced (Nothhaft & Zerfass, 2023), which partly explains why PR pedagogy does not seem to catch up quickly enough with the needs of the industry (Chmiel & Moise, 2024). On the one hand, the demand for new or updated PR skills is strong, but on the other, theory-led, applied scientific evidence is still scarce to help practitioners in their everyday tasks, which would help them appreciate the value of academic theorising.

Recently, the attention of practitioners, as well as scholars in the field of PR, has been captivated by challenges related to the practice of PR that reflect an array of recently emerged societal phenomena – for example, topics related to wellbeing, EDI, fake news, and artificial intelligence (Chmiel, 2025; Thompson, 2020; Topić & Lodoforos, 2021; Verčič et al., 2025). Although these issues immediately suggest multidisciplinary approaches, practitioners often tackle these issues by including the psychological perspective only as a historical background. It seems that one building block of the puzzle has started disappearing from the jigsaw puzzle: the human individual. For some thinkers, there could be an irresistible charm to proposing upward-directed higher-level explanations of phenomena that appear to be societal only. For example, the problem of fake news proliferation can be explained as driven by societal polarisation. Climate change can be looked at as stemming from inequalities between the poor and the rich and powerful (Islam & Winkel, 2017). AI can be investigated as a phenomenon affecting the problems of the global economy, policy, and politics (Liu, 2021). All of the above are valid lines of investigation that advance the understanding of the respective challenges. However, they should be supported by a psychological perspective related to attitude formation, judgement, and decision-making, as well as wellbeing and mental health.

One possible explanation for the limited involvement of psychological science in addressing 21st-century challenges faced by PR can be directly linked to psychology and its limited ability to promote itself. It is a paradoxical situation: the word 'psychology' is often used in public discourse, and many people claim to be good psychologists, yet the understanding of psychology as a scientific discipline is poor. Many erroneous, simplified, or simply incorrect definitions of psychology and social psychology circulate in the popular mindset, too. Although social psychology's definition as the study of human behaviour in its social context is universally used by scholars in the field (e.g. Sutton & Douglas, 2013), significant confusion, misconceptions, and distortions still exist, even in scholarly publications (e.g. Crawford & Novak, 2024). For several reasons, which I will partly address in this book, the individual-level perspective of an audience member and the bottom-up approach of psychological inquiry have been somewhat neglected by PR.

Psychological Aspect of Public Relations' Identity: the Case of Missing Question(s)?

One particular element of the modern PR landscape makes the present volume timely and relevant: an unprecedented growth of the epistemic power of the individual. The new power to control their information environment or exert influence, which manifests in the way audience members handle or mishandle information can be seen, for example, when the concepts of fake news sharing are discussed. This new power has arrived with the development of social media and has been facilitated by (almost) permanent access to them via mobile phone technology. On the one hand, it has limited the role of traditional information handlers, and that includes not only journalists and governments but also PR practitioners. With the ability to share information that suits personal likings and satisfies needs rather than is simply credible, the need to investigate the individual from the perspective of the industry that uses communication to build relationships seems more pressing.

For a psychologist, it is easy to see the applied value of individual-level analyses when it comes to understanding phenomena related to processing and acquiring information, evaluating people, forming opinions, and the behaviour of individuals and groups. Additionally, professional communicators should be aware that the act of communication is instrumental in achieving other goals. Not surprisingly, these phenomena have been the focus of psychology since the conception of the discipline. However, because psychology has developed its own lexicon, as well as the terms and concepts it uses may differ from those used in the popular discourse (as well as from other disciplines that have influenced the practice and the theory of PR), strong links between psychology and PR have not developed to the extent that psychology's role would be immediately recognised in the current PR context.

Some of the reasons behind this diagnosis may be fairly obvious and simply a matter of tradition that is followed without much deliberation.

In most scholarly accounts, the 'social' aspect of PR theory has been firmly attached to macro-level sociological investigations (e.g. Edwards & Ihlen, 2023). Merriam-Webster defines social science as a branch of science that deals with the institutions and functioning of human society, as well as the interpersonal relationships of individuals as members of society (Merriam-Webster, n.d.). Although the 'social' element in PR theorising fulfils the promise of the first half of the definition, the individual and relationship aspects seem to be missing. For comparison, a dictionary definition of psychology in the Cambridge Dictionary of Psychology defines social psychology as

> 'the branch of psychology that specialises in studying processes of social interaction among humans, including ways the thoughts, feelings, and beliefs of the individual are affected by the real or imagined presence of others. This includes the study of attitudes, affiliation, mass communication, compliance, conformity, cross-cultural issues, authority, social roles and status, interpersonal attraction, group processes, social attribution, altruism, and nonverbal communication'
>
> *(Matsumoto, 2009, p. 504)*

Surprisingly for a social psychologist like myself, bringing insights into their discipline to advance PR, the vast majority of contemporary PR scholarship that discusses the social aspect of PR focuses on institutions, society, and various forms of relations (not to be confused with relationships), but not individuals as members of the society. While a plethora of psychological findings and theories could be easily applied to PR phenomena, the psychological perspective in PR should reach beyond demonstrating the mere applicability of theories and findings to PR practice and education. Particular topics of interest in psychology, like attitudes, information processing, judgement formation, social evaluation, and needs or wellbeing, could inform the practice and theory of PR immediately. For example, neuroimaging techniques could increase the understanding of human needs and opinion formation, or recent advances in research about moral outrage are helpful in explaining the spread of fake news. However, going beyond the simple, functional application of specific experimental findings and explaining their relevance is necessary to establish that 'social' in PR also means psychological. Social psychological concepts, the philosophy of the discipline, and its history should be first debated and mapped onto the current PR theoretical landscape.

The sociological dominance of the 'social' in PR has already been discussed. Wehmeier (2009) noticed two trends in PR after analysing opinions of academics and practitioners collected in 2005 and 2006. On the one hand, practical PR focuses on communication management; on the other, the academic discipline has been heavily steered towards a sociological perspective. Questions asked by Wehmeier about the status of PR seem very relevant today: 'Is it an academic discipline? Is it an interdisciplinary field of research? Which methodology does it follow?' (p. 266). In 2025, the status of PR as an academic discipline still varies from country to country. What also seems to play a role is how PR degrees are taught, especially in those countries where university education is not free. The marketisation of university degrees and ill-perceived convergence has led single-honour undergraduate PR degrees in the UK to disappear from the market (Chmiel & Moise, 2024).

Goal-Centred Approach to Developing Theory Informing PR Practice

Taken together, the practice of PR necessitates transdisciplinarity, while PR scholarship requires interdisciplinarity. For these two related conditions to occur, PR needs psychology. While occasionally scholars explicitly borrowed from the rich psychological scholarship of social psychology (Chmiel, 2023, 2024; Chmiel et al., 2025; Grunig & Grunig, 2008; Kim & Grunig, 2011), especially nowadays, these attempts appear to be an isolated practice, which often leads to criticism, maintaining that micro and meso level of domains of social science does not deal well with the current societal challenges of the macro PR environment.

One of the potential sources for integrating disciplinary achievements within the field of PR is axiology. Which shared values are held by PR practitioners and academic scholars? Democracy, the pursuit of the wellbeing of individuals and the public, improving the conditions of the society, and sustainability? From a more pragmatic standpoint, what are the goals of routine PR practice? The central objective of this monograph is to formulate an argument that supports the identification of a comprehensive perspective within the domain of PR scholarship and practice, the psychology of PR. Even though the proposed perspective is not entirely novel, it could be argued that in the field of PR, psychology is an older, less practically focused aunt. I aim to propose an alternative perspective and provide a detailed exposition of theories that have the potential to address the challenges faced by PR comprehensively. In this sense, the introduction of a new perspective should not give rise to tensions with existing paradigms. Instead, it may offer a more comprehensive understanding of PR phenomena, providing answers to questions from a micro-, intra-, and interindividual level of analysis. In the field of psychology, a plethora of perspectives exist that seek to explain human behaviour. These include cognitive, behavioural, evolutionary, and developmental. The underlying philosophy that guided their identification was to seek explanations for common psychological questions that would complement rather than compete with each other. My intentions are consistent with this approach. It is evident that psychology has the capacity to address the practical goals of PR and facilitate the development of theories that would assist in achieving these goals or informing relevant actions.

In psychology, goal setting is one of the most widely researched concepts (Aarts et al., 2005; Bargh, 1994; Dijksterhuis et al., 2006; Kruglanski et al., 2018; Moskowitz et al., 2004; Shah et al., 2002). Goals are defined as mental representations of desired end states. Goals can be events, processes, or outcomes – the results of an activity. I will use this psychological definition to explain where I see the potential for information in the practice of PR. Practitioners pursue goals every day. These could involve understanding an issue better, writing a press release, making a phone call, or changing the attitudes of audience members. In the pursuit of those goals, they need tools of tested efficacy. From the academic standpoint, the best test ground of efficacy is provided by theory. In the next section, I will briefly explain which areas of practical importance would benefit from infusing psychology.

The abandonment of psychology by PR – in my view – has been present at three stages relevant to the practice of the profession. The first stage is analysis, which involves seeking evidence to inform decisions. In this stage, the causality of human behaviour and its explanatory power in determining the input of PR activities has been approached in a fragmented manner. Too often, qualitative or correlational evidence is gathered instead of identifying the causes behind the investigated effects. The second problematic stage appears to be planning the object of PR, which often confuses outputs with outcomes. Because of the ill-defined object, the practice of PR often focuses on producing content and evaluating content production, while outcomes (opinions, attitudes, and relationships) remain vague and, at best, implied. The last issue is the topic of audiences in principle. Too little is known about contemporary audience members, their needs, and their role in communication management processes. As a consequence of these fallacies, modern PR rarely investigates relationships with audiences and almost completely ignores the unintended consequences of PR programmes. Identifying the exact reasons for the lack of application of psychological thought in PR could be largely speculative; therefore, a more fruitful approach would be to demonstrate the relevance of psychology to the practice and theory of PR.

In order to improve the practice of PR, four psychological tenets are necessary. Firstly, evidence-based thinking and decision-making should be based on quantitative methods of inquiry. Secondly, psychological and mental processes need to be incorporated into explanations of any phenomenon. Thirdly, the evaluation of PR programmes needs to become more routine, and a basic understanding of attitudes as outcomes of PR activity is necessary. Lastly, PR requires interdisciplinarity (the integration of knowledge

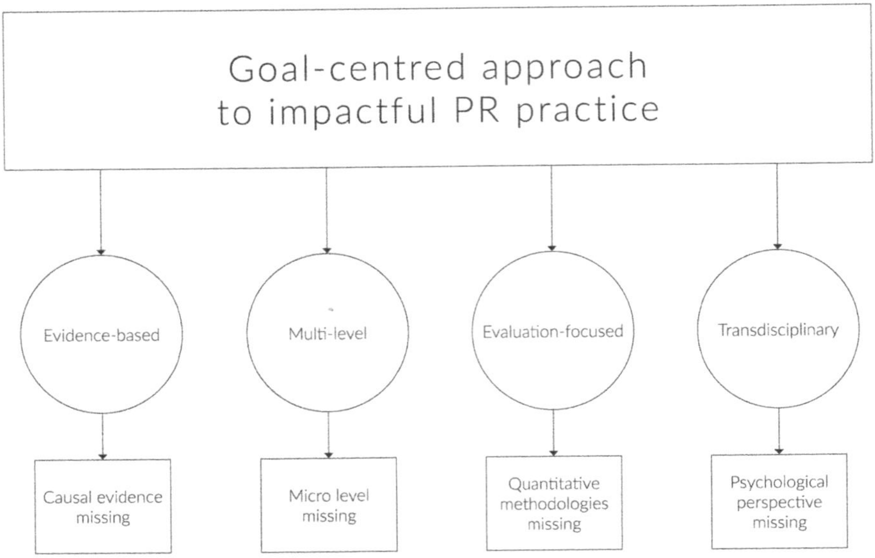

FIGURE 1.2 Goal-Centred approach to PR practice.

from different disciplines) as well as transdisciplinarity, understood as the co-creation of solutions that involve practitioners and other stakeholders. In that sense, psychology can contribute to establishing a common lexicon and standards of evaluation that the practice of PR can benefit from. These elements are currently missing or only partially developed (see Figure 1.2).

Grunig was notably the first PR scholar who appreciated the role of the science of cognitive psychology in PR. At some point, his theory was faced with – in my view – unjust criticism (Grunig, 2006). Using Grunig's terminology, the attempt made in this volume is to provide content for furnishing the edifice constructed by Grunig's work. Psychological evidence, although used in PR on multiple occasions, is inserted in PR theorising as isolated concepts or fragments of larger theories. I will approach my task with a different motivation, trying to demonstrate the context and background of the discussed terms.[2] The aim of the monograph is anchored in the definition of PR suggested by White (2000) and concentrates on the following questions:

1 Is PR an applied social psychology?
2 Can PR be studied using psychological methods and evidence?
3 What is missing in the contemporary scholarship and evidence-informed practice of PR, and how can the missing element be aided by psychology, understood here as modern experimental science?

I will provide answers to these questions in the next seven chapters.

Outline of the Book

Chapter 2 will provide an overview of social psychology as a discipline, exploring how human behaviour is influenced by its social context. I intend to provide a scaffolding for understanding how mental processes contribute to a partial explanation of societal-level effects. The disambiguation will be offered to distinguish between different definitions and accompanying traditions of studying social psychological phenomena from different disciplinary viewpoints: social psychology, sociological social psychology, and microsociology. While there may be different theoretical advantages to adopting one perspective over another, one emerging theme is the goal shared by different perspectives: to explain social phenomena as driven by the behaviours of individuals. The social psychological tradition will be examined through the perspective of the popularity of some theories gained among the general public. The evidence presented in Chapter 2 is expected to justify the usefulness of approaching the practice of PR as an applied behavioural discipline. It will contest some outdated views about psychology in PR scholarship, which see psychology only as a study of persuasion or consider methods of psychology mainly through laboratory science, which is not concerned with real-life problems and human behaviour.

Chapter 3 will begin by discussing the historical heritage of psychology in PR and the writings of Edward Bernays. Regardless of the state of knowledge in psychology in the early 20th century, he made excellent use of the arrival of the new, exciting discipline and was committed to incorporating it into his publicity and PR campaigns. What Bernays meant by psychology is also interesting. Some of his views demonstrated great insight into matters related to human thinking, while in other instances – especially when group psychology was discussed – his thinking was more sociological than psychological, even at the time he wrote. Next, it will be argued that modern, applied psychological science can be integrated with PR to help understand individual-level mechanisms of human behaviour and to propose interventions to solve the challenges PR practitioners face. Recent areas of research interest in social psychology, understood as a field of science with practical applications, will be examined based on quantitative, bibliographic data.

Chapter 4 begins by discussing the relevance of the concept of evidence to the practice of PR. PR needs to analyse the environment and be able to draw conclusions from available data. Practitioners also need evidence to understand if their programmes work, and for that, they need methodological tools that psychology is particularly well-suited for. People do not live in clean laboratory settings, and methods of investigating their behaviours should not be constrained to artificial settings. However, every practitioner should have a grasp of the concepts of causality and avoid confusing them with correlations. They should also be able to identify which evidence can be generalised to other situations and help develop successful campaigns in the future. That is why it is paramount to adopt a single definition of truth in PR and see that principles adopted in psychology work well when it comes to understanding why people lie, even though they know they do. Pinker (2021) defines rationality as 'the use of knowledge to attain goals' and rejects the idea that human cognition is 'heffalump trap of biases and delusions' (p. 47), which is a good summary of some 70 years of discussion about human rationality in psychology and one of the topics of Chapter 4.

Next, I will argue that by identifying a psychological perspective in PR scholarship and practice, tangible benefits can be achieved for both theory and practice. For example, appreciating the emotional components of attitudes can help practitioners evaluate their campaigns more effectively. Adopting quantitative methodologies of measurement will lead to establishing clear 'cause-and-effect mechanisms' of Public Relations' impact on society. In Chapter 5, an argument will be provided that challenges some of the criticism levelled at functionalist and positivist thinking in the field of PR. For instance, Wehmeier's (2006) observations highlighted the limitations of positivist approaches to PR planning and execution, noting their inability to account for irrationality and uncertainty, as well as their failure to describe social processes adequately. Indeed, a significant contribution of social psychology over the past 70 years has been the analysis of human irrationality.

Additionally, it has investigated the experience and consequences of uncertainty. Furthermore, it has made social processes the main objects of its inquiry. Therefore, when Wehmeier observed an absence of rationality in organisational decision-making, as evidenced by a scarcity of information, divergence of interests, and the potential for opposition, his implied definition of irrationality was that of a 19th-century nature. Furthermore, while the attribution of decision-making capacity to organisations may be interpreted as a mental shortcut or a useful metaphor for describing organisational behaviour, it is essential to note that organisations do not possess mental states in and of themselves. The responsibility for decision-making lies with humans, defined here as individuals in managerial or occupational roles who possess the cognitive capacity to collect, process, and interpret information. In such cases, the rationality of the subjects in question must be subjected to rigorous scrutiny. By the social psychological understanding of rationality outlined in Chapter 4, the value of defining the psychological object of PR will be discussed. Furthermore, the benefits of focusing on the individual micro-level of analysis will be explored.

Psychology has undergone interesting progress in the role of including context to understand human behaviour and to arrive at the conclusion that humans operate in an environment and have been equipped with tools to deal with actual, and not laboratory-conceived, problems and mental processes are a result of interaction (transaction) with external world (Mesquita et al., 2010; Mischel & Shoda, 2010). One of these tools is epistemic motivation. This is why, in Chapter 6, I will focus on the need for information and the human epistemic needs of individuals in general. I will contextualise relevant individual-level findings against the characteristics of an environment rich in information, in which audience members need to operate efficiently. Although PR has proposed its theory of information processing (as explained in greater detail in Chapter 3), today, these theories can be seen as anchored in disciplines less suited to investigate particularities of the human mind (e.g. politics) or were inspired by historically interesting but largely outdated psychological concepts (e.g. from the 1960s and 1970s). More worryingly, the words 'information processing' strike a bad note outside the science of psychology, which may cause a complete neglect of this area as not 'social enough'. They may remind us of a period when quantitative methods of analysis of behaviour were equated with laboratory settings, which partly ignored the role of context. In today's communication landscape, rich in information, which quickly depletes mental resources, it is particularly important to understand what motivates audience members to seek information, how they use it, and when they process it in a biased manner. In some instances, it happens because there are too many mental tasks to deal with the information, but increasingly, other needs also play a role. This will also be discussed in Chapter 6.

In Chapter 7, the practical value of involving insights from several disciplines will be discussed in relation to two significant PR-relevant phenomena: fake news and artificial intelligence. As much as PR is not just about communication, it also should not be about content creation only. Although content creation is considered one of the major practical tasks of the PR function, overreliance on content can have severe consequences for both audiences and the profession of PR. That is why the dangers associated with contributing by communication professionals to a content-abundant information landscape will be discussed. Generative artificial intelligence has become one of the key agents of the landscape, and the consequences of creating irrelevant content of low quality, as well as treating it as a goal rather than a tool, are explored in detail. Quantitative-type risks of content abundance will provide a springboard for a qualitative analysis of another phenomenon: the spread of fake news. A transdisciplinary approach to understanding why fake news are shared online by contemporary audience members will be advanced along with the critical analysis of seemingly similar notions of misinformation, disinformation, and malinformation. The two-way symmetrical model of PR will be argued to be the most accurate perspective to approach the goal of limiting the spread of fake news in society.

Chapter 8 will investigate the transdisciplinarity of PR as a dialogue between disciplines, as well as between theory and practice. For transdisciplinarity to develop fully, the value of PR education needs to be recognised, and practitioners and pedagogues should work closely to achieve this. Psychologists have been known to respond to questions, particularly those posed by the media, with a standard retort of 'it depends'. While providing a direct and straightforward answer to a question can be seen as a virtue and a sign of intellect, the witty phrase also highlights a specific object of inquiry in psychology: human behaviour. Psychologists are trained to understand that explanations of human behaviour can rarely be understood in terms of a single factor or simple mechanism. In psychology, complexity is recognised, and a variety of perspectives are encouraged. I will use evidence from previous chapters to explain how the goals of PR practice can be achieved by fostering dialogue between disciplines, as well as educators, practitioners, and professional associations. I will (partly) argue that a new grand theory of PR is rarely a necessity, and instead, transdisciplinary (versus multidisciplinary or interdisciplinary) is an idea worth exploring with attention in the context of PR. Chapter 8 will not call for a paradigm shift or transformation of PR. It also will not suggest that PR needs to evolve into a new, fuller, and somewhat better discipline, like PR 2.0. However, to initiate the transdisciplinary dialogue, psychology should be accurately represented at the decision-making table. The book will finish by integrating themes from previous chapters and suggesting educational, practical, and societal challenges for the profession of PR.

In conclusion, the goal of this book is to offer a contemporary social psychological perspective on PR grounded in the social cognitive approach, goal-directed theories of behaviour, and the basic epistemic needs and characteristics of audience members. In the chapters that follow, I will try to demonstrate that recent advancements in social psychology provide a consistent framework for understanding the meaning-construction process of members of publics, dialogical communication building based on knowledge formation processes of individuals, and societal-level analysis of influences of public communication. It is hoped that additional benefits of adopting a social psychological perspective will also help address misconceptions about PR: the discipline that requires talent but also knowledge and science-underpinned expertise. In the current media and communication landscape, psychological elements appear as the missing cog for understanding the practicalities of the mechanism of building symmetrical relationships between organisations and individuals – members of publics. This book, at the very least and to be succinct – could be summarised by a modification of White's (2000) assertion, which sees PR as applied psychology. For what matters, PR is also applied psychology. The next chapter provides a necessary psychological scaffolding and discusses the development of psychology as a discipline that inspired the birth of PR.

Note

1 Partly, the topic has been addressed by Russell and Lamme (2016) in their work on the human agency of publics in PR.
2 Readers across different geographical locations may be familiar with IKEA's PAX system, which comprises multiple customisable furniture elements. While its look may not be to everyone's taste, one should also appreciate that for certain purposes and at a certain stage in life, using a combination of elements of one type that are characterised by visual consistency, making them fit well, can efficiently produce a coherent and aesthetic furnishing of a dwelling. The purpose of integrating psychological theories for PR edifice's purpose is this PAX philosophy.

References

Aarts, H., Custers, R., & Wegner, D. M. (2005). On the inference of personal authorship: Enhancing experienced agency by priming effect information. *Consciousness and Cognition*, *14*(3), 439–458. https://doi.org/10.1016/J.CONCOG.2004.11.001

Bargh, J. A. (1994). The Four Horsemen of Automaticity: Awareness, Efficiency, Intention, and Control in Social Cognition. In R. S. Wyer & T. K. Srull (Eds.), *Handbook of Social Cognition* (2nd ed., Vol. 1, pp. 1–40). Lawrence Erlbaum Associates, Inc.

Bernays, E. L. (1923). *Crystallizing Public Opinion*. Boni & Liveright.

Bernays, E. L. (1928). *Propaganda*. Horace Liveright.

Bernays, E. L. (1940). *Speak Up for Democracy*. Viking Press. https://www.abebooks.co.uk/servlet/BookDetailsPL?bi=31178300650&ref_=o_3_ac

Bernays, E. L. (1986). *The Later Years: Public Relations Insights 1956-1986*. Howard Penn Hudson Assc Inc.

Bowen, S. A. (2003). "I thought it would be more glamorous": Preconceptions and misconceptions among students in the public relations principles course. *Public Relations Review*, *29*(2), 199–214. https://doi.org/10.1016/S0363-8111(03)00012-2

Brown, R. E. (2014). *The Public Relations of Everything: The Ancient, Modern and Postmodern Dramatic History of an Idea*. Routledge.

Chmiel, M. (2023). Social Cognitive Psychology of Corporate Reputation. In U. Bihler (Ed.), *Wirkungsmechanismen im Reputationsmanagement* (pp. 67–82). Springer. https://doi.org/10.1007/978-3-658-41204-3_6

Chmiel, M. (2024). Societal impact of Brand Public Relations on gender equality: Evidence for a mediation-type mechanism. *Corporate Communications: An International Journal*, 29(6), 796–817. https://doi.org/10.1108/CCIJ-04-2024-0059

Chmiel, M. (2025). Loneliness, office space arrangement and mental well-being of Gen Z PR professionals. Falling into the trap of an agile office? *Journal of Communication Management*, 29(3), 379–400. https://doi.org/10.1108/JCOM-03-2024-0046

Chmiel, M., Fatima, S., Ingold, C., Reisten, J., & Tejada, C. (2025). Climate change as fake news. Positive attribute framing as a tactic against corporate reputation damage from the evaluations of sceptical, right-wing audiences. *Corporate Communications: An International Journal*, *30*(2), 388–407. https://doi.org/10.1108/CCIJ-12-2023-0190

Chmiel, M., & Moise, R. (2024). Undergraduate public relations education in the United Kingdom: Quo Vadis? *Public Relations Inquiry*, *13*(3). https://doi.org/10.1177/2046147X241230055

Crawford, L. A., & Novak, K. B. (2024). *Individual and Society: Sociological Social Psychology* (3rd ed.). Routledge.

Cutlip, S. M. (1994). *The Unseen Power: Public Relations: A History (Routledge Communication Series)*. Routledge.

Dijksterhuis, A., Bos, M. W., Nordgren, L. F., & Van Baaren, R. B. (2006). On making the right choice: the deliberation-without-attention effect. *Science*, *311*(5763), 1005–1007. https://doi.org/10.1126/SCIENCE.1121629

Edwards, L., & Ihlen, Ø. (2023). Social theory in public relations: Insights and directions. *In Public Relations Theory III: In the Age of Publics*. https://doi.org/10.4324/9781003141396-15

Gras, N. S. B. (1945). Shifts in public relations. *Business History Review*, *19*(4), 97–148. https://doi.org/10.1017/S0007680500008266

Grunig, J. E. (1997). A situational theory of publics: Conceptual history, recent challenges and new research. In D. Moss, T. MacManus, & D. Vercic (Eds.), *Public Relations Research: An International Perspective*. (pp. 3–48). International Thomson Business Press.

Grunig, J. E. (2006). Furnishing the Edifice: Ongoing Research on Public Relations as a Strategic Management Function. *Journal of Public Relations Research*, *18*(2), 151–176. https://doi.org/10.1207/s1532754xjprr1802_5

Grunig, J. E., & Grunig, L. A. (2008). Excellence theory in public relations: Past, present, and future. In J. E. Grunig and L. A. Grunig *Public Relations Research: European and International Perspectives and Innovations* (pp. 327–347). Wiesbaden: VS Verlag für Sozialwissenschaften. https://doi.org/10.1007/978-3-531-90918-9_22

Gruning, J. (2013). Situational Theory of Publics. In R. Heath (Ed.), *Encyclopedia of Public Relations* (Vol. 2, pp. 778–780). Sage Publications.

Hambrick, D. C., & Mason, P. A. (1984). Upper echelons: The organization as a reflection of its top managers. *The Academy of Management Review*, *9*(2), 193. https://doi.org/10.2307/258434

Islam, S. N., & Winkel, J. (2017). *Climate Change and Social Inequality*. 1–30. DESA Working Paper No. 152 ST/ESA/2017/DWP/152 https://www.un.org/esa/desa/papers/2017/wp152_2017.pdf

Kim, J. N., & Grunig, J. E. (2011). Problem solving and communicative action: A situational theory of problem solving. *Journal of Communication*, *61*(1). https://doi.org/10.1111/j.1460-2466.2010.01529.x

Kruglanski, A. W., Dechesne, M., Orehek, E., & Pierro, A. (2018). Three decades of lay epistemics: The why, how, and who of knowledge formation. *In The Motivated Mind: The Selected Works of Arie Kruglanski*. https://doi.org/10.4324/9781315175867

L'Etang, J. (2004). *Public Relations in Britain: A History of Professional Practice in the 20th Century*. Routledge.

Lasswell, H. D. (1979). *Propaganda and Communication in World History: The Symbolic Instrument in Early Times*. University of Hawaii Press.

Ławniczak, R. (ed.) (2001) *Public Relations Contribution to Transition in Central and Eastern Europe: Research and Practice*. Printer.

Ławniczak, R. (2004). Intermezzo. The transitional approach to public relations. In B. van Ruler & D. Verčič (Eds.), *Public Relations and Communication Management in Europe* (pp. 217–226). De Gruyter Mouton. https://doi.org/10.1515/9783110197198.217

Ławniczak, R. (2005). *Introducing Market Economy Institutions and Instruments: The Role of Public relations in Transition Economies* (R. Ławniczak, Ed.). Piar.pl.

Ławniczak, R. (2009). Re-examining the economic roots of public relations. *Public Relations Review*, *35*(4). https://doi.org/10.1016/j.pubrev.2009.08.009

Liu, Z. (2021). Sociological perspectives on artificial intelligence: A typological reading. *Sociology Compass*, *15*(3), e12851. https://doi.org/10.1111/SOC4.12851

Matsumoto, D. (2009). *The Cambridge Dictionary of Psychology*. Cambridge University Press & Assessment.

Merriam-Webster. (n.d.). Social science. Retrieved May6, 2025, from https://www.merriam-webster.com/dictionary/social%20science

Mesquita, B., Barrett, L. F., & Smith, E. R. (2010). *The Mind in Context*. The Guilford Press.

Mischel, W., & Shoda, Y. (2010). The Situated Person. In B. Mesquita, L. F. Barrett, & E. R. Smith (Eds.), *The Mind in Context* (pp. 149–173). The Guilford Press.

Moskowitz, G. B., Li, P., & Kirk, E. R. (2004). The implicit volition model: On the preconscious regulation of temporarily adopted goals. *Advances in Experimental Social Psychology*, *36*, 317–413. https://doi.org/10.1016/S0065-2601(04)36006-5

Nothhaft, H., & Zerfass, A. (2023). Public Relations in an Postdisciplinary World: On the Impossibility of Establishing a Constitutive PR Theory within the Tribal Struggles of the Applied Communication Disciplines. In C. Botan (Ed.), *Public Relations Theory III: In the Age of Publics* (pp. 247–266). Routledge. https://doi.org/10.4324/9781003141396-17

Pinker, S. (2021). *Rationality: What It Is, Why It Seems Scarce, Why It Matters*. Penguin Books.

Russell, K. M., & Lamme, M. O. (2016). Theorizing public relations history: The roles of strategic intent and human agency. *Public Relations Review*, 42(5), 741–747.

Shah, J. Y., Friedman, R., & Kruglanski, A. W. (2002). Forgetting all else: On the antecedents and consequences of goal shielding. *Journal of Personality and Social Psychology*, *83*(6), 1261–1280. https://doi.org/10.1037/0022-3514.83.6.1261

Stichweh, R. (2015). Scientific Disciplines, History of. *In International Encyclopedia of the Social & Behavioral Sciences: Second Edition*. https://doi.org/10.1016/B978-0-08-097086-8.03048-8

Sutton, R., & Douglas, K. (2013). *Social Psychology*. Red Globe Press.

Thompson, G. (2020). Post-Truth Public Relations. Routledge. https://doi.org/10.4324/9780429429125

Topić, M., & Lodoforos, G. (Eds.) (2021). *The Sustainability Debate: Policies, Gender and the Media (Critical Studies on Corporate Responsibility, Governance and Sustainability)*. Emerald Publishing Limited.

Verčič, D. (2005). PR is champion of democracy. *In Speech to AGM of the Institute of Public Relations (now the Chartered Institute of Public Relations) in London*. https://www.researchgate.net/publication/261135446_PR_is_champion_of_democracy

Verčič, D., & Grunig, J. E. (2000). The Origins of Public Relations Theory in Economics and Strategic Management. In D. Moss, D. Verčič, & G. Warnaby (Eds.), *Perspectives on Public Relations Research* (pp. 9–58). Taylor and Francis. https://doi.org/10.4324/9780203192924-8

Verčič, D., Selaković, M., Hung-Baesecke, F., Cheng, Y., Tkalac Verčič, A., Ljepava, N., & Stavreva, S. (2025). *Ethical Standards and Guidelines for the Use of Artificial Intelligence in Public Relations*. The International Public Relations Association and University of Ljubljana, Faculty of Social Sciences. https://www.dlib.si/details/URN:NBN:SI:DOC-DZGEHGBN

Wehmeier, S. (2006). Dancers in the dark: The myth of rationality in public relations. *Public Relations Review*, *32*(3), 213–220. https://doi.org/10.1016/j.pubrev.2006.05.018

Wehmeier, S. (2009). Out of the fog and into the future: Directions of public relations, theory building, research, and practice. *Canadian Journal of Communication*, *34*(2), 265–282. https://doi.org/10.22230/CJC.2009V34N2A2033

White, J. (2000). Psychology and public relations. In D. Moss, D. Verčič & G. Warnaby (Eds.), *Perspectives on Public Relations Research*. (pp 161–172) Routledge.

2

THE INSPIRATION

Contemporary Social Psychology and Its Potential for Informing PR Theory and Practice

Brief Historical Overview

The first mention of the word 'psychology' dates back to the 16th century and appears in (now lost) writings of a Croatian poet and two German philosophers (Klempe, 2020). Although traditionally, the origins of the discipline psychology are located around the year 1879, when Wundt opened his experimental psychology laboratory in Leipzig, the first book arguing that psychology can be studied in the same way as physics ('Psychologia Empirica') was published much earlier – in 1732 by Christian Wolf (Brysbaert & Rastle, 2021). For comparison, the first public relations course was offered in 1920 (University of Illinois) and the first programme – in 1948 (University of Boston) (Watson & Wright, 2011). The 150-year difference between the actual and popularly acknowledged birth of psychological science is interesting for at least two reasons. The first one is straightforward: psychology's history as a discipline is more extended, and the year 1879 marks the start of the institutional development of the discipline. From the perspective of internal dynamics and within disciplinary processes, one can argue that the lessons psychology has to offer to PR are not only concerned with a partly overlapping object of the discipline. The theoretical breadth of applied findings related to human thoughts, emotions, and behaviours can inspire PR research and has inspired scholars, as well as practitioners, to search for tools to facilitate their practice. In parallel to the practical and theoretical toolbox offered by psychology, the evolution of psychology as a science, the history of its internal tensions, the relationship between theory and practice, real and assumed criteria of scientific success, and the potential for being distorted in the popular mind – all could inform and help avoid crises. The second

DOI: 10.4324/9781003610403-2

implication is as relevant as it is perplexing. The criterion of adopting a theoretical perspective does not depend solely on the quality of the perspective itself. As was the case with Wundt, the popularity of his school of thought and the attribution of the discipline's birth to his name can also be attributed to his promotional work. Wundt enabled American students to study in his laboratory, and this led to spreading his school of thought after returning to the home country and, subsequently, their students. It is believed that by 1892, at least 20 institutes of psychology were established in the US as a consequence of Wundt's teaching (Van Biervliet, 1892 as cited in Brysbaert & Rastle, 2021).

In the first textbook on social psychology, McDougall (1919) positioned the discipline as an essential foundation for all other social sciences (e.g. economics, political history, and sociology) but was well aware of the existence of critics of the approach and those who completely ignored psychology altogether. One assertion he made resonates quite well with the current 'state of affairs' of psychology in relation to more complex fields: 'psychology will before long be accorded in universal practice the position at the base of the social sciences which the more clear-sighted have long seen that it ought to occupy' (McDougall, 1919, p. 14). The enthusiasm of McDougall is praiseworthy, but perhaps a misreading of the manner in which he positioned psychology in relation to other disciplines made the integration of psychology with other disciplines, especially those dealing with human behaviour, difficult and occasionally discouraging. Ultimately, we can only speculate what McDougall meant by 'the base of the social sciences'.

Social Psychology – Definition and Scope

Historically, psychologists have focused on understanding individual human behaviour, particularly how it is affected or how it affects other people. The field of social psychology saw a surge of interest in the aftermath of the Second World War, driven by applied research in areas such as persuasion (Hovland et al., 1953), voting behaviour (Festinger, 1954), and the study of attitudes (Katz, 1960; Markus, 1979). Considering the motivations of scholars, psychology, and social psychology in particular, can be examined through the lens of their efforts to bring about meaningful change in individuals and society. Today, major global phenomena continue to inspire new waves of psychological research: wars and global conflicts (Scharbert et al., 2024), social movements (Eagly et al., 2012), the rise or fall of ideologies (Duckitt et al., 2002), terrorism and its implications, as well as other global phenomena like the recent pandemic of SARS COV 2 (Van Bavel et al., 2022).

Sutton and Douglas (2013) provide the following succinct definition of social psychology: 'a branch of psychology dedicated to the study of how people think about, influence and relate to each other' (p. 3) and add that 'much of social psychology focuses on real-world questions and issues' (Sutton & Douglas, 2013). Social psychologists study people's lives in relation to one another. Today, the discipline is focused on how human beings take shape through their ongoing interactions in the world. Many social psychologists are particularly interested in understanding and seeking solutions to problems faced by increasingly diverse, multicultural, and globally interconnected societies (Hodgetts et al., 2010). Since its conception, Psychology has undergone a methodological evolution, expanding its repertoire of techniques and has grown to appreciate the role of context and external factors in explaining human behaviour.

In the 1970s, some behavioural psychologists began to change their view that environmental stimuli and accompanying behavioural responses (S-R) were sufficient information for explaining human behaviour. In the 1980s, Cosmides (1985) challenged the behaviourists' understanding that the human learning process is non-specific and domain-independent. This is not to say that the primacy of the behaviourist approach, which ignored the role of mental processes, content, and context, was not contested by other researchers much earlier. For example, Piaget (1926) had already recognised the link between mental processes and behaviour at the beginning of the 20th century. Piaget emphasised the role of thought content by introducing a three-component formula for cognitive development. Also, one of the most famous publications by the Russian psychologist Vygotsky, first published in 1934, was titled 'Thought and Speech' (later changed to 'Thought and Language'). Vygotsky appreciated the relationship between thinking and language, treating them not as systems but as interrelated activities. The change in psychological methods and approaches that began to proliferate at the end of the 1980s led to several important changes. Not only did content and context begin to be investigated more seriously, but also more quantitative methodological rigour was introduced in areas previously considered qualitatively. In 1986, Bandura proposed Social Cognitive Theory, which suggested a dynamic character of behaviour and the interplay of personal and environmental factors and viewed learning as a cognitive (mental) process rather than a simple behavioural response. The process of learning can involve observing and imitating others, such as peers, family, or social groups. At the beginning of the 21st century, the European Association of Experimental Social Psychology (EAESP) dropped the 'experimental' from its name to suggest that social psychology appreciates different methods as long as they are scientific.

The prevailing view among theorists of social cognition is that the cognitive representations which underpin social judgements and human behaviour are abstract and unchanging. The processes responsible for activating them were considered relatively automatic and context-independent. However, recent studies indicate that social-cognitive processes can be adaptable, adjusting to an individual's immediate goals, the communicative environment in which they are operating, as well as their physical and bodily states. The authors of experiments confirming these relationships assume that the traditional school of social cognitive psychology does not adequately explain the mechanisms of these phenomena. A better model they advocated for is known as situated social cognition (Barsalou, 1999; Smith & Semin, 2004). Smith and Semin's (2004) seminal work established the basis for situated social cognition, marking a paradigm shift in the way we understand the relationship between cognition and action. Their work introduced a change in the metaphor explaining this relationship and a shift from computational to biological models. According to the proposed paradigm, cognition has an adaptive function in relation to behaviour, and cognitive representations are functionally oriented and dependent on the nature of the actions taken. Human cognition is also embodied, dependent on both the mind and sensorimotor abilities, as well as the environment in which it operates. The world is recognised not only through mental processes but also through the human environment, including the groups to which a person may belong. As researchers of the situated social cognition approach argue, treating the context in which a person is located as noise and a factor disrupting the study of basic cognitive processes is a mistake (Smith & Semin, 2007). The context and content are pivotal in determining the adaptive nature of cognitive processes. They should not be regarded as mere moderators or additives to cognitive processes but rather as their essential elements. Psychological laws are not abstract principles that can be universally applied to understand behaviour. Instead, they are developmental rules that suggest the direction of changes that occur as a result of interaction with the environment, social surroundings, and other people.

As humans have survived and prospered by sensing subtle changes in their environment and adapting to them, the mind, as the organ responsible for this adaptation, cannot be adequately described in static terms. The human mind is capable of pairing known stimuli with completely new responses, as well as extracting residual characteristics of stimuli and adapting to them cognitively (Mischel & Shoda, 2010). Mischel also presents his concept of understanding human personality based on the primary assumptions of the situated cognition approach. In this view, the *situated person* is a constructor of meanings that are skilfully extracted from the context of various situations thanks to their knowledge of culture, similar genetic code, and individual learning history. The conclusions drawn from Mischel's research work and that of his colleagues concern the relationship between context, the level of cognitive representation, and the diverse goals of the individual. The theory of the situated person is based on the assumption that situational characteristics can activate cognitive representations (constructs, expectations, and goals) based on an individual's previous experience with identified characteristics. As Barrett et al. (2010) noted, ignoring context is a mistake. In their anti-essentialist argument, these researchers demonstrated the extent to which contemporary psychology, influenced by the scientific tradition of Western civilisation, ignored the influence of context. In their framework, emotions, memory, the self, and attitudes are considered distinct entities, each governed by its own unique set of rules. As another proponent of contextualism, Schwarz (2010) has highlighted that the variability of human behaviour is rooted in the varying availability of particular pieces of information in the human memory system. A wide range of possible behavioural acts is, therefore, influenced by the context, knowledge, and experience of the current state. Schwarz's position was that human actions cannot be predicted solely based on the content of a person's thoughts. He also contended that actions can be predicted based on reflections arising from a person's subjective experience of those thoughts.

Today, most social psychologists agree that social psychology is an empirical, scientific discipline that uses both quantitative and qualitative methods to investigate how the interaction between an individual's mental processes and the environment produces behaviour. Unfortunately, definitions that distort and bias the understanding of social psychology also exist. One explanation for that could be the nature of questions asked by psychologists and other adjacent disciplines.

Investigating the 'Social': Psychology and Sociology

Two disciplines, despite their differing perspectives, appear particularly well-positioned to address questions concerning human behaviour in social contexts: psychology and sociology. The first known use of the word 'psychology' was in the 15th century, while the term 'sociology' was first used by August Comte in the 19th century. The sociological perspective on human behaviour and the roots of motivation to analyse it differed from psychology. Historically, while psychology has been keen to identify the connection between the mind and the body and understand how the former governs the latter, early sociologists assumed the animal nature of human beings and the need for regulating human behaviour by society and its institutions. Today, some sociologists identify a consistent psychological line of inquiry in sociological research and argue that social psychology is overly focused on laboratory experiments, ignoring the context and malleable nature of human experience. In their view, large parts of social psychology are, in fact, sociological (Crawford & Novak, 2024). Although approaching the questions of human behaviour in social contexts from multiple perspectives is necessary to develop a better understanding of social phenomena, and dialogue between disciplines is needed, this should not lead to sociologists claiming large parts of social psychology.

This misunderstanding can be explained by three different traditions that social psychology has evolved around. One of them has roots in psychology, and the other two in sociology. The starting point for the argument developed by Crawford and Novak (2024) is a paper from 1977 by House: 'Three faces of social psychology'. House identified a crisis in social psychology and argued that it reflected 'the division of the field into three increasingly isolated domains or faces: (1) psychological social psychology, (2) symbolic interactionism, and (3) psychological sociology (or social structure and personality)' (House, 1977, p. 161). While he acknowledged that social psychology was a psychological discipline, he noted the interest in this area from sociologists, although he observed that their area of specialisation was 'less intellectually and organizationally secure and coherent' than psychology (House, 1977, p. 162).

The roots of the sociological tradition of investigating social psychological phenomena were identified with Mead (1934). The following excerpt from Mead's Mind, Self and Society will be particularly instrumental for grasping the difference between sociological and psychological approaches in general:

> We are not in social psychology building up the behavior of the social group in terms of the behavior of the separate individuals composing it, rather we are starting out with a given social whole of complex group activity, into which we analyze (as elements) the behavior of each of the separate individuals composing it.
>
> *(Mead, 1934, p. 7)*

Mead's social psychology began with a group or society as the unit of analysis, deducing how individuals might act or think (by seeing the small through the big). In contrast, psychology begins with an individual and proposes how mental processes, goals, and needs might lead to different effects when two or more individuals interact (seeing the big picture through the small details). To differentiate between different traditions, House used the adjectives 'psychological' and 'sociological' to denote different 'faces' of social psychology. While his papers resonated well among sociologists, it does not seem to have changed the fact that today, mainstream social psychology does not require the use of additional qualifiers: social psychology is a subdiscipline of psychology. Nevertheless, it is interesting to observe how some sociologists seem to be tempted to hijack traditional areas of psychological research by suggesting that, for example, prejudice and discrimination, social influence, social control, collective behaviour, or mental health are topics of 'sociological' social psychology (Crawford & Novak, 2024). In fact, they are not, and have been studied passionately by social psychologists – a subdiscipline of psychology (e.g. Crisp et al., 2024; Pratkanis, 2007; Sutton & Douglas,

2013; Vallacher & Gollwitzer, 2025). Public relations also suffers from similar hijacking attempts. In the context of higher education, media and communication programmes borrow topics from PR to attract students (Chmiel & Moise, 2024). The interest of sociology in psychological areas of investigation does not mean that sociology cannot be behavioural. This can happen in the context of practice, for example, when tasks typically associated with PR are attached to marketing or advertising functions. A good example is brand public relations, which is not a new area of research and, in the practical context, sees a large portion of PR practitioners: 'a type of consumer stakeholder-oriented PR, which is focused (but not limited) on co-creating (with marketing) the strategy and tactics of communication, their monitoring and measurement, as well as the responsibility for their outcomes and impact' (Chmiel, 2024, p. 798). Brand PR, especially when linked to business functions, is expected to produce a behavioural change. In that context, too, psychology and sociology can make valuable contributions to a better understanding of the effects on audience members, as well as on society.

Ritzer's (1975) definition captures the spirit and aspirations of behavioural sociology succinctly. It is the 'theoretical effort to apply the principles of psychological behaviorism to sociological questions' (p. 145). For Michaels and Green (1978), behavioural sociology was interested in the principles of operant conditioning borrowed from behaviourism (i.e. rewards and punishments) to explain two phenomena jointly: human behaviour and macro-level sociological phenomena. To clarify why behavioural analysis is relevant to sociology, the aforementioned authors provide several reasons, but two of them seem particularly relevant for identifying distinct sociological contributions. First, behavioural analysis provides a 'more complete understanding of organisations and communities' (p. 25). In addition to that, they pinpointed two important benefits of sociological macro-look into behaviour that – according to authors – had not been well explained by operant conditioning: the inclusion of culture as a factor influencing the behaviour of individuals, as well as the characteristics and processes of social systems that were not captured by the individual level of learning. This approach has caused some controversy among sociologists, and adherence to the definition of behavioural sociology as relying on operant conditioning and neglecting mental processes has led to suspicions. Again, the key questions of human nature and free will, about which behaviourism apparently was providing a negative view, led many sociologists to dismiss behavioural sociology altogether (Michaels & Green, 1978). In parallel with Michaels and Green (1978), Stolte et al. (2001) also acknowledged the long history of the sociological social psychology tradition. At the same time, they understood its discontinuous character and uncertain position. Their definition of the goal of sociological social psychology is to see how interpersonal situations explain 'broader social forces, properties and processes' (p. 388). These authors saw sociological social psychology not as social psychological but instead as a form of microsociology and further elaborated that this would refer to 'the examination of large-scale social issues by means of the investigation of small-scale social situations' (p.388). The assumption of miniaturism, as proposed by Stolte et al. (2001), is attractive and offers a good foundation for the postulate of transdisciplinarity. For Good (2022) too, social psychology is an interdisciplinary field and, as a discipline, it 'emerged from the cross-fertilisation of psychology and other human sciences, including sociology' (Moscovici, 1990, p. 67).

Although the distinctions between sociological social psychology, micro-sociology, and psychological social psychology may be intellectually stimulating and entertaining from a scholarly perspective, their practical applications are less clear for the practice of public relations. After all, advocates of each of the disciplines discussed previously share one common interest: explaining human behaviour in its social context and appreciating all, that is, both internal and external factors that shape it. On the one hand, the developments that followed from early 20th-century theoretical discussions about the scope and definition of sociology and psychology can be seen as disciplinary turf wars and can be explained in terms of efforts to define basic concepts and advance unique theories that would help the disciplines mature and establish clear academic identities. On the other hand, scholars have traditionally asked very similar questions about human nature, but they differ in the importance assigned to internal constructs (e.g. motivation, information processing, memory, attention) versus external forces (e.g. family, society, nation) in shaping it. However, the consensus is that all those factors are necessary to understand how people behave. With the common question set, different variants of psychology also differed in their methods of pursuing answers and engaged in (often heated) debates about methodological limitations. This can explain why 'clean' laboratory-based approaches have been criticised for their limited external validity – partly missing the point of experimentation, which brings the advantage of isolating singular factors in mapping internal processes. It would seem that much of the confusion about the scope and definition of psychological versus sociological social psychology could have been avoided if the power struggle element was removed and the focus was placed on the specific questions of shared interest and the choice of methods and evidence. In the remaining parts of the book, I shall adhere to using the term 'social psychology' as a psychological discipline.

Applied psychology deals with contextualised settings (Howitt, 1991), and the applications of the discipline can be seen in many spheres of professional and everyday life. For example, clinical psychology focuses on the wellbeing and the prevention of mental disorders. In business settings, occupational psychology is applied in various aspects of organisational functioning, such as recruitment, career planning, and change management. Human resources departments often recruit graduates from psychological educational backgrounds, appreciating their theoretical knowledge and statistical dexterity. These two areas seem to be primarily associated with practical applications of psychology, yet the potential of 'looking through the small to understand the big' seems much bigger. This can be seen in another area of common interest of sociologists and psychologists.

To address the gap between social and political psychology, Himmelweit and Gaskell (1990) introduced a new subdiscipline: societal psychology and defined it as the 'study of social phenomena in their own right as they affect, and are affected by, the members of the particular society' (p. 9). Howarth et al. (2013) explain that societal psychology 'was first proposed by Hilde Himmelweit in 1985 to address the 'crisis' in social psychology in the 1970s and 1980s over the irrelevance of social psychological research to the world outside the discipline' and further note that it was 'a return to the original ambitions of social psychology' (Howarth et al., 2013, p. 366). The need to propose a new approach within social psychology, one with a name and a distinctive scope, sheds some light on the inner dynamics of the discipline in the 1990s. Proponents of societal psychology understood well that the overreliance on laboratory experiments shifted the object of study of psychology from what the discipline had originally been preoccupied with: explaining human behaviour in its social context. Societal psychologists defined context broadly to include social constructions of various phenomena, such as race and identity, as well as the impact of culture. The choice of the label 'societal' was a deliberate attempt to demonstrate its attachment with the discipline of psychology (and not sociology), differentiate its focus from applied psychology, as well as appreciate that individual thoughts and feelings and environmental factors, culture, and institutions play a role in explaining human behaviour (Himmelweit, 1990). Societal psychologists have investigated sociological phenomena through the lens of individual-level processes and experience, for example, the impact of societal dynamics on a child's cognitive development (Doise, 1990), variability of personality as a function of culture and society (Brown, 1990), morality and social orientation (Deutsch, 1990), and macroeconomic processes (Strümpel, 1990). For Parker, psychology should also be ideological and politically engaged, but this can come with the risks of being accused of subjectivity and a lack of academic rigour. Misinterpretation of evidence can happen, especially when scientific psychological findings are taken out of context or interpreted by non-expert audiences.

Criticism of Applied Psychology

Even non-political applications of psychology can be met with criticism. The critique that applied psychology occasionally receives from critical scholars can be exemplified by how critical scholars view psychological contributions in the field of organisational psychology. The argument taken from Mcdonald and Bubna-Litic (2012) is illuminating:

> The adherence to an individualistic ontology (e.g. Thompson, 2003, p. 1) effectively separates the individual worker from their organisational and social context. Its singular emphasis on the individual locates the social inside the workers mind (Burr, 2002; Moscovici, 1972), effectively delegitimizing the historical, social, cultural, political, and economic forces that influence and shape organisational behaviour.

Two claims made in the passage deserve scrutiny as they incorrectly interpret (applied) psychological understanding of organisational psychology. The fallacies of the criticism also seem applicable to explaining why psychological theories are often misinterpreted and psychological approaches to PR are dismissed as less relevant. The first claim is incorrect, and the second assertion effectively operates as an implicature.

Organisational psychology, underpinned by social psychological theories, does not separate the worker from context. The multiple definitions of social psychology discussed in this chapter provide evidence contrary to Mcdonald and Bubna-Litic (2012). Social psychology is precisely focused on understanding human behaviour in its social context, comprehensively appreciating multiple social factors: other people, groups, language, and various forms of social influence. It is not only the classical theory of social learning (Bandura, 1977) that now explains human behaviour as a joint influence of the experience of observing significant others (family, peers, notable groups), as well as culture and society. More recent theories of social cognitive psychology (Bandura, 1989), situated social cognition (Smith & Semin, 2007), situated person (Mischel & Shoda, 2010), and mind in context (Mesquita et al., 2010) are far from neglecting external influences on human thought and action and have done the job in quite the opposite direction. As a result, a distorted picture of psychology and its application to PR may emerge: a discipline being ignorant and self-absorbed. The second assertion of an outwardly incorrect nature would be equally difficult to defend, especially when the argument was to be examined logically. First, to state the obvious, extant research and theoretical evidence in psychology emphasise social, cultural, and economic conditions to explain human action, and the works cited earlier provide evidence for this. Although psychology rarely investigates factors that are labelled as historical, a conclusion cannot follow that it ignores historical factors – processes of social learning (that may include historical facts) and memory, knowledge and knowledge availability (about history or experience) in the processes of judgement formation and decision-making have been central to social psychological thought for at least four decades (Kruglanski et al., 2018). Psychology fully appreciates historical, economic, and political factors, also in organisational context. Secondly, logically, the absence of specific thematic cues in specific writings is evidence for delegitimising them. Considering plausible explanations of misreading applied psychology by critical scholars, one more line of inquiry could be entertained. It could be argued that critical scholars can operate on a more indirect level of argumentation and evidence, following their established habits when exploring psychological work that leads to confusion. It would seem that modern psychological scientific writing and evidence take a more literal form. Meanings seem to be more explicit than implied. When psychologists focus on one level of analysis –micro – it does not undermine phenomena from other levels: class, race, society, or power. Equally, neither does it provide evidence for their importance (or unimportance). Focus on one level of analysis does not legitimise or delegitimise other potential sources of influence.

Another line of criticism can be found when Mcdonald and Bubna-Litic (2012) write that occupational psychology 'ignores significant workplace phenomena such as unions and the power relations that exist between workers and owner managers' and that 'the questions of mainstream applied social psychologists is not whether modes of authority and the structures that maintain them are fair and equitable' (Mcdonald & Bubna-Litic, 2012, p. 856). This is precisely correct and not necessarily a bad thing that psychology has never aspired to investigate phenomena that do not occur naturally. What psychology is interested in is how power is individually experienced, what the concept of power may be mentally linked to, and what the implications of experiencing power or abusing it may be. In this sense, psychology is not ignorant – it simply leaves the space for moral interpretations and prescriptive explanations of societal dynamics to be explored by sociology and philosophy. This apparent lack of understanding of how disciplines from different levels could complement each other is quite pervasive. Mcdonald and Bubna-Litic (2012) elaborate as follows: 'Issues related to historical, social, political and economic forces are viewed as the domain of sociologists, political scientists, and economists (Thompson, 2003, p. 2); this is despite their significant influence on the day-to-day social and psychological experience of work for many workers (e.g. Bourdieu, 1998; Gorz, 1999; McDonald, Wearing, & Ponting, 2008; Sennett, 1998)'. In response to the argument, we can conclude that by saying that certain phenomena (e.g. economic forces) are investigated by sociology and not psychology should not be considered a sign of ignorance or disregard. I believe it is quite the opposite – leaving those phenomena to be investigated by more suitable disciplines and methodologies suggests openness to discussion and appreciation of a multi-level investigation requirement in the pursuit of understanding human behaviour.

There are also benefits to the existing criticism of applied psychology, which can be beneficial for the development of practice and theory in PR. In my view, when a critical line of inquiry was discovered for PR scholarship, PR underwent a paradigm shift, which led to emphasising the importance of macro-level phenomena as important factors PR should take accountability for. What followed was equipping PR with methods and tools for investigating causal relationships between PR activities and societal-level phenomena. One good source of those tools would be psychology, with its vast repertoire of quantitative methods and statistical techniques. With them, producing credible evidence of relationships between public relations activities and societal-level outcomes would be possible. Instead, criticism of meso-level PR theory emerged, whereby, for example, Grunig's excellence theory does not address societal-level problems and is overly focused on organisational goals. This kind of criticism typically involves arguments misconstrued similarly to Mcdonald and Bubna-Litic (2012) and can be refuted very briefly: treating PR as a management function should not mean that PR does not impact society.

So far, the history of psychology has been discussed through the lens of interdisciplinary discussions, occasional tensions, and turf wars. Moving away from the theoretical realm, psychology, like any other scholarly field, is interested in building a dialogue with lay audiences and promoting positive societal change. Psychology may be particularly well-suited for these efforts: the subject of psychology is relevant to all people. The science of social psychology is also a history of changes in folk understanding of what social psychology is and what its findings mean for lay members of the public. In the case of psychology, it may lead to miscommunicating findings and misunderstandings. Unlike other disciplines of science (e.g. medicine or physics), many people would call themselves 'good psychologists' despite lacking knowledge and relevant training.

Psychology in the Popular Mind

Although there is nothing more practical than a good theory, the term *theory* can be understood differently within academia and outside of it. For academics, a theory can be defined 'as a system of constructs and variables in which the constructs are related to each other by propositions and the variables are related to each other by hypotheses. The whole system is bounded by the theorist's assumptions' (Bacharach, 1989, p. 498). The appeal of the word *theory* can be much different to practitioners, as well as to lay audiences. Theories can be viewed as abstract and, hence, not practical or even vague. As a consequence, practice is often juxtaposed with theory to indicate the detachment of academic work from the 'real world'. While this is not true, and any proper theory has, in fact, a direct value for explaining physical as well as social phenomena, theoretical findings typically need 'help': when it comes to communicating them effectively and ensuring they impact important decisions of policymakers or members of the society. Something interesting happens when select scientific findings cross the invisible barrier between theory and practice and gain popular support. While several factors may contribute to successful science communication, one of them is relevance. Much like in marketing, when an eminent popular need is addressed, a scientific theory gains a different meaning and becomes evidence of its credibility.

In the history of psychology, some 'psychological' ideas are particularly problematic.[1] Some scientific findings seem to have the potential to gain attention from the general public more than others, and this happens especially when science is said to provide quick solutions to issues of universal importance. Wellbeing of children is one of them. Famously, in the US, one Georgia governor wanted to add a CD or cassette tape with classical music to a goodies bag for mothers with the aim of stimulating the brain development of infants ("Georgia's Governor Seeks Musical Start for Babies," 1998). His motivation was based on a famous paper suggesting that listening to classical music can positively impact spatial reasoning skills (Rauscher et al., 1993). Although the Mozart effect is controversial and the impact of classical music on reasoning is very limited and constrained in time (Jenkins, 2001), the idea that a simple activity of listening to classical music can impact children's intelligence captivated many hearts at the beginning of the 21st century. In the popular discourse, psychology seems to be shrined in mystery, and whenever a new discovery 'uncovers' a hidden factor influencing human actions, it has the potential to attract attention.

Historically, the fight for gaining popular attention for their achievements has probably accompanied most psychologists, who wanted to make a positive change with their ideas. The name of Sigmund Freud is probably the one that is associated with psychology most easily, and his work on unconscious thought has changed the way we think about human motivations and the role of past experience in shaping human actions. However, from the contemporary, scientific psychological perspective, psychoanalysis is deemed unscientific and considered a pseudoscience (Cioffi, 1998; Eysenck, 2018; MacMillan, 1997; Webster, 1995). Although supporters of Freud's psychoanalysis do exist today (e.g. Mitchell & Black, 2016), more scientifically oriented scholars generally find three problems with psychoanalysis: its testability, falsifiability, and methodology. In essence, theoretically, it is impossible to design a methodological approach that would test and falsify Freud's predictions. Also, one of the major weaknesses of Freud's idea is the assumed objective nature of a psychoanalyst and observation-theory dichotomy (e.g. implied in psychoanalysis). Information gathered during therapy is never pure or separate from the observer's (psychoanalyst's) interpretation. Consequently, a therapist is not able to interpret their patient in separation from their own 'theory'-driven expectations or frames.

Freud's example is illuminating as it also signals some of the problems academia suffers from to this day. The pursuit of knowledge and truth is (fortunately) occasionally accompanied by self-esteem and success motivations, which can obscure scholars' achievements. The motivations of those working in science do not seem to be selfish; however, the pursuit of truth is only fully realised when scientific discoveries can be implemented for the benefit of the public. However, to achieve that, scientific discovery must go a long and arduous way from academia to the popular discourse. On this journey, scholars not only need to communicate the truth accurately but also demonstrate the relevance of their work to lay audiences. In the process of translating the often complex and hermetic language of science, simplifications and errors occur. Audiences typically need straightforward answers to complex problems, and this is when science communication can go wrong. Regardless of the criticism of Freud's ideas, as a person, he can be considered a brilliant marketer (Gellner, 1985) and, by some, called a propaganda genius (Eysenck, 2018). Part of the problem with Freud's idea, however, is not only the theory's failure to meet the standards of modern science. Freud is also said to have falsified some of his significant findings, most notably the account of his discovery of the Oedipus complex (Cioffi, 1998). Although Freud believed that he laid the foundation of psychology, and his work should be appreciated from a historical perspective, Freudian psychoanalysis should not be considered the historical heritage of modern scientific psychology. In fact, as explained by Tavris (2003), psychoanalysis and empirical psychology never managed to complement one another, and when it first became popular in 1920, scientific psychologists regarded psychoanalysis as a 'popular craze' (p. xiv). In summary, today, psychoanalysis has the status of pseudo theory, and its links with PR can only be considered as inspiration for Bernays' interest in the human mind, as well as a promotional wagon that helped Bernays attract clients.[2]

Unfortunately, ideas that gain popularity among the general public are rarely the ones that have good scientific backing. Much like the folk medicine's snake oil potions, believed to cure various diseases between the 18th and 20th centuries, folk psychology also had its inventions offering rapid solutions to a multitude of mental problems throughout the 20th century. To some extent, organisational practice and marketing have been affected by similar psychology-related problems. For example, HR is still being incentivised to use projective tests (Carter et al., 2013; Janetius et al., 2019), despite their use being associated with considerable validity and reliability issues (Hunsley et al., 2015). To put the problem succinctly, interpreting an ink-formed shape is not a reliable measure or predictor of an employee's success at work, as no evidence exists to support it. In fact, the validity of all personality tests in predicting job performance has been called into question (Morgeson et al., 2007). The semi-mysterious lure of a psychological component is also evident in one famous marketing hoax invented by Vicary in the 1950s. As a market researcher himself, Vicary claimed that presenting visual stimuli ('Drink Coca-Cola' and 'Eat popcorn') for a brief period so that consumers would not consciously register them would lead to increased sales

(Pratkanis, 1992). Although the concept of subliminal advertising has been criticised, and only partially supportive evidence has been produced to suggest the impact of subliminal primes on consumers only when they have an unsatisfied need consistent with the prime (Karremans et al., 2006), the appeal of hidden influences on human decisions seems to be continually appealing. The problematic reputation of psychology as a science of hidden forces, offering shortcuts to success, continues to permeate the first three decades of the new millennium. Today, especially on social media, pseudo-psychological approaches and advice are presented as psychological promises to change life if a person 'manifests' wealth as if a simple act of thinking about a goal magically led to its attainment. Unfortunately, academia is not entirely free from dark deeds (and neither of minor demeanours), and occasionally, the temptation to achieve status or power wins out among academics. This can put in question the validity even of some of the most famous psychological experiments.

In the second half of the 20th century, misreporting or omission errors occurred, especially when psychological findings had the potential to alter perceptions of human nature or provide simple explanations for pressing issues. Zimbardo's 1972 prison study is a notable example of capturing public attention, as it posited that every human being is capable of committing acts of violence and evil. In the original experiment, Zimbardo recruited participants for a study – a simulation of a prison environment – in which he randomly assigned participants to roles of guards and prisoners (Zimbardo, 2008). The experiment was designed to analyse group identity processes, authority, and powerlessness. Famously, it had to be terminated after six days, and striking findings stirred public opinion. Every person is capable of evil, abuse, and dehumanising behaviour, which can be instigated when specific circumstances arise. Previous evidence had already suggested methodological flaws in the study's setup and subtle omissions in the reporting of the experimental procedure. For example, recruitment to the experiment can be considered problematic because the advertisements in the Palo Alto Times and Stanford Daily partially revealed the scope. The ad read: 'Male college students needed for psychological study of prison life. $15 per day for 1–2 weeks beginning August 14[...]'. Therefore, those who agreed to participate could exhibit sensation-seeking behaviours prior to the experiment, so they should not be considered typical or average representatives of the population, and their motivation was not just to make money (Zimbardo, 1972), which can imply self-selection bias (Carnahan & McFarland, 2007). Subsequent BBC study – a replication of the experiment conducted by Haslam and Reicher (Haslam & Reicher, 2006, 2012), already cast doubt on the nature of Zimbardo's original findings and led to a joint statement from Zimbardo, Haslam, and Richer which explained that behaviours observed in both experiments: 'were a function of many factors, including roles, norms, leadership, social identification, group pressure, and individual differences, not all of which are necessarily mutually exclusive. It is only natural that explanations of social behaviour will be complex and multifactorial' (Haney et al., 2018). More worryingly, a recent analysis of the archive material and interviews with participants conducted by Le Texier (2019) uncovered additional evidence of training and instructions given to 'guards' in the experiment, as well as a lack of realism, which suggests that prisoners – contrary to Zimbardo reporting – never fully immersed in the prison simulation (e.g. noises of photocopiers, discussions from the upper floor and ringing phones were audible). The famous Milgram experiment (Milgram, 1974), designed to study obedience orders, produced similarly disturbing evidence and, comparably, is not free from methodological criticism. In this well-known study, Milgram tested the extent to which participants who assumed the role of teachers would obey the experimenter's directions to administer an electric shock to alleged subjects ('students') when they failed to learn. The message that came from the experiment was similarly disturbing to Zimbardo's original findings: people can be extremely cruel in the presence of authority (65% of participants delivered the maximum shock). However, subsequent investigations into Milgram's study revealed that participants might have been coerced into applying electric shocks and did not fully believe in the experimental setting (Perry et al., 2020).

Even when researchers endeavour to ensure that their findings are communicated accurately and without bias, distortions and misinterpretations can still occur. Some scientific findings are intuitively insightful and novel, and as a result, they are trusted by the general public and desired by professionals for financial gain. Popular culture, for instance, is replete with the notion that non-verbal communication holds greater significance than verbal expression. When reviewing LinkedIn profiles of social skills trainers, it remains evident that a significant proportion assert that body language constitutes 70%, 80%, or occasionally even 90% of effective communication. However, this is not the case. In the 1990s, the use of formulae in Hollywood movies was very prevalent, particularly in business-related scenes. These formulae allocated 10% of the weight to the verbal channel and 90% to non-verbal cues, focusing on the importance of persuasive non-verbal skills in business environments. However, this formula, which appears to be scientifically sound, is the result of a misreading of two research papers published in the 1960s (Mehrabian & Ferris, 1967; Mehrabian & Wiener, 1967). Findings reported in the two publications were selectively used by soft skills trainers interested in making a profit from teaching non-verbal communication. The author of the original research project, psychologist John Mehrabian, had originally been interested in the consequences of communication inconsistency between verbal and non-verbal cues in a specific case of forming basic attitudinal impressions about people. The design of the experiments was reasonably simple. A participant was asked about the attitude of a fictitious person (A) towards another person (B). Participants were shown messages coming from person A in the three different formats (channels): a facial expression in three versions: positive, neutral, or negative (channel 1), three groups of words: positive (honey, thanks, dear), neutral (maybe, really, oh), and negative (Don't, brute, terrible) (channel 2) and with varying tone of voice (positive, neutral, negative). Subsequently, they were instructed to disregard the tone, disregard the meaning, or consider both. The sample size of both experiments was very small, and the design involved exposing different combinations of stimuli to the same group of participants. Despite the limitations of the studies, the so-called '7-38-55' formula, which placed minimal importance on verbal communication, gained traction in popular discourse, contributing to the surge in popularity of non-verbal communication training in the 1990s and the early 2000s. Despite Mehrebian's attempts to clarify the objectives of his research and its limitations, some people still believe that only 7% of meaning is conveyed through verbal communication. For better or worse, much of psychology can be presented as a history of winning public attention.

In the context of the discussion on the role of psychology in PR, both Zimbardo's and Milgram's studies, as well as the history of the popularity of Freud's ideas, highlight a more pertinent question posed by psychology since the discipline's inception, and by philosophers for much longer. In what ways can human actions be considered free or determined, and to what extent are they a result of our actions? In the proposed politics–economy–individual triangle, the answer to the question can produce different implications for the practice of PR. Firstly, if any controllable influences on human behaviour are possible, PR should be considered a behavioural science and should operate differently by monitoring or influencing members of the public. Should external or internal constraints of the human will exist, however, changing how people think and act is not a possibility. Monitoring it, however, to understand the result would be of interest. For instance, Freud's perspective would fall somewhere along the continuum from absolute determinism (or random impulses) to absolute mathematical control of all factors affecting human actions. Freud believed that repressed thoughts could influence human behaviour and that psychoanalysis was the only way to uncover these thoughts. For comparison, behaviourism – if erroneously defined – would be located on a different part of the continuum (behaviourists used to believe that people's mental states are not necessary to understand their behaviour and are fully a function of situations; therefore, any investigation of people's attitudes would not be required). Nowadays, psychology has accepted a complex type of explanations and mechanisms of human behaviour, which are a function of mental states and situations in which they participate, as well as larger societal forces (including institutions). While this does not make the task of understanding behaviour easy, it does allow for more in-depth explanations and avoids superficial justifications.

Furthermore, it is possible to influence and change behaviours, provided that the causes of actions are established. Crucially, there is a difference between behaviourism, an approach in psychology that historically did not require knowledge of mental processes to explain human behaviour, and the adjective 'behavioural', which means related to or involving behaviour. Consistently, in this monograph, I will advance a perspective which proposes that, to some extent, the motives behind human actions can be learned and behaviours of members of publics can be altered. This implies that PR is, to a large extent, based on behavioural science and PR is a behavioural field of practice.

In conclusion, one observation that can be seen as both useful and challenging is the scope of contemporary scientific psychology, particularly its social domain. A wide range of topics within the field of social psychology has been the focus of extensive research over the past 50 years. These include information processing, knowledge formation mechanisms, judgement formation, persuasion, motivation, attitudes, stereotypes, group identity, and emotions and relationships. Despite this, a consistent psychological thought is absent from PR scholarship. The reasons for this absence that I have outlined so far could include a misunderstood definition and methods of psychology, a misplaced object of psychological investigations, tensions and competition between academic disciplines, and, from the perspective of external observers, the complicated status of social psychology, which is underpinned by three different traditions within the subdiscipline. The nature of public relations, which originated as a professional field of practice, also appears relevant in this context. Public relations, as a field of professional practice, involves building and maintaining positive relationships between organisations and their various audience members. Any theory that is going to be used in practice needs to be able to explain three levels of phenomena: audience members (micro), organisations and their stakeholders (meso), and society (macro). However, there are significant and unavoidable obstacles to this. When changes in audience members, organisations, and society occur rapidly, the scientific cycle of producing and testing theories has the difficult task of keeping up. Consequently, rather than developing a PR theory (a consistent set of premises), theoretical 'patches' are sometimes produced with the expectation of providing immediate responses to pressing industry questions and challenges. However, these patches fail to address the issues comprehensively. I suggest a different approach, which is more effective in the field: transdisciplinarity. This approach involves the use of theories, findings, and methods from different levels of analysis and integrating them carefully under the theme of achieving practical PR goals. Chapter 3 will examine the psychological contributions to PR from this perspective and identify potential synergies and current areas of overlap.

Notes

1 The word *ideas* is used here deliberately instead of *theory* to avoid confusing established scientific evidence with pseudoscientific approaches or disproven ideas that gained traction and were found to be appealing to the general public.
2 Chiefly for that reason, scarce influences of psychoanalysis on PR scholarship will not be covered in the next chapter.

References

Bacharach, S. B. (1989). Organizational theories: Some criteria for evaluation. *The Academy of Management Review*, *14*(4), 496. https://doi.org/10.2307/258555
Bandura, A. (1977). *Social Learning Theory*. Prentice-Hall.
Bandura, A. (1989). Human agency in social cognitive theory. *American Psychologist*, *44*(9). https://doi.org/10.1037/0003-066X.44.9.1175
Barrett, L. F., Mesquita, B., & Smith, E. R. (2010). *The Context Principle* In B. Mesquita, L. F. Barrett, & E. R. Smith (Eds.), The mind in context (pp. 1–22). The Guilford Press.
Barsalou, L. W. (1999). Perceptual symbol systems. *Behavioral and Brain Sciences*, *22*(4), 577–660. https://doi.org/10.1017/S0140525X99002149
Bourdieu, P. (1998). The essence of neo-liberalism. In *Le Monde diplomatique*, 4–5.
Brown, L. (1990). The culture and personality theorist's approach to societal psychology. In H. T. Himmelweit & G. Gaskell (Eds.), *Societal Psychology* (pp. 138–154). Sage Publications, Inc.
Burr, V. (2002). *The Person in Social Psychology*. Routledge.
Brysbaert, M., & Rastle, K. (2021). *Historical and Conceptual Issues in Psychology*. Pearson Education.
Carnahan, T., & McFarland, S. (2007). Bulletin personality and social psychology revisiting the Stanford prison experiment: Could participant self-selection have led to the cruelty? *Social Psychology Bulletin*, *33*, 603–614. https://doi.org/10.1177/0146167206292689
Carter, N. T., Daniels, M. A., & Zickar, M. J. (2013). Projective testing: Historical foundations and uses for human resources management. *Human Resource Management Review*, *23*(3), 205–218. https://doi.org/10.1016/J.HRMR.2012.12.002
Chmiel, M. (2024). Societal impact of Brand Public Relations on gender equality: Evidence for a mediation-type mechanism. *Corporate Communications: An International Journal*, 29(6), 796–817. https://doi.org/10.1108/CCIJ-04-2024-0059
Chmiel, M., & Moise, R. (2024). Undergraduate public relations education in the United Kingdom: Quo Vadis? *Public Relations Inquiry*, *13*(3). https://doi.org/10.1177/2046147X241230055
Cioffi, F. (1998). *Freud and the Question of Pseudoscience*. Open Court. https://www.karnacbooks.com/product/freud-and-the-question-of-pseudoscience/5310/#
Cosmides, L. (1985). *Deduction or Darwinian Algorithms? An explanation of the "elusive" Content Effect on the Wason Selection Task*. Harvard University.
Crawford, L. A., & Novak, K. B. (2024). *Individual and Society: Sociological Social Psychology* (3rd ed.). Routledge.
Crisp, R. J., Turner, R. N., & Meleady, Rose. (2024). *Essential Social Psychology*. Sage Publications.
Deutsch, M. (1990). Forms of social organization. Psychological consequences. In H. T. Himmelweit & G. Gaskell (Eds.), *Societal Psychology* (pp. 157–176). Sage Publications.

Doise, W. (1990). Individual cognitive functioning: societal aspects. In H. T. Himmelweit & G. Gaskell (Eds.), *Societal Psychology* (pp. 92–111). Sage Publications, Inc.
Duckitt, J., Wagner, C., Du Plessis, I., & Birum, I. (2002). The psychological bases of ideology and prejudice: Testing a dual process model. *Journal of Personality and Social Psychology*, *83*(1), 75–93. https://doi.org/10.1037/0022-3514.83.1.75
Eagly, A. H., Eaton, A., Rose, S. M., Riger, S., & McHugh, M. C. (2012). Feminism and psychology: analysis of a half-century of research on women and gender. *The American Psychologist*, *67*(3), 211–230. https://doi.org/10.1037/A0027260
Eysenck, H. (2018). Decline and fall of the freudian empire. Routledge. https://doi.org/10.4324/9780203793688
Festinger, L. (1954). A theory of social comparison processes. *Human Relations*, *7*(2). https://doi.org/10.1177/001872675400700202
Gellner, E. (1985). *The Psychoanalytic Movement: The Cunning of Unreason*. Paladin.
Georgia's Governor Seeks Musical Start for Babies. (1998, January 15). The New York Times. https://www.nytimes.com/1998/01/15/us/georgia-s-governor-seeks-musical-start-for-babies.html?pagewanted=1?pagewanted=1
Good, J. M. M. (2022). Social psychology: Exemplary interdiscipline or subdiscipline. In D. McCallum (Ed.), *The Palgrave Handbook of the History of Human Sciences* (pp. 1005–1034). https://doi.org/10.1007/978-981-16-7255-2_78
Gorz, A. (1999). *Reclaiming Work: Beyond the Wage-Based Society* (C. Turner, Trans.). Polity Press.
Haney, C., Haslam, A., Reicher, S., & Zimbardo, P. (2018). *Consensus Statement on the Stanford Prison Experiment and BBC Prison Study*. https://www.researchgate.net/profile/Craig-Haney/publication/328826436_Dealing_with_toxic_behavior/links/66d9b07d2390e50b2c5415d2/Dealing-with-toxic-behavior.pd
Haslam, S. A., & Reicher, S. (2006). Stressing the group: Social identity and the unfolding dynamics of responses to stress. *Journal of Applied Psychology*, *91*(5), 1037–1052. https://doi.org/10.1037/0021-9010.91.5.1037
Haslam, S. A., & Reicher, S. D. (2012). When prisoners take over the prison. *Personality and Social Psychology Review*, *16*(2), 154–179. https://doi.org/10.1177/1088868311419864
Himmelweit, H. T. (1990). Societal Psychology: Implications and scope. In H. T. Himmelweit & G. Gaskell (Eds.), *Societal Psychology* (pp. 17–45). Sage Publications, Inc.
Himmelweit, H. T., & Gaskell, G. (Eds.). (1990). *Societal Psychology*. Sage Publications, Inc.
Hodgetts, D., Drew, N., Sonn, C., Stolte, O., Waimarie Nikora, L., & Curtis, C. (2010). *Social Psychology and Everyday Life*. Palgrave Macmillan.
House, J. S. (1977). The three faces of social psychology. *Sociometry*, *40*(2), 177. https://doi.org/10.2307/3033519
Hovland, C. I., Janis, I. L., & Kelly, H. H. (1953). *Communication and Persuasion*. Yale University Press.
Howarth, C., Campbell, C., Cornish, F., Franks, B., Garcia-Lorenzo, L., Gillespie, A., Gleibs, I., Goncalves-Portelinha, I., Jovchelovitch, S., Lahlou, S., Mannell, J., Reader, T., & Tennant, C. (2013). Insights from societal psychology: The contextual politics of change. *Journal of Social and Political Psychology*, *1*(1), 364–384. https://doi.org/10.5964/jspp.v1i1.64
Howitt, D. (1991). *Concerning Psychology: Psychology applied to social issues*. Open University Press.
Hunsley, J., Lee, M. C., Wood, J. M., & Taylor, W. (2015). Controversial and Questionable assessment techniques. In S. O. Lilienfeld, S. Jay Lynn, & M. J. Lohr (Eds.), *Science and Pseudoscience in Clinical Psychology* (2nd ed., pp. 83–112). Guilford Press.

Janetius, S. T., Pooja, V., & Shilpa, S. (2019). Projective tests in human resource management and hiring process: a challenge and a boon. *The International Journal of Indian Psychology*, *7*(4), 259–265.
Jenkins, J. S. (2001). The Mozart effect. *Journal of the Royal Society of Medicine*, *94*(4), 170. https://doi.org/10.1177/014107680109400404
Karremans, J. C., Stroebe, W., & Claus, J. (2006). Beyond Vicary's fantasies: The impact of subliminal priming and brand choice. *Journal of Experimental Social Psychology*, *42*(6), 792–798. https://doi.org/10.1016/J.JESP.2005.12.002
Katz, D. (1960). The functional approach to the study of attitudes. *Public Opinion Quarterly*, *24*(2). https://doi.org/10.1086/266945
Klempe, S. H. (2020). The origin of psychology in the humanities. *Oxford Research Encyclopedia of Psychology*. https://doi.org/10.1093/ACREFORE/9780190236557.013.473
Kruglanski, A. W., Dechesne, M., Orehek, E., & Pierro, A. (2018). Three decades of lay epistemics: The why, how, and who of knowledge formation. In A. Kruglanski (Ed.), *The Motivated Mind: The Selected Works of Arie Kruglanski* (pp. 19–59). Routledge.
Le Texier, T. (2019). Debunking the Stanford prison experiment. *The American Psychologist*, *74*(7), 823–839. https://doi.org/10.1037/AMP0000401
MacMillan, M. (1997). *Freud Evaluated: The Completed Arc*. The MIT Press.
Markus, G. B. (1979). The political environment and the dynamics of public attitudes: A panel study. *American Journal of Political Science*, *23*(2). https://doi.org/10.2307/2111006
Mcdonald, M., & Bubna-Litic, D. (2012). Applied social psychology: A critical theoretical perspective. *Social and Personality Psychology Compass*, *12*(6), 853–864. https://doi.org/10.1111/spc3.12004
McDonald, M., Wearing, S., & Ponting, J. (2008). Narcissism and neo-liberalism: Work, leisure and alienation in an era of consumption. *Loisir et Societe (Society and Leisure)*, *30*, 489–510.
McDougall, W. (1919). *An Introduction to Social Psychology* (14th ed.). Methuen & Co. Ltd.
Mead, G. H. (1934). *Mind, Self and Society*. University of Chicago Press.
Mehrabian, A., & Ferris, S. R. (1967). Inference of attitudes from nonverbal communication in two channels. *Journal of Consulting Psychology*, *31*(3), 248–252. https://doi.org/10.1037/h0024648
Mehrabian, A., & Wiener, M. (1967). Decoding of inconsistent communications. *Journal of Personality and Social Psychology*, *6*(1), 109–114. https://doi.org/10.1037/h0024532
Mesquita, B., Barrett, L. F., & Smith, E. R. (2010). *The Mind in Context*. The Guilford Press.
Michaels, J. W., & Green, D. S. (1978). Behavioral sociology: Emergent forms and issues. *The American Sociologist*, *13*(1), 23–29.
Milgram, S. (1974). *Obedience to Authority: an Experimental View*. Harper & Row, Publishers.
Mischel, W., & Shoda, Y. (2010). The situated person. In B. Mesquita, L. F. Barrett, & E. R. Smith (Eds.), *The Mind in Context* (pp. 149–173). The Guilford Press.
Mitchell, S. A., & Black, M. J. (2016). *Freud and Beyond: A History of Modern Psychoanalytic Thought*. Basic Books, a member of the Perseus Books Group.
Morgeson, F. P., Campion, M. A., Dipboye, R. L., Hollenbeck, J. R., Murphy, K., & Schmitt, N. (2007). Reconsidering the use of personality tests in personnel selection contexts. *Personnel Psychology*, *60*(3), 683–729. https://doi.org/10.1111/j.1744-6570.2007.00089.x
Moscovici, S. (1972). Society and theory in social psychology. In J. Israel & H. Tajfel (Eds.), *The Context of Social Psychology* (pp. 17–68). Academic Press.

Moscovici, S. (1990). The generalised self and mass society. In H. T. Himmelweit & G. Gaskell (Eds.), *Societal Psychology* (pp. 66–91). Sage Publications, Inc.
Perry, G., Brannigan, A., Wanner, R. A., & Stam, H. (2020). Credibility and Incredulity in Milgram's Obedience Experiments: A Reanalysis of an Unpublished Test. *Social Psychology Quarterly*, *83*(1), 88–106.
Piaget, J. (1926). *Language and thought of the Child*. Routledge.
Pratkanis, A. R. (1992). The cargo-cult science of subliminal persuasion. *Skeptical Inquirer*, *16*, 260–272.
Pratkanis, A. R. (2007). *The Science of Social Influence: Advances and Future Progress*. Psychology Press.
Rauscher, F. H., Shaw, G. L., & Ky, C. N. (1993). Music and spatial task performance. *Nature*, *365*(6447), 611–611. https://doi.org/10.1038/365611a0
Ritzer, G. (1975). *Sociology: A Multiple Paradigm Science*. Allyn and Bacon.
Scharbert, J., Humberg, S., Kroencke, L., Reiter, T., Sakel, S., Ter Horst, J., Utesch, K., Gosling, S. D., Harari, G., Matz, S. C., Schoedel, R., Stachl, C., Aguilar, N. M. A., Amante, D., Aquino, S. D., Bastias, F., Bornamanesh, A., Bracegirdle, C., Campos, L. A. M., … Back, M. D. (2024). Psychological well-being in Europe after the outbreak of war in Ukraine. *Nature Communications*, *15*(1), 1–12. https://doi.org/10.1038/s41467-024-44693-6
Schwarz, N. (2010). Meaning in context: Metacognitive experiences. In B. Mesquita, L. F. Barrett, & E. R. Smith (Eds.), *The Mind in Context* (pp. 105–125). The Guilford Press. https://psycnet.apa.org/record/2010-09987-006
Sennett, R. (1998). *The Corrosion of Character: The Personal Consequences of Work in the New Capitalism*. Norton.
Smith, E. R., & Semin, G. R. (2004). Socially situated cognition: Cognition in its social context. *Advances in Experimental Social Psychology*, *36*, 53–117. https://doi.org/10.1016/S0065-2601(04)36002-8
Smith, E. R., & Semin, G. R. (2007). Situated social cognition. *Current Directions in Psychological Science*, *16*(3), 132–135. https://doi.org/10.1111/J.1467-8721.2007.00490.X
Stolte, J. F., Fine, G. A., & Cook, K. S. (2001). Sociological miniaturism: Seeing the big through the small in social psychology. *Annual Review of Sociology*, *27*, 387–413.
Strümpel, B. (1990). Macroeconomic processes and societal psychology. In H. T. Himmelweit & G. Gaskell (Eds.), *Societal Psychology* (pp. 193–211). Sage Publications, Inc.
Sutton, R., & Douglas, K. (2013). *Social Psychology*. Red Globe Press.
Tavris, C. (2003). The widening scientist-practitioner gap: A view from the bridge. In S. O. Lilienfeld, S. J. Lynn, & J. M. Lohr (Eds.), *Science and Pseudoscience in Clinical Psychology* (pp. ix–xvii). Guilford Press.
Thompson, L. L. (2003). Organizational behavior: A micro perspective. In L. L. Thompson (Ed.), *The Social Psychology of Organizational Behavior: Key Readings* (pp. 1–6). Psychology Press.
Vallacher, R. R., & Gollwitzer, P. M.. (2025). *Social Psychology: Exploring the Dynamics of Human Experience*. Routledge. https://www.routledge.com/Social-Psychology-Exploring-the-Dynamics-of-Human-Experience/Vallacher-Gollwitzer/p/book/9781032553269
Van Bavel, J. J., Cichocka, A., Capraro, V., Sjåstad, H., Nezlek, J. B., Pavlović, T., Alfano, M., Gelfand, M. J., Azevedo, F., Birtel, M. D., Cislak, A., Lockwood, P. L., Ross, R. M., Abts, K., Agadullina, E., Aruta, J. J. B., Besharati, S. N., Bor, A., Choma, B. L., … Boggio, P. S. (2022). National identity predicts public health support during a global pandemic. *Nature Communications*, *13*(1), 1–14. https://doi.org/10.1038/s41467-021-27668-9
Van Biervliet, J. J. (1892). La psychologic experimentale: L'Institut de M. Wundt a Leipzig [Experimental psychology: Wundt's Institute at Leipzig]. *Revue de l'Instruction Publique (Superieure et Moyenne) en Belgique*, *35*, 177–192.

Watson, T., & Wright, D. K. (2011). History and development of public relations education in North America: A critical analysis. *Journal of Communication Management*, *15*(3), 236–255. https://doi.org/10.1108/13632541111151005
Webster, R. (1995). *Why Freud Was Wrong: Sin, Science and Psychoanalysis*. HarperCollins.
Zimbardo, P. G. (1972). Pathology of Imprisonment. *Society*, *9*(6), 4–8.
Zimbardo, P. G. (2008). *The Lucifer Effect: How Good People Turn Evil* (22nd ed.). Rider.

3

THE PAST

Historical Heritage of Psychology in PR

The Origins of Psychology in PR

Edward Bernays was clearly under the influence of the new science of psychology, specifically the position of the individual:

> Public relations covers the relations of a man, institution, idea, with its publics. Any efficient attempt to improve these relations depends on our understanding of the behavioral sciences and applying them-sociology, social psychology, anthropology, history, etc. The social sciences are the foundation of public relations. If the behavioral sciences have made any contribution to our knowledge of behavior, it is obvious that a knowledge of them is basic to a consultant.
>
> *(Bernays, 1986, p. 2)*

He also seems to have been proud of his ability to integrate it with his work as a publicist and press agent. In his memoir, he considered himself a social scientist who employed 'psychology, sociology, psychological sociology and sociological physiology' for the benefit of his clients (Bernays, 1965, p. 86) and appeared to be particularly flattered when others appreciated him for using psychological insights. The title of the interview, which was published in Musical America in 1917, read: 'How the Press Agent Creates Music Lovers. Psychology as a Working Basis' and Bernays explained that 'a press agent must regard his calling as an art and a science, a science in that it employs the elementary laws of psychology' (Bernays, 1965, p. 92). Bernays treated both Public Relations and psychology as relatively new fields ('psychology was just a word', p. 157), and he saw the role of both as elements of

DOI: 10.4324/9781003610403-3

progress that played their part in advancing democracy and making everyday life fairer. The influence could come not only from being a double nephew of Sigmund Freud but also from Edward Titchener, one of the founding fathers of American psychology, his university lecturer at Cornell. His enduring respect for psychology is also evident in his note of the educational background of his son-in-law, Richard Held, who, after obtaining a PhD at Harvard, became a professor of experimental psychology at MIT.

Bernays' memoir is rich in references to psychology and its 'basic laws', which he argued should provide a greater understanding of the American mind. It is interesting to see Bernays' use of the word psychology as a key to capturing the spirit of the contemporary audience members: dealing with the consequences of depression, the rise of divisions and racism, (ethnic) in-group identification, the consequences of rumours, and the encroachment of fascism. American psychology could, for example, explain 'mores and thought patterns' and 'arrogant disposition to do things their own way' (Bernays, 1965, p. 730). He criticised hate in the media as it 'expose individuals who might otherwise not have been exposed to the disease [hate] and in that way inoculates them and broadens the field of the disease and its incidence' and argued that 'not seeking out haters for public platform is not suppression of free speech but good judgment and sense in the interests of preserving our democracy' (Bernays, 1965, p. 688). In essence, Bernays' psychology involved understanding what audience members needed, what they feared, and how they attributed success and failure in their personal lives – very much in tune with the contemporary definition of psychology, which is simply about understanding human behaviour.

The role of psychology in the development of the practice of PR is evident in Bernays' definition of a key aspect of his professional activities: gauging and changing the attitudes of audiences. His wartime work for the Committee on Public Information (CPI) in 1918 and the campaign for Lithuania's independence, funded by the Lithuanian National Council, led him to realise that the arts and entertainment industry was not the only domain where clients could benefit from his talents. In an interview reported in Cutlip (1994), Bernays remembered that 'efforts comparable to those applied by the CPI to affect the attitudes of the enemy, of neutrals, and people of this country could be applied with equal facility to peacetime pursuits' (Cutlip, 1994, p. 168). Interestingly, in 1919, when Bernays pursued the interests of his first post-World War I clients, his work was more applied psychology than that of PR. He later recalled that he was not familiar with the term *public relations* at that time, and he was not aware of Ivy Lee's work. Bernays considered the term *publicity* to be too vague. In his terms, he described his then-current activity as 'publicity direction' and defined it as 'directing the actions of a client to result in the desired publicity' (Bernays, 1965, p. 288). After introducing the term public relations, he emphasised its interactive and dynamic character and juxtaposed it with one-way persuasion associated with press agentry and publicity. The psychological and attitude-centred aspects of his actions were at the core of his professional journey early on from his press agentry work for entertainment clients when he 'tried to evaluate [his] audience by hunch and insight' and 'determined people's economic status by looking at them' (Bernays, 1965, p. 402). When recalling numerous case studies from his rich career, the initial attitudes – towards an organisation, a brand, a person, an idea, or a country – are the reference point around which his public relations counsel activities are strategised. Quite early, he recognised the problems brought by misuse or incorrect research of attitudes, especially in the 1940s, and the impact of polls that shaped public opinion but were based on misinterpreted data.

Although it is somewhat evident that, for Bernays, studying psychology was essential to becoming good at PR or succeeding as a publicist, his reliance on psychology was neither absolute, nor was psychology expected to provide a solution to all the problems faced by Americans of the era. Bernays' psychology was used not only as a means to an end but also as a promotional vehicle for his business. The use of psychology in his writings seems to have an evocative function. Psychology is a science, but it is also a mystery that only a few wise counsellors can use. Whether Bernays viewed psychology as an exact science or not is difficult to determine. On the one hand, he declared that psychology is a field of science and can provide insights into the mechanisms of human behaviour. On the other hand, however, he thought that psychology could not account for all explanations of human behaviour because of the multitude of factors that influence behaviour that were beyond propagandists' control (today, we would say that the number of variables that affect human judgement and behaviour is beyond control or impossible to monitor).

Regardless of the above, Bernays should be credited for many observations that appreciated the role of psychology in explaining human behaviour, as well as for identifying principles that are valid today. First, he appreciated the need for novel information and news: 'In popular psychology it has come to be a crying primal want of the mind, like hunger of the body' (Bernays, 1923, p. 180). He criticised behaviourists and saw the human mind as something more than merely an individual machine, 'a system of nerves and nerve centers, reacting with mechanical regularity to stimuli, like a helpless, will-less automaton' (Bernays, 1928, p. 53). Related to that, he saw the impact of unconscious processes: 'Men are rarely aware of the real reasons which motivate their actions' (Bernays, 1928, p. 51), although the sources of unconscious action are understood differently by contemporary scientific psychological approaches: 'A thing may be desired not for its intrinsic worth or usefulness, but because he has unconsciously come to see in it a symbol of something else, the desire for which he is ashamed to admit to himself'

(Bernays, 1928, p. 52). Some of his advice would fit very well with the contemporary concepts of latitude acceptance and latitude of rejection of the Social Judgment Theory (Sherif & Hovland, 1961): 'A fundamental study of group and individual psychology is required before the public relations counsel can determine how readily individuals or groups will accept modifications of viewpoints or policies, which they have already imposed upon their respective mediums' (Bernays, 1923, p. 97). Much of his work seems to be based on the normative social influence and laid the foundations for the modern idea of influencers: 'mind retains the patterns which have been stamped on it by the group influences' (Bernays, 1923, p. 49).

In line with his universal insights, he also held views that have not stood the test of time. Idealistically, Bernays expected that there were matters about which ordinary men should not have an opinion ('the training and experience of no average man can qualify him to have any opinion upon them at all' (Bernays, 1923, p. 64). In fact, people can have opinions about anything – just like they can have attitudes towards any topic. It is, however, a different type of problem whether opinions (or attitudes) about matters requiring scientific judgement should not compete for attention (consider a difference between having an opinion about the safety of vaccination versus using an average man's opinion to decide whether to introduce vaccination or not. Someone's lay opinion should not be used as evidence. However, people are entitled to have them (in fact, it is partly the responsibility of a PR professional to be able to mould such opinions in a direction congruent with the scientific consensus).

Ivy Lee could be seen as a counteract to Bernays. While Bernays was influenced by Freud's psychoanalysis and the role of the unconscious, Lee's ideas seem more in line with the thinking of behaviourists. An even more vigorous opposition between reason and emotions than in Bernays's view of the crowd can be found in Ivy Lee's writings:

> Reason, we are told, developed late in the structure of the human animal. It is still woefully feeble and untrustworthy because of its habit of abdicating to the passions. The emotions, on the other hand, are built on the foundation of primitive man's earliest responses. They are powerful, but they, too, are untrustworthy because they are so easily swayed, because they are changeable, and because, being powerful, they can only be excited for a comparatively short time.
>
> *(Lee & St John III, 2017)*

Parallel to the opposition between reason (rational thought) and emotion, another division was implied by Lee: between the individual and the crowd. This is interesting as the outcome of the crowd was derationalising individuals and making them animal instinct-driven creatures ('It is unanimously agreed that the crowd debases the individually mentally and excites him emotionally' (Lee & St John III, 2017)). In support of this, Lee explained Lippmann's (1922) understanding of public opinion as being driven by reason as long as emotions were not interfering. The emotions of the crowds could make a publicist's job difficult, as they impeded control: crowds could become bloodthirsty, hysterical, and driven by fear. Viewing Lee's and Bernays' approaches to PR, a subtle distinction between two competing schools of psychological thought could be made. While for Bernays, it was the psychoanalytical unconscious (repressed, unrealised) that constituted the psychological aspect of the profession, for Lee, it would be behaviourism. To explain how Napoleon III altered the perception of himself and Napoleon I, Lee employs the behaviourist term 'conditioning' to describe communication tactics aimed at changing public views.

Ironically, reading Bernays' early views on the role of psychology occasionally elucidates more of a sociological rather than psychological approach, and this is supported by the choice of thinkers that influenced Bernays: Trotter, Le Bon, Wallas, and Lippmann. Bernays also considered a group of people as having different mental characteristics from an individual. While this idea might have been accurate in the 1920s, today, psychology does not subscribe to this view. Although several effects can account for the change in behaviour of individuals when other people are present, for example, systematic biases exist to explain errors made by groups, a group mind today is – at best – a metaphor that describes what happens when people jointly deliberate on issues rather than a real object – an entity that emerges, when people are gathered around a common goal. This is perhaps why Bernays referred to mass psychology as the discipline best suited to aid propagandists in their efforts to manipulate public opinion. Some of Bernays' observations about human nature have remained valid; however, psychology has provided alternative explanations for others. Despite the understandable limitations in his understanding of human psychology, which align with historical scientific accounts, all the topics investigated by Bernays – attitudes, persuasion, communication, and normative social influence – continue to be critical for effective PR practice in today's context. Common to Bernays and Lee were their views on crowd psychology; however, this concept would fit better into sociological investigations than into a psychological understanding of a group. Lee's *crowd*, comprising individuals who had been depleted of reason, began to act in a way that was no longer conceivable through the sum of individual experiences and needs. This new unit of analysis changed the optics. Much like Mead's sociological approach, whereby individuals are assessed through the group they belong to rather than by aggregating. Although psychology was a major source of inspiration for Bernays, it is expected that his understanding of human psychology differed a hundred years ago from what it is today, which explains the somewhat diluted psychological-sociological perspective. In Propaganda (1928), Bernays wrote that 'the group has mental characteristics distinct from those of the individual, and is motivated by impulses and emotions which cannot be explained based on what we know of individual psychology' (Bernays, 1928, pp. 41–42). Today, scientific psychological thinking about the role of unconscious thought is more nuanced. Unconscious processes could be a result of previous learning of repeated responses from environmental stimuli (e.g. Bargh, 1994), as well as a symptom of operations of the hot, impulsive system (Strack & Deutsch, 2004).

As little as the questions asked by early psychoanalysts had to do with real science, so too did the connection between early PR writings have little grounding in the scientific method. Nevertheless, rather than criticising the beginnings of PR as having little to do with notions of truth and the scientific method, one can appreciate the early acknowledgement of the complexity of factors influencing the relationship between an organisation and its publics. It appears that one of the fundamental assumptions of Bernays' work was recognising the impact of psychology on public opinion, particularly the role of motivation and other people as sources of information. It could be argued that the rise of the profession of PR would not have been possible without the achievements of psychological science; however, the direct influence of psychology on PR is not as visible as one would expect. The reluctance to view psychology as more than just an inspiration (or starting point) in PR is almost as old as the discipline itself. Psychology informs the practice of PR more than the scholarship.

Fragmented Nature of Psychological Applications

In 2000, McKie observed PR's insularity from other scholarly fields, despite many thematic overlaps, and resolutely explained that 'if a field is not already part of the public relations canon of accepted feeder disciplines (e.g., management and decision theory, marketing, communication theory), then it has difficulty in gaining recognition regardless of its appropriateness or logical relevance' (McKie, 2001, p. 34). His work on introducing postmodern theory to PR has enriched the discipline, and the success of McKie and others seems evident. However, instead of establishing a more paradigmatic nature of the field of PR, some of his views seem reductionist – something he saw as a negative sign of the 'old science'. First, integrating psychology with PR would not bring reductionism to the field, and psychology's 'experience' with neuroscience is a good example of just the opposite. For instance, psychology recognises that investigating the brain and collecting neural data alone is insufficient for understanding the brain–behaviour link and, specifically, the processes governing behaviour (Krakauer et al., 2017). Likewise, identifying causal mechanisms on a neural level alone will not allow us to understand why these relationships exist and how they modulate behaviour. Accepting psychology as an evidence-barer should be viewed merely as an act of rebalancing and achieving equilibrium between three levels of analysis. That seems necessary, given the trend to equate social aspects of PR phenomena with sociological and critical perspectives. Apart from some notable exceptions (e.g. Van Ruler & Vercic, 2005; White, 2000), social psychological influences on PR have often been considered only a collection of loosely connected tactics. The individual level of analysis and the popularity of mid-20th-century psychological theories left their mark on the perception of psychological thought. The distorted or incomplete perception of psychology often implicated a non-dialogic, information-based, and non-societal level approach to understanding publics influenced by PR activities and programmes (see Ihlen et all., (2009) for a review of key social theoretical approaches).

Following the divergence of mass communication research and social psychology in the 1960s, the role of psychology in the practice of PR has been less acknowledged. Still, several concepts were used, but without much scrutiny placed on their psychological aspects. For example, opinions were considered as expressions of attitudes by Seitel (1989), who defined them as evaluations of problems or issues. Seitel also explained several characteristics of attitudes, including personal, cultural, educational, familial, religious, social, and racial. The social-psychological perspective of information processing and the concept of cognitive dissonance as a driver of cognition and action were mentioned in the works of Grunig, Hunt, and Seitel (Grunig & Hunt, 1984; Seitel, 1989). Applied psychological research has led to the identification of several psychological components that the practice of PR can benefit from. In the fifth edition of Exploring Public Relations, which is the authoritative source of learning for PR students in the UK, Topić-Rutheford (2021), reviews the psychological knowledge base and suggests that the following are relevant: cognitive dissonance (Festinger, 1957), theory of planned behaviour (Ajzen, 1985), dual process theories of persuasion (Chaiken, 1980; Petty & Cacioppo, 1986), and most recently, the nudge theory (Thaler & Sunstein, 2008). While these theories have a significant value for the practice and theory of PR, it seems that more could be said about psychology when preparing them for the practice of PR. As noted by White (2000),

> students of public relations – academics and practitioners – draw piecemeal from psychology. While this is productive of insights, it means that exposure to all that psychology has to offer is limited and raises questions about the criteria used in any search through the psychological literature.
> *(p. 151)*

Indeed, more than just a few psychological theories have been used to explain PR phenomena and are core to several 'big ideas' in PR. In 2001, DiFonzo and Toth wrote an 'Annotated bibliography of recent and significant psychological research of import to public relations practitioners'. In this publication of the Institute for Public Relations, examples of applications of psychological research on attitude formation and change, cognitive processing, consumer behaviour, framing effects, intergroup relations, political attitudes, persuasion, personality rumours, and social identity were briefly summarised. On the one hand, it demonstrated the applicability of psychology to the practice of PR. On the other hand, however, the title of the bibliography revealed one of the major failings of integrating a psychological perspective in PR. Psychology was an 'import', which suggests a separate disciplinary 'country' which is governed by different laws and requires 'translation' for its 'treasures' to be discovered.

However, the potential for applying psychological concepts is evident. Psychology constitutes a significant portion of the rationale behind Macnamara's (2024) framework of organisational listening. Coombs based his situational crisis communication theory on one of the most well-known psychological concepts: attribution theory (Coombs, 2007). Cognitive dissonance could also be said to have inspired many PR scholars (e.g. Waters, 2009). Not only cognitive and social but also evolutionary perspectives can be applied in the PR context (Nothhaft & Seiffert-Brockmann, 2023; Seiffert-Brockmann & Thummes, 2017). Most recently, individual-level analyses have begun to develop a better understanding of the mental health and wellbeing of PR and communication professionals, as the global pandemic paused businesses from normal operations and altered organisational environments, likely forever. The impact of physical distancing measures was immense (Fancourt et al., 2021), particularly as relationships between individuals became strained due to isolation policies. PR professionals were also affected by this, and individual wellbeing became a subject of more intense focus in PR scholarship and professional practice. Topić-Rutheford began researching the wellbeing of PR professionals early in 2021 and reported that life satisfaction largely depends on job satisfaction, which, among surveyed communication professionals, was a function of job enjoyment, job enthusiasm, and shared work values (Topić-Rutheford & Chmiel, 2024). Topić-Rutheford and Chmiel's (2024) report also highlighted the importance of networking and a flexible, accommodating work environment, a theme echoed in another project led by Anton and Moise (2025). Topić-Rutheford and Meng have recently devoted a special issue in the Journal of Communication Management to this topic, and professional associations have also increased their interest in the wellbeing of PR professionals (CIPR et al., 2024; PRCA et al., 2022).

The key takeaways from psychological inquiries into the nature of human thinking processes seem to have been acknowledged. Communication is accepted as a means of changing cognitions, beliefs, and attitudes. The process of persuasion is seen as involving two types of processes or two types of outcomes, which helps understand why people never rely only on rational evidence and systematically analyse arguments before making a judgement. Occasionally, it takes a while to accept psychological definitions, and persuasion is a good example. What psychology sees as a process of changing attitudes had a different reception in PR. Persuasion was considered unethical manipulation until Pfau and Wan (2006) explained that changing the behaviour of individuals does not necessarily mean manipulating (the confusion about the definition of persuasion could be one of the reasons why some PR practitioners refuse to see PR as a behavioural discipline: 'if persuasion is unethical and I do not want to be unethical then I will not use persuasion at all'). When psychological theories received popular acclaim, the enthusiasm of other disciplines was clear. The nudge theory, which provides a basis for the existence of two types of cognition, hot and cold, is a good example of how popular culture has helped reduce resistance and criticism (although not completely: Sunstein (2014)). Nudge appears to be a significant contributor to demonstrating, through practical examples, that hot cognition is automatic (but not animalistic) and dependent on prior experience and memory. Cold cognition involves the generation of new knowledge, is more demanding, and requires time. An important aspect of those theories is also the appreciation of the role of motivation, which can engage individuals in the laborious processing of information, while a lack of it simplifies these processes and makes their outcome superficial. One of the failings of psychology in PR is the lack of demonstrating its relevance in explaining its complex phenomena, which involve internal and external factors, which include the context of human cognition and behaviour. This large body of knowledge, which was discussed in Chapter 2, has not been utilised well in PR scholarship. One of the areas of psychological investigation seems to have a considerable potential for informing PR theory: motivation to process information and its behavioural consequences. The concept of motivation has been tackled in several places, but most notably in Grunig's Situational Theory of Publics.

Past Inspirations and Benefits of Psychological Updates: The Case of STP

Grunig explains that he 'developed the situational theory of publics [STP] as a theory of individual communication behavior and decision making' and explains its evolution as 'the theory later moved to a collective level of analysis as the concepts in the individual-level theory were used to explain and identify who are publics of organisations, as that term is used in public relations' (Grunig, 1997) (Kim & Grunig, 2011, p. 120). Grunig predicted that depending on how the publics (1) recognised the problem, (2) perceived constraints to solve it, (3) their level of involvement, and (4) the presence of a referent criterion, different effects could be expected: a change of attitudes or a behavioural act (Grunig, 1997; Grunig & Ipes, 1983). STP is an interesting theory as it seems to have been informed by insights from several disciplines, including psychology. The information processing perspective, especially popular in the 1960s and 1970s, appears to be one of the sources of inspiration.

Building on STP, Kim and Grunig (2011) developed the Situational Theory of Problem Solving (STOPS) based on the assumption 'that most human behavior is motivated by problem solving' (Kim & Grunig, 2011, p. 123). While STP relates well to the evidence from social psychology, STOPS has a few weaknesses. From the perspective of PR, STOPS a is a well-developed, internally consistent proposition. However, although the concept of problem-solving has been applied to consumer decision-making (Stankevich, 2017), decisions of consumers that involve comparing different (available) alternatives and recognising what the goal of this process is seem to differ from the type of judgements made by the public about issues. An issue does not always entail problem-like features, whereby a set of alternatives is available.

Additionally, an issue is rarely associated with a single solution. While some issues could be represented as problems, not all issues are problems in a psychological sense. It would seem that a psychological definition of an attitude fits this notion of evaluating an issue: 'a psychological tendency that is expressed by evaluating a particular entity with some degree of favor or disfavor' (Eagly & Chaiken, 1993, p.1). The issue is the entity that undergoes the evaluation process. Even when the theory of problem-solving is applied to solving societal issues, solving a problem requires wisdom: 'using one's abilities and knowledge toward a common good, by balancing one's own, others', and higher interests over the long and short terms through the infusion of positive ethical values' (Sternberg et al., 2019, p. 3). In light of this definition, evaluations are rarely made by members of publics, as they typically lack the required abilities and knowledge. In that sense, STOPS is an idea that appreciates the subjective experience of members of publics, who can think about themselves as problem solvers. STOPS should be appreciated for its introspective value. Grunig (1971, 1972, 1997) and later Grunig and Kim's (2011) theory is appreciative of the audiences' self-perceptions of their communicative actions: the experience of solving a problem is the key consideration in their idea. However, the goal of the STP and STPS seems to be explaining the behaviour of audiences as a means to identify different publics, rather than describing the feelings of audiences associated with the information they receive. So, although Kim and Grunig's (2011) theory looks at the task of evaluating an issue from the perspective of an internal observer and acknowledges their feelings, psychology would suggest that the process of judgement and attitude formation shows a better fit that allows comprehensive and systematic scrutiny of what is happening in the mind of a member of publics. In addition, treating this process as a type of evaluative judgement enables the discovery that a specific type of epistemic motivation monitors the process of acquiring information and compares it with internal beliefs.

Psychology considers the process of judgement involved in the formation of attitudes to be knowledge-based. Contrary to Kim and Grunig's (2011) assumptions, all human judgements can be seen as rational when the concept of human ecological rationality is taken into consideration (see Chapter 4). People gather knowledge in a purposive manner. The primary goal is to satisfy the need for stimulation and exploration of the environment (see Chapter 6). The epistemic motive is, in a colloquial sense, never at rest. Some authors suggest that knowledge acquisition is the basis for every decision we make (Kruglanski, 1989; Popper, 1959). Every decision is controlled by motivation, and the motivational force that is said to be responsible for that is the Need for Cognitive Closure (NFCC) (Webster & Kruglanski, 1994). It has been defined as a preference for a definite answer and an intolerance for ambiguity. NFCC has been embedded in the theory of Lay Epistemics (Kruglanski, 1989; Kruglanski et al., 2009), which looks at motivation and cognition as one system (motivation as cognition) and sees the search for knowledge as the fundamental process of human cognition. The search for knowledge, which involves collecting information and testing it in a quasi-scientific manner, is governed by epistemic motivation: NFCC. It is the NFCC that explains the extent and direction of the search for information. Two phases of the information collection process are postulated: seizing and freezing (Kruglanski & Webster, 1996). In the seizing phase, a person collects available information. During freezing, although the collection may continue, an initial choice for information has been made, and new information is compared against the anchored bit. Increasingly often, the amount of information exceeds our optimal levels of stimulation. A substantial body of psychological scholarship on epistemic needs exists (see Chapter 6) and could be utilised to explore the motivational aspects of Grunig and Kim and Grunig's theory (Grunig, 1997, 2005; Kim & Grunig, 2011), with significant benefits for practitioners.

Psychology in the 21st Century and PR – Potential for Synergy?

Is there a place for psychology in PR? The rapid overview of the keywords used in the top ten psychology scholarly journals suggests that the potential for synergies is considerable (see Tables 3.1–3.3). Tables 3.1–3.3 reveal the focus on several areas of interest. Personality is the prevailing topic of psychological inquiry. Although it may seem that this concept is purely psychological, a deeper examination of psychological theories reveals that, for example, extroversion and openness to experience are related to distinct patterns of behaviour among social media users (Chen, 2014; Correa et al., 2010). In turn, a recent investigation by Chmiel and Thompson (2024) into another dimension of personality, narcissism, suggests that this trait may be responsible for sharing fake news. Narcissism is related to self-esteem, which can be indicative of a range of behaviours observed on social media among

TABLE 3.1 Top 10 Psychological Journals Based on H5 Index Median as of November 2024

	H5-Index	*H5-Index median*	*Impact Factor*	*Number of publications*
Personality and Individual Differences	98	134	4.3	6117
Journal of Personality and Social Psychology	82	120	7.6	1361
Social Psychological and Personality Science	62	102	3.6	1260
Cyberpsychology, Behaviour, and Social Networking	62	99	4.2	1425
Personality and Social Psychology Bulletin	60	84	4.38	1465
Journal of Personality	57	86	5.12	859
Journal of Experimental Social Psychology	53	79	3.53	1329
European Journal of Social Psychology	48	71	2.22	966
Journal of Social and Personal Relationships	47	69	3.12	1403
British Journal of Social Psychology	45	64	2.87	747

members of publics who seek attention and power. Also, other concepts related to personality, for example, sociopathy, can be investigated as a potentially interesting correlate of leadership.

Each of the keywords in Tables 3.1–3.3 open up significant areas for investigating concepts relevant to the practice and theory of PR. The biggest obstacle would be the need for specialised psychological expertise. In many instances, keywords listed in this section may not immediately sound meaningful to scholars operating in different disciplines or to practitioners unless they have a background in psychology. While the concept of wellbeing, which has been identified as the second most investigated topic in psychology over the last ten years, bears immediate relevance for the practice of PR in the post-COVID world, many other concepts require a better introduction to PR. The outlook, however, should be positive. The field of psychology has the potential to make a significant contribution to the realm of PR, extending beyond the established concepts of communication, attitudes, and persuasion. Apart from the content of psychological theories, the approach that involves focusing on understanding relevant phenomena rather than developing particular theories could be a source of inspiration for the metatheoretical model of the discipline's development.

TABLE 3.2 Top 10 Author Keywords in the Top 10 Psychological Journals 2015–2024

2015	*2016*	*2017*	*2018*	*2019*	*2020*	*2021*	*2022*	*2023*	*2024*
personality	personality	personality	personality	personality	personality	COVID-19	COVID-19	COVID-19	personality
narcissism	self-esteem	narcissism	psychopathy	wellbeing	wellbeing	personality	personality	personality	wellbeing
self-esteem	narcissism	psychopathy	narcissism	narcissism	narcissism	narcissism	wellbeing	wellbeing	morality
wellbeing	wellbeing	wellbeing	self-esteem	romantic relationships	self-esteem	wellbeing	romantic relationships	narcissism	romantic relationships
psychopathy	depression	prejudice	motivation	self-esteem	psychopathy	stress	narcissism	romantic relationships	narcissism
morality	mindfulness	romantic relationships	prejudice	motivation	romantic relationships	romantic relationships	meta-analysis	morality	depression
depression	psychopathy	self-esteem	wellbeing	emotion regulation	big five	psychopathy	psychopathy	social identity	social identity
machiavellian-ism	gender	gender	morality	psychopathy	prejudice	social support	depression	loneliness	big five
romantic relationships	prejudice	morality	machiavelli-anism	social identity	motivation	big five	self-esteem	stress	person perception
motivation	adolescence	motivation	depression	gender	social identity	self-esteem	social media	social media	social media

Note:

Total number of publications: 16932
Total number of keywords: 78640
Total number of unique keywords: 24777

TABLE 3.3 Top 25 Author-selected Keywords in the Top 10 Psychological Journals 2015–2024

Keyword	*Count*
Personality	982
Wellbeing	470
Narcissism	455
Psychopathy	347
Self-esteem	341
Romantic relationships	317
Motivation	267
Depression	265
Morality	263
COVID-19	260
Prejudice	255
Big five	246
Gender	241
Social support	240
Machiavellianism	231
Stress	222
Social identity	218
Social media	211
Dark triad	199
Anxiety	199
Life satisfaction	198
Individual differences	194
Social cognition	193
Aggression	185
Self-regulation	183

One of the leading journals covering research in social psychology, the Journal of Personality and Social Psychology (5-year Impact Factor: 9.2), invites papers that investigate attitudes and social cognition, interpersonal relations and group processes, and personality and individual differences. The boundaries of those investigations are drawn by topics or problems rather than a pursuit or advancement of a particular theoretical paradigm. The topic- or goal-centred approach the journal's editors seem to have taken is further strengthened by methodological openness and an appreciation of traditional as well as new methods, including biological, neuroscientific, and big data approaches (Journal of Personality and Social Psychology, n.d.). A brief examination of the titles of papers published in 2025 provides a good demonstration of the approach. 'A worldwide test of the predictive validity of ideal partner preference matching' (Eastwick et al., 2025), 'Dispositional optimism and wealth accumulation across the income spectrum' (Gladstone & Pomerance, 2025), 'Frontal alpha asymmetry as a marker of approach motivation?' (Paul et al., 2025), 'The vicious cycle of status insecurity' (Hoff et al., 2025), 'Probing connections between social connectedness, mortality risk, and brain age' (Kahhale et al., 2024), 'How people (fail to) control the influence of affective stimuli on attitudes' (Hütter & Sweldens, 2025) or 'False face stereotypes emerge from a few exemplars and persist via insufficient sampling' (Bai et al., 2025) are just a few examples of papers that show the breadth of social psychological interest in topics that link internal, micro-level processes with a plethora of social phenomena, including interactions with other individuals, groups, and wider society.

The evidence presented in the previous paragraph can be used to make two observations. Firstly, at the close of the first quarter of the 21st century, social psychology has a broad interest in understanding human behaviour and its links with the immediate social environment, including people, groups, social or organisational status, and culture. The methods of social psychology are related and subject to the investigation of problems, as opposed to theoretical paradigms (the latter would, in fact, constitute a form of biased thinking). The aforementioned points suggest a certain degree of vertical flexibility. To understand human behaviour, evidence from the nano-level (represented here by neuroscience), the micro-level (encompassing human behaviour and mental capacities), and the mezzo-level can be utilised – and oriented towards a specific goal: answering a particular question or solving an issue (as opposed to advancing a single theory). As an interdisciplinary field, PR draws on theoretical concepts from related disciplines to develop a cohesive body of knowledge. It is true that PR benefits from contributions from other disciplines, but I have reservations about the necessity for a distinct PR theory that would offer comprehensive answers to all inquiries from all three levels of analysis. While the notion of a unifying theory may appear intriguing, the intricacies of the social realm necessitate a collaborative effort across diverse disciplines and an acknowledgement of multiple perspectives. PR has performed well in terms of developing a comprehensive body of knowledge. However, there appears to have been an oversight in conducting a thorough investigation of the lower, micro-level phenomena, which are typically within the remit of psychology.

Based on the evidence presented so far, I see three issues that could impede the integration of psychological findings in PR. Firstly, psychological concepts are introduced into PR in a limited way, and the context and intended use of psychological theories are sometimes misinterpreted. This can happen unintentionally when psychological concepts are examined with the conceptual and methodological apparatus of other scientific fields. Secondly, definitions of psychological concepts (or constructs) are rooted in the theoretical contexts at the point of their inception and are not updated. The previous issue outlines a scenario where a psychological concept, such as motivation or persuasion, is adopted from psychology to inform a PR investigation and is subsequently utilised in its original form and context, disregarding developments, studies, and the evolution of psychology. Third is the problem of complex societal phenomena, which often overlook the individual level of mental characteristics as a significant source of evidence and interindividual (between-person) variability.

Edwards and Hodges (2011) advocates of the sociocultural approach in PR, list several benefits of moving away from the dominant functional-normative paradigm in PR. Grunig's works lead the way here (Grunig, 1992; Grunig & Grunig, 2008), mainly thanks to its insightful understanding of the practical challenges PR practitioners face. It would also be difficult to undermine Grunig's influence on the understanding of the definition of PR, especially recognising that publicity and PR are not synonyms, and treating them as such significantly impoverishes and limits the discipline. The historiographic work of Grunig, which traced the evolution of PR from models based on publicity through the agency model to models of two-way (symmetrical and asymmetrical) communication, served not only as a springboard for developing a more coherent academic approach to studying the discipline but also, perhaps more importantly, helped identify ethical challenges for practitioners. Grunig's ideas, however, have been accepted with some criticism. Edwards and Hodges (2011) reflect on Grunig's work, concluding that it has been an inspiration for the scholarly development of the discipline. They also acknowledge that it would be challenging to understand PR without answering the question of what the profession means in practice. However, functionalist orientation and organisational focus are said to have their drawbacks as they could lead to ignoring the social environment or organisations. As Grunig (1992) asserts, the success of PR practice is a function of the organisation achieving its goals and meeting the needs of its stakeholders.

As a consequence, the impact of PR practice on shaping the social and cultural needs and values of its audiences may be overlooked: PR communication often prioritises specific values and groups – depending on the organisational goals adopted (Edwards & Hodges, 2011). In my view, this criticism is only partly justified. It is possible that practitioners operating at the organisational level do not have the societal context of the organisation as their primary focus, but this does not mean that Grunig's theory encourages such neglect.

The psychological approaches presented in this book align well with the epistemological and ontological shift in the way we define and study PR, as advocated by Edwards and Hodges (2011). The praxis, processes, and outcomes of PR activities are phenomena that are dependent on definitions and context. In other words, the practice of PR is a matter of agreement. Most commonly, however, the social nature of those definitional agreements points to group- and societal-level processes rather than individual-level ones. I will argue that by virtue of integrating approaches, societal phenomena and societal effects can be better understood when psychological evidence is assorted. For example, consider how Edwards and Hodges (2011) define PR from a broad social perspective, stating that it is about creating, maintaining, and regulating meanings through which we communicate and develop knowledge and attitudes. The psychological perspective of an individual proposed in this book aligns well with the above definition, focusing on information processing and the construction of social knowledge at the individual level. The theoretical, social-cognitive perspective of psychology captures the human being as a naive scientist who, in constructing knowledge about the surrounding reality, acquires and compares information to reach the best possible judgement (Kruglanski, 1989). The detailed assumptions of this theoretical system, which effectively links motivation and cognition and provides a formal explanation of errors in judgement and decision-making, will be presented later in the book. Psychology can provide a complementary and competitive perspective on problems and challenges identified by critical scholars. However, it does not mean that each investigation should encompass a comprehensive analysis of individual mental processes. Such an expectation would not only be too ambitious but also impossible unless conducted by an interdisciplinary team of scholars. Psychological processes should, at the very least, be acknowledged to understand societal processes in their complexity.

Although Edwards and Hodges (2011) highlight the social nature of the definitional processes through which groups construct their understanding of reality, the role of the individual as a receiver, transformer, and exchanger of information appears to have been overlooked. The authors suggest a certain base of theoretical approaches that seem essential for developing a sociocultural perspective. They mention cultural studies, sociology, anthropology, and political economy, among others, without directly referring to the psychological component. For a psychologist, this may come as a surprise, as it is not irrelevant who constructs social meanings, under what conditions, and what psychological processes are involved. In turn, Taylor explains how the failure of excellence theory to address the technological advances of the 1990s and early 2000s opened the door of PR at that time to new perspectives of relationship management, dialogue building, critical and other macro-level sociological theories (Taylor, 2023), which marked a sociological turn in PR (Edwards, 2018). The evolution of PR scholars' interests from the application of communication studies through functional (excellence) approaches to co-creational (Botan & Taylor, 2004) and macro-level societal (Ihlen & van Ruler, 2007) could be interpreted as an upward trend. Initially focused on the organisation's communication with its publics, PR has evolved and expanded to identify societal-level phenomena and discuss the contribution of PR to the distribution of power in society. Ultimately, the upward trend left the lower-level discipline of psychology somewhat neglected despite its potential to offer significant benefits. One interpretation of the abandonment of psychology by PR could stem from the analyses of Weick. In 1969, he explained that 'the organisational member is simultaneously individual and socialised' (p. 30), but 'investigators seem to resist defining their concepts in terms of observable actions by individuals in the mistaken belief that, in doing so, they will have to explain the actions psychologically' (Weick, 1969, p. 31). Building on Weick's argument, it is reasonable to assume that no discipline has a monopoly on answering the questions that arise in the context of interactions between individuals and the groups to which they belong. However, what seems to be a necessity for PR scholarship today is establishing 'a consensual starting point' so that 'anyone who looks at the same set of observations can build an explanation' (Weick, 1969, p. 32).

A more in-depth look at psychological contributions to PR suggests that while psychology in PR exists and its concepts have been used to inform both theory and practice, a comprehensive level of analysis – the psychology of PR – has not yet emerged. It can be argued that today, psychological contributions to the discipline of PR can be regarded as a tactical repertoire of isolated psychological findings that are predominantly used to guide the efforts of practitioners. That is why, in Chapter 2, I discussed the definition of contemporary social psychology and suggested several advantages of a more comprehensive integration of psychology and PR. PR, as an interdisciplinary field of study, should be open to integrating social psychological theory that would entail going beyond the simple, functional application of specific experimental findings. The following chapters aim to demonstrate the applicability and benefits of psychological evidence and methodology from both practical and theoretical perspectives. The psychological and social scientific approach will help me define the psychological object of PR and demonstrate that the outcomes and the interdisciplinary object of PR can be better defined using psychological thinking. One of the missing links between psychology and PR will be elaborated in Chapter 6: epistemic motivation. It will be important to demonstrate how epistemic motivation qualitatively and quantitatively alters the process of information processing, as this can help in understanding how audiences and publics are constituted. The central component of the process – content – will be used to explain divisions and the propensity of some publics members to share fake information. Lastly, I will conclude that incorporating psychological concepts can be used to define the broader purpose of PR.

References

Ajzen, I. (1985). From intentions to actions: A theory of planned behavior. In J. Kuhl & J. Beckmann (Eds.), *Action Control: From Cognition to Behavior* (pp. 11–39). Springer. https://doi.org/10.1007/978-3-642-69746-3_2

Anton, A., & Moise, R. (Eds.) (2025). *Gender and Freelancing in the Communication Industries*. Emerald Publishing.

Bai, X., Uddenberg, S., Labbree, B. P., & Todorov, A. (2025). Learning too much from too little: False face stereotypes emerge from a few exemplars and persist via insufficient sampling. *Journal of Personality and Social Psychology*, *128*(1), 61–81. https://doi.org/10.1037/PSPA0000422

Bargh, J. A. (1994). The four horsemen of automaticity: Awareness, efficiency, intention, and control in social cognition. In R. S. Wyer & T. K. Srull (Eds.), *Handbook of Social Cognition* (2nd ed., Vol. 1, pp. 1–40). Lawrence Erlbaum Associates, Inc.

Bernays, E. (1923). *Crystallizing Public Opinion*. Boni & Liveright.

Bernays, E. L. (1928). *Propaganda*. Horace Liveright.

Bernays, E. L. (1965). *Biography of an Idea: Memoirs of Public Relations Counsel*. Simon and Schuster.

Bernays, E. L. (1986). *The Later Years: Public Relations Insights 1956-1986*. Howard Penn Hudson Assc Inc.

Botan, C. H., & Taylor, M. (2004). Public relations: State of the field. *Journal of Communication*, *54*(4), 645–661. https://doi.org/10.1111/j.1460-2466.2004.tb02649.x

Chaiken, S. (1980). Heuristic versus systematic information processing and the use of source versus message cues in persuasion. *Journal of Personality and Social Psychology*, *39*(5), 752–766. https://doi.org/10.1037/0022-3514.39.5.752

Chen, G. M. (2014). Revisiting the social enhancement hypothesis: Extroversion indirectly predicts number of Facebook friends operating through Facebook usage. *Computers in Human Behavior*, *39*, 263–269. https://doi.org/10.1016/J.CHB.2014.07.015

Chmiel, M., & Thompson, G. (2024). Gen Zs seeking companionship. Loneliness, individual and collective narcissism as predictors of sharing fake news. In D. Verčič, A. Tkalac Verčič, & K. Sriramesh (Eds.), *Public Relations and Human Well-being: Book of Abstracts of the 31st International Public Relations Research Symposium BledCom* (pp. 52–53). University of Ljubljana.

CIPR, Opinium, & PRCA. (2024). Mental Wellbeing Audit 2023/2024. https://www.cipr.co.uk/common/Uploaded%20files/Policy/Mental%20Health/Workplace_Mental_Wellbeing_Audit_2023-24.pdf

Coombs, W. T. (2007). Attribution theory as a guide for post-crisis communication research. *Public Relations Review*, *33*(2), 135–139. https://doi.org/10.1016/J.PUBREV.2006.11.016

Correa, T., Hinsley, A. W., & de Zúñiga, H. G. (2010). Who interacts on the Web?: The intersection of users' personality and social media use. *Computers in Human Behavior*, *26*(2), 247–253. https://doi.org/10.1016/J.CHB.2009.09.003

Cutlip, S. M. (1994). *The Unseen Power: Public Relations: A History (Routledge Communication Series)*. Routledge.

DiFonzo, N., & Toth, E. (2001). *Annotated Bibliography of Recent and Significant Psychological Research Of Import to Public Relations Practitioners*. The Institute for Public Relations.

Eagly, A. H., & Chaiken, S. (1993). *The Psychology of Attitudes*. Harcourt Brace Jovanovich College Publishers. https://psycnet.apa.org/record/1992-98849-000

Eastwick, P. W., Sparks, J., Finkel, E. J., Meza, E. M., Adamkovič, M., Adu, P., Ai, T., Akintola, A. A., Al-Shawaf, L., Apriliawati, D., Arriaga, P., Aubert-Teillaud, B., Baník, G., Barzykowski, K., Batres, C., Baucom, K. J., Beaulieu, E. Z., Behnke, M., Butcher, N., … Coles, N. A. (2025). A worldwide test of the predictive validity of ideal partner preference matching. *Journal of Personality and Social Psychology*, *128*(1), 123–146. https://doi.org/10.1037/PSPP0000524

Edwards, L. (2018). *Understanding Public Relations*. SAGE Publications Ltd, https://doi.org/10.4135/9781473983571

Edwards, L., & Hodges, C. E. M. (2011). Introduction: Implications of a (radical) socio-cultural "turn" in public relations scholarship. In L. Edwards and C. E. M. Hodges (Eds.), *Public Relations, Society & Culture: Theoretical and Empirical Explorations* (pp 1–14). Routledge.
Fancourt, D., Steptoe, A., & Bu, F. (2021). Trajectories of anxiety and depressive symptoms during enforced isolation due to COVID-19 in England: a longitudinal observational study. *The Lancet Psychiatry*, *8*(2), 141–149. https://doi.org/10.1016/S2215-0366(20)30482-X
Festinger, L. (1957). *A Theory of Cognitive Dissonance*. Stanford University Press.
Gladstone, J. J., & Pomerance, J. (2025). A glass half full of money: Dispositional optimism and wealth accumulation across the income spectrum. *Journal of Personality and Social Psychology*, *128*(1), 147–195. https://doi.org/10.1037/PSPP0000530
Grunig, J. E. (1971). Communication and the economic decision-making processes of Colombian peasants. *Economic Development and Cultural Change*, *19*(4). https://doi.org/10.1086/450514
Grunig, J. E. (1972). Communication in community decisions on the problems of the poor. *Journal of Communication*, *22*(1). https://doi.org/10.1111/j.1460-2466.1972.tb00127.x
Grunig, J. E. (Ed.). (1992). *Excellence in Public Relations and Communication Management*. Routledge.
Grunig, J. E. (1997). A situational theory of publics: Conceptual history, recent challenges and new research. In D. Moss, T. MacManus, & D. Vercic (Eds.), *Public Relations Research: An International Perspective*. (pp. 3–48). International Thomson Business Press.
Grunig, J. E. (2005). Situational theory of publics. *In Encyclopedia of Public Relations* (Issue 2).
Grunig, J. E., & Grunig, L. A. (2008). Excellence theory in public relations: Past, present, and future. In A. Zerfass, B. Ruler, & K. Sriramesh (Eds.), *Public Relations Research: European and International Perspectives* (pp. 327–347). Weisbaden, Germany: VS Verlag für Sozialwissenschaften.
Grunig, J. E., & Hunt, Todd. (1984). *Managing Public Relations*. Holt, Rinehart and Winston.
Grunig, J. E., & Ipes, D. A. (1983). The anatomy of a campaign against drunk driving. *Public Relations Review*, *9*(2), 36–52. https://doi.org/10.1016/S0363-8111(83)80004-6
Hoff, M., Galinsky, A. D., & Rucker, D. D. (2025). The vicious cycle of status insecurity. *Journal of Personality and Social Psychology*, *128*(1), 101–122. https://doi.org/10.1037/PSPI0000473
Hütter, M., & Sweldens, S. (2025). How people (fail to) control the influence of affective stimuli on attitudes. *Journal of Personality and Social Psychology*, *128*(1), 38–60. https://doi.org/10.1037/PSPA0000426
Ihlen, Ø., Fredrikson, M., & Van Ruler, B. (Eds.). (2009). *Public Relations and Social Theory*. West Sussex: Routledge/Taylor and Francis Group.
Ihlen, Ø., & van Ruler, B. (2007). How public relations works: Theoretical roots and public relations perspectives. *Public Relations Review*, *33*(3), 243–248. https://doi.org/10.1016/j.pubrev.2007.05.001
Journal of Personality and Social Psychology. (n.d.). Retrieved February5, 2025, from https://www.apa.org/pubs/journals/psp
Kahhale, I., Puccetti, N. A., Heller, A. S., & Hanson, J. L. (2024). Probing connections between social connectedness, mortality risk, and brain age: A preregistered study. *Journal of Personality and Social Psychology*. https://doi.org/10.1037/PSPI0000465
Kim, J. N., & Grunig, J. E. (2011). Problem solving and communicative action: A situational theory of problem solving. *Journal of Communication*, *61*(1). https://doi.org/10.1111/j.1460-2466.2010.01529.x

Krakauer, J. W., Ghazanfar, A. A., Gomez-Marin, A., MacIver, M. A., & Poeppel, D. (2017). Neuroscience needs behavior: Correcting a reductionist bias. *Neuron, 93*(3), 480–490. https://doi.org/10.1016/J.NEURON.2016.12.041/ASSET/480659E0-DC57-42F2-91F1-D940EEEB904A/MAIN.ASSETS/GR4.JPG

Kruglanski, A. W. (1989). *Lay Epistemics and Human Knowledge: Cognitive and Motivational Bases*. Springer US.

Kruglanski, A. W., Dechesne, M., Orehek, E., & Pierro, A. (2009). Three decades of lay epistemics: The why, how, and who of knowledge formation. *European Review of Social Psychology, 20*. https://doi.org/10.1080/10463280902860037

Kruglanski, A. W., & Webster, D. M. (1996). Motivated closing of the mind: "seizing" and "freezing." *Psychological Review, 103*(2), 263–283. https://doi.org/10.1037/0033-295X.103.2.263

Lee, I. Ledbetter., & St John III, Burton. (2017). *Mr. Lee's Publicity Book: A Citizen's Guide to Public Relations*. PR Museum Press.

Lippmann, W. (1922). *Public Opinion*. Harcourt, Brace & Co.

Macnamara, J. (2024). *Organizational Listening II*. Peter Lang Verlag. https://doi.org/10.3726/B21160

McKie, D. (2001). Updating public relations: "New science" research paradigms and unevendevelopments. In R. L. Heath (Ed.), *The Handbook of Public Relations* (pp. 75–91). ThousandOaks, CA: Sage.

Nothhaft, H., & Seiffert-Brockmann, J. (2023). From costly signals and competitive niches to reciprocity, memes, and memory traces: Evolutionary psychology and strategic communication. *International Journal of Strategic Communication, 17*(3), 151–162. https://doi.org/10.1080/1553118X.2023.2227958

Paul, K., Beauducel, A., Hennig, J., Hewig, J., Hildebrandt, A., Kührt, C., Lange, L., Mueller, E. M., Osinsky, R., Porth, E., Riesel, A., Rodrigues, J., Scheffel, C., Short, C. A., Stahl, J., Strobel, A., & Wacker, J. (2025). Frontal alpha asymmetry as a marker of approach motivation? Insights from a cooperative forking path analysis. *Journal of Personality and Social Psychology*, 128(1), 196–210. https://doi.org/10.1037/pspp0000503

Petty, R. E., & Cacioppo, J. T. (1986). *Communication and Persuasion: Central and Peripheral Routes to Attitude Change*. Springer-Verlag.

Pfau, M., & Wan, H.-H. (2006). Persuasion: An intrinsic function of public relations. In C. H. Botan & V. Hazleton (Eds.), *Public Relations Theory II* (pp. 101–136). Lawrence Erlbaum Associates Publishers. https://psycnet.apa.org/record/2006-03628-004

Popper, K. R. (1959). *The Logic of Scientific Discovery*. Basic Books. https://psycnet.apa.org/record/1961-02882-000

PRCA, CIPR, & Opinium. (2022). Workplace Mental Wellbeing Audit 2022. https://cipr.co.uk/common/Uploaded%20files/Policy/Mental%20Health/Mental_Wellbeing_in_Public_Relations_%202022.pdf

Seiffert-Brockmann, J., & Thummes, K. (2017). Self-deception in public relations. A psychological and sociological approach to the challenge of conflicting expectations. *Public Relations Review, 43*(1), 133–144. https://doi.org/10.1016/j.pubrev.2016.12.006

Seitel, F. P. (1989). *The Practice of Public Relations*. Merrill Publishing Company.

Sherif, M., & Hovland, C. (1961). *Social Judgment; Assimilation and Contrast Effects in Communication and Attitude Change*. Yale University Press. https://archive.org/details/socialjudgmentas0000sher

Stankevich, A. (2017). Explaining the consumer decision-making process: Critical literature review. *Journal of International Business Research and Marketing, 2*(6), 7–14. https://doi.org/10.18775/jibrm.1849-8558.2015.26.3001

Sternberg, R. J., Nusbaum, H., & Glück, J. (2019). *Applying Wisdom to Contemporary World Problems* (1st ed.). Palgrave Macmillan. https://doi.org/10.1007/978-3-030-20287-3

Strack, F., & Deutsch, R. (2004). Reflective and impulsive determinants of social behavior. *Personality and Social Psychology Review*, *8*(3). https://doi.org/10.1207/s15327957pspr0803_1

Sunstein, C. R. (2014). *Why Nudge: The politics of libertarian Paternalism*. Yale University Press.

Taylor, M. (2023). Reflections on the evolving theories of public relations. In C. H. Botan, & E. J. Sommerfeldt (Eds.), *Public Relations Theory III* (pp. 523–537). Routledge.

Thaler, R. H., & Sunstein, C. R. (2008). *Nudge: Improving Decisions about Health, Wealth, and Happiness*. Penguin Books.

Topić, M. (2021). Public relations theories: communication, relationships and persuasion. In R. Tench & S. Waddington (Eds.), *Exploring Public Relations and Management Communication* (5th ed., pp. 147–174). Pearson.

Topić, M., & Chmiel, M. (2024). Life satisfaction, job satisfaction and well-being in the public relations and communication industry in the United Kingdom. https://ir.ua.edu/handle/123456789/13666

Van Ruler, B., & Vercic, D. (2005). Reflective communication management, future ways for public relations research. *Annals of the International Communication Association*, *29*(1), 239–274.

Waters, R. D. (2009). Examining the role of cognitive dissonance in crisis fundraising. *Public Relations Review*, *35*(2), 139–143. https://doi.org/10.1016/J.PUBREV.2008.11.001

Webster, D. M., & Kruglanski, A. W. (1994). Individual differences in need for cognitive closure. *Journal of Personality and Social Psychology*, *67*(6), 1049–1062. https://doi.org/10.1037/0022-3514.67.6.1049

Weick, K. E. (1969). *The Social Psychology of Organizing*. Addison-Wesley Pub. Co.

White, J. (2000). Psychology and public relations. In D. Moss, D. Verčič & G. Warnaby (Eds.), *Perspectives on Public Relations Research* (pp. 161–172). Routledge.

4

THE EVIDENCE

Psychology and Everyday Practice of PR

The Need for Evidence-Based Decision-Making in Public Relations

Ivy Lee's declaration of principles stated that publicists should 'frankly and openly, on behalf of business concerns and public institutions, [...] supply to the press and public of the United States prompt and accurate information concerning subjects which it is of value and interest to the public to know about' (Ivy Lee's Declaration of principles, Morse, 1906, p. 460, in Russell & Bishop, 2009, p. 98).[1] The text of the declaration may be seen as a positive step change when we compare it to the ethics of communication of P.T. Barnum, who advertised one of his exhibits in the 1840s in the following way:

> Fejee Mermaid, which was exhibited in most of the principal cities of America, in the years 1840, '41, and '42, to the wonder and astonishment of thousands of naturalists and other scientific persons, whose previous doubts of the existence of such an astonishing creation were entirely removed.

However, the relationship between public relations and how evidence is produced and used to support clients' interests is more nuanced and somewhat troubled. P.T. Barnum, in his days as a travelling showman, is said to have sent letters to local newspapers that were seemingly voices from members of the public, both supporting and criticising his ventures. The evolution of the practice of PR from less ethical to more ethical use of evidence does not seem to be linear, either (Russell & Myers, 2019). PR used to be practised ethically in the past, but unethical examples of fabricated stories and invented

DOI: 10.4324/9781003610403-4

evidence still occur today. However, it can be more challenging to spot them – especially if stories are presented as if they are backed up by science, especially by psychology.

In 2004, one psychologist from Wales was commissioned by a travel company to calculate a formula for the most depressing day of the year. The formula, which led to 'Blue Monday' becoming a global cultural phenomenon, was calculated based on factors such as weather, debt, monthly salary, time since Christmas, and the 'time since the failure of New Year's resolutions' (Burnett, 2012). This is a good example of using pseudoscience to create publicity, apparently to address the low number of holiday packages sold in the first weeks of the year. There is no evidence to suggest that the third Monday of January is the most depressing day of the year. Sound scientific research supports the idea that mood does not vary depending on a particular day of the week (Stone et al., 1985, 2012). Public relations is also said to have played a role in even more serious impediments to truth and fabrication of evidence in support of the military intervention in Iraq (Hiebert, 2003; Rampton & Stauber, 2003).

Although Blue Monday may appear an innocent lie, it could have more serious consequences for people who experience mental health issues and could feel even more overwhelmed with negative thoughts when bombarded with news about the most depressing time approaching. The problematic use and production of evidence is not only the domain of PR but a much broader issue. Some authors argue that expert evidence is being weaponised today to serve political agendas (Russell & Patterson, 2025). The reasons for that are manifold, but one applies to PR practice: in the process of making evidence-based decisions, data is seldom presented alone, and it exists in conjunction with its interpretation.

Larger companies, such as Procter & Gamble, typically involve Public Relations in the process of developing their external-facing communications. Experts from different organisational functions, including legal, regulatory, and external relations, review existing evidence or commission new research to ensure it is used to communicate truthfully and comply with existing regulations and laws. This is to ensure that, for example, advertisements not only have a persuasive effect but also are sensitive to context (e.g. national, religious, or cultural) and do not cause harm to audience members. Less triumphed and talked about, but good examples of companies using evidence also exist. For example, Unilever surveyed 3,200 women from 10 countries to understand the concept and perception of beauty, which informed Dove's 'Real beauty' campaign (Etcof et al., 2004).

Whether the evidence is gathered and used correctly would fall under three general categories of explanations. These relate to the definition of rationality, the concept of truth, and whether it matters to audience members, as well as the choice of research methods.

Rationality and the Nature of Evidence Derived from Audience Members

Before research begins, the central question concerns the type of evidence being sought. If the opinions of audience members are of interest, a decision should be made about what the limits are to the audience's capacity to respond. This is a fundamental question because it helps weigh the extent to which audience members can make accurate judgements about reality. For example, if you ask a group of consumers if they see their wellbeing as improving, should their judgement be trusted more than the appraisal of an external expert? Are audience members capable of gathering information and producing credible judgements? These questions feed into the debate about human rationality.

When Tversky and Kahneman (1974) observed that people make predictable mistakes and identified the bias in their thought process, the definition of heuristics (shortcuts) seemed highly pejorative. They explained that people make mistakes because they cannot cope with the amount of information they receive and are unable to select the right ones and assess their usefulness in the decision-making process. The prevailing notion of heuristics as a negative phenomenon is attributed to the incapacity of individuals to effectively process and assimilate the deluge of information that inundates them, consequently impeding their ability to make well-informed decisions. As Simon (1955) noted, an individual's rationality is constrained by both external and internal forces, and as a result, rational actions are seldom performed. Consequently, the concept of heuristics had been initially regarded as a factor that resulted in erroneous decision-making. Although the importance of Kahneman and Tversky's works cannot be overstated for the development of modern psychology of decision-making and other branches of science, with economics at the forefront, such a perspective, in which people often come to erroneous conclusions, seemed unattractive to some researchers. They asked the following questions: Do we always make bad decisions when taking shortcuts? Do we always have to be right? Are we truly unfit to handle everyday problems?

The approach of Payne, Bettman, and Johnson (1993) was also based on the desire to study and describe heuristics in detail. However, they suggested that humans have developed a repertoire of specialised cognitive mechanisms as a result of interaction with the environment as a purposive adaptation. These mechanisms contain instructions for inference and reasoning in specific situations. More often than not, it means considering less rather than more information. In the decision-making process, which often involves choosing a particular alternative or product or taking a position in an argument, people are faced with the need to acquire and compare information about the available alternatives. Depending on the cognitive resources available, the motivation to carry out the task, and external conditions (e.g. time pressure, noise), a person may use the available information in different ways. Intuitively, since the human species has successfully adapted to the demands of its environment for a considerable period, the tool responsible for efficient navigation within it (the brain) should be free from inherent flaws. In experimental studies, Gigerenzer and Todd (1999) demonstrated that not all shortcuts necessarily lead to incorrect solutions.

Furthermore, there are circumstances in which employing a heuristic decision-making model is advantageous, given that the weight of the decision is negligible and the savings in terms of time and cognitive resources are substantial. In light of these considerations, a proposal has been put forward to define the human species as *a mechanic of reality*, endowed with a specialised set of tools (heuristics) that facilitate efficient navigation of the decision-making scenarios encountered. This assertion challenges the prevailing view that human rationality is inherently constrained. While constraints exist, these limitations do not necessarily impede daily living and have an adaptive function. It is, therefore, human, ecological rationality (Chase et al., 1998; Gigerenzer et al., 1999).

From a social psychological perspective, knowledge formation processes have been said to be inherent in every act of human behaviour. While secular in nature, people require knowledge to successfully navigate and resolve the challenges they encounter in daily life. Humans produce and test knowledge by collecting information and comparing it with their existing knowledge. This is a logical process, but it has its limitations because not all information is available and can be processed in a manner that satisfies needs other than being objectively correct. The knowledge formation process, as interpreted by Kruglanski (1989), can be applied to explain various phenomena on an individual level (e.g. the use of heuristics in decision-making, goal planning and attainment, stereotype formation and loyalty towards brands), on a group level (e.g. fake news sharing, collective narcissism, choice of group leaders); and on a societal level (e.g. tolerance towards immigrants, preference for authoritarian leaders). Audience members are, in a sense, rational lay scientists. They gather evidence to formulate judgements. This explains why evidence derived from human participants is quasi-objective. Although attention should be paid to understanding what audience members think or feel, these thoughts or feelings do not constitute an objectively existing reality. For example, a large group of people might believe that the inauguration of Donald Trump drew the most significant number of visitors in the history of the ceremony. However, their perception of attendance will not change the objectively verified number of spectators on that day. The attitudes and opinions of audience members are rational insofar as they result from a logical process of gathering available information and testing it. One of the mechanisms proposed to explain how much information is used and how long the process of deliberation takes is the construct of the need for cognitive closure NFCC (Webster & Kruglanski, 1994).

Psychology proposes and tests hypothetical mental processes that are said to help us find regularities in human behaviour. The fact that psychology views those separate phenomena as useful means that they are capable of comprehensively capturing and explaining human behaviour. However, it does not mean that there exist discreet physical or physiological processes that fully and comprehensively correspond to them, such that with the advancement of investigation techniques, they could be captured in their physical manifestations. Occasionally, however, scientists fall prey to the nominalist bias (Forgas et al., 2020), which leads to assuming the existence of a phenomenon or process based solely on evidence from observing associated behaviour. In other words, one can argue that the need for cognitive closure exists because we can observe its impact on the judgement process, whereby higher NFCC leads to reliance on information and evidence, and a lower need for cognition explains reliance on heuristics or peripheral cues (e.g. an expert's appearance or the source of information). To an extent, theoretical phenomena are useful and 'exist' as long as they can explain behaviour, but it does not prove their existence itself.

Truth and PR

Public relations – first and foremost – deals with subjective evidence and not facts. Consider the following statements: 'Eighty-nine per cent of people think their governments should do more to fight global warming' (Andre et al., 2024), '70% of stimulant drug overdoses involve fentanyl' (Drug Overdose Deaths: Facts and Figures | National Institute on Drug Abuse (NIDA), n.d.) or 'Google Pixel 9 is the best Android phone' (Scott & Whitwam, 2025). In the above examples, the evidence is subjective and is based on the opinions and attitudes of individuals (how to objectively determine if governments should do more to fight global warming or how to determine which Android phone is the best objectively?). PR lacks the competencies and instruments to assess the quality of political action or the extent to which it effectively addresses the rise in temperatures. This work should be performed jointly by climate change experts, politicians, and public servants – and even when disciplinary experts are involved, the outcome of the evaluation will be an approximation. Similarly, a political PR advisor's work should neither be about determining the percentage of deaths caused by fentanyl nor about determining the origin of fentanyl entering the US. Relevant medical professionals and secretaries (ministers) of homeland security are, among others, the right fit for this job. Even though attitudes and opinions are not sources of objective knowledge, scientific principles of data collection and interpretation should still be employed to determine what audience members think on topics when opinions, rather than facts, are of interest. Subjective perceptions, feelings, and evaluations are at the heart of what PR aims to influence.

Consequently, PR should build more expertise in two relevant areas: assessing attitudes and opinions and producing credible evidence to change them.

Let us consider the following PR scenario that outlines the potential challenges encountered by a public relations consultant. A high-profile race driver celebrity has been apprehended for exceeding the stipulated speed limit. The police issue a ticket, which the celebrity driver refuses to accept. The story gained attention from the public because the celebrity race driver is known for his advocacy of responsible and safe driving. The celebrity refuses to accept the ticket and contests the decision, ultimately initiating a court case. The police assert with conviction that the vehicle was operating at an elevated velocity, and the substantiating evidence derives from two sources: the patrol car speed camera and the stationary speed radar. The PR and legal teams of the race driver team investigated the matter, learning that the speed camera feeds information from the police vehicle (which itself may have been speeding) and that the stationary radar had not been adequately certified. How should the PR consultant proceed? Part of the problem with suggesting an answer is how contemporary publics perceive the concept of truth: a characteristic that can be decided by each individual depending on their own needs and goals.

The notions of truth and knowledge have continued to be a point of interest in academic discourse, at least since the moment Kellyanne Conway, Donald Trump's advisor, first used the expression *alternative facts*, inspiring the everyday public to contest the traditional notion of a lie. Subsequent scandalous manipulations by companies such as Cambridge Analytica confirmed the shift in attitudes towards what had been considered objectively truthful but is now subject to a democratic, popular vote. In response to this shift, numerous authors have sought to explain the factors underpinning the waning trust in experts, the diminution of academic achievement, and the disregard for objective knowledge (e.g. Nichols, 2017; Sloman & Fernbach, 2017; Sunstein, 2017).

Traditionally, knowledge and truth were considered important as they could be used to distinguish Public Relations from propaganda (L'Etang, 2008). PR practitioners and academics generally agree that truth is important in public relations, although the definition of truth varies depending on the theoretical orientation of scholars. As observed by Bentele and Seidenglanz (2008), contemporary societies, which are reliant on knowledge and information, have become increasingly dependent on non-immediately verifiable facts. Consequently, the role of trust and credibility is now considered a prerequisite for effective communication. Furthermore, it appears that methods of verifying information have evolved, and the correspondence theory of truth – a stance that requires a degree of similarity between a statement and external reality – is neither essential nor necessary for most matters discussed in public discourse. Emotions appear to play a role in determining what is factual and what is not, and – clearly – the consequences of openly lying have become minimal.

Somewhat disturbingly, academia is partly to blame for introducing confusion about the nature, role, and need for truth. One of the culprits, which has continued to play a role in how various audiences define truth, is postmodernism: 'a late 20th-century movement characterised by broad scepticism, subjectivism, or relativism; a general suspicion of reason; and an acute sensitivity to the role of ideology in asserting and maintaining political and economic power' (Postmodernism | Definition, Doctrines, & Facts | Britannica, n.d.). Postmodernism questioned the existence of objective reality and suggested that truth is a construction (Lyotard, 1984). As much as truth is construed, the language used in the process of construction is said – by postmodernists – to be an instrument of power, leading to the creation of regimes of truth (Foucault, 2000). The criticism of the obsession of postmodernists with the notion of power as well as all-capable function of language as a tool for constructing reality was well explained in Pluckrose and Lindsay (2020) who demonstrate the cynicism of postmodern thinking as characterised by the 'denial of objective knowledge or truth and commitment to cultural constructivism, and belief that whatever it is we call truth is nothing more than a construct of the culture' (Pluckrose & Lindsay, 2020, p. 59). The increasing popularity of postmodern thought, as much as it is inapplicable to many practical PR and communication problems, might have led to confusion not only among audience members but also among PR practitioners. Does truth exist? Is it negotiable? Does it depend on power?

Producing evidence in a world where anyone can decide what is true, depending on their wants, needs, and emotions, should be problematic for PR practitioners. If anyone can decide the credibility of a topic, why should PR be bothered with research and liaising with experts at all? I argue that social psychology and individual-level analyses could bring much-needed realism to the practice of PR. In the psychological, propositional view of truth, statements (beliefs, attitudes, judgements) are true as long as they correspond to an element of reality. The race driver from the previously used scenario was speeding because speed can be measured. Whether he felt he was not speeding or considered the notion of speed as tied to the regime of truth imposed by the state and police should be of secondary importance. Social psychology is a scientific discipline in a positivist sense and relies on the correspondence theory of truth. The discipline also handles apparent inconsistencies in truth-related judgements well. Let us consider how often people, especially on social media, formulate opinions about topics that should be decided through academic judgement, especially recently, when non-experts discussed the efficacy of COVID-19 vaccination or questioned the existence of the pandemic. Psychology investigates the formal nature of attitudes of evaluations that involve objectively incorrect statements. The role of those investigations is not to cast doubt on scientifically proven phenomena but instead to understand causes of disbelief and formulate recommendations for efficient communication with audience members whose opinions differ from the academic consensus or facts. In conclusion, the responsibility of a researcher is to acknowledge their own doubts, cognitive biases, judgement errors, and motivations. To do so, psychology views people as ecologically rational and investigates instances where people hold attitudes towards matters of fact while also acknowledging the existence of objective elements of reality.

To say that truth is unimportant to contemporary audience members would be an exaggeration. It would miss an important aspect of the psychological characteristics of audience members. Truth seems to be important to them, but only to the extent that it aligns with the existing system of beliefs of an audience member. This is why people who are brought up listening to one internally consistent set of beliefs tend to adhere more to information that would not violate their attitudes and support their choices. This phenomenon has been defined as alternative epistemologies (ways of learning about the environment) and alternative epistemic realities (systems of perceiving the world and concepts that are true or false, e.g. Lewandowsky et al. (2017)). The development of alternative epistemologies can challenge the need to produce credible evidence. Some people will only believe evidence if it comes from sources they trust, regardless of the appropriateness of the methods used. However, this does not absolve the practice of PR from being familiar with the basics of producing truthful evidence and credible communication. Audiences expect organisations (as well as politicians) to exercise due diligence when communicating evidence. For example, PR communicators should not expect that collecting data from 60 participants will reveal whether a product is the number one choice of British consumers. The following section provides a brief overview of the quantitative methods required in PR practice.

Methodology of Psychological Research

The interdisciplinary character of PR scholarship can be a source of methodological confusion. In my view, the symptoms of confusion that affect the practice of PR include a preference for qualitative over quantitative methods, disregard for experimentation, a limited understanding of the concept of causality, confusion about the requirements of external versus internal validity, and incorrect sampling techniques. Although qualitative research provides a more in-depth understanding of analysed phenomena, the generalisability and predictive power of its outcomes are complemented by quantitative methodologies (Stacks, 2010). Stacks argues that simple quantitative tools commonly employed by practitioners are very good sources of knowledge about a company's perception, image, or reputation, which enable the evaluation of the effectiveness of campaigns (Stacks, 2010). With the (occasional) adoption of quantitative methods in everyday PR practice comes a relative lack of enthusiasm towards using this methodology to advance PR scholarship – at least where a perspective other than Grunig's management function is favoured.

At the heart of understanding the relationship between the various contents and structures of mental processes and observable behaviour is the notion of causality. In both public relations and psychology, it relates to the question of determining whether one process, person, or activity affects another. Whenever a word like *affects*, *leads to*, or *impacts* is used, scientific methodology prescribes a set of conditions that should be met to establish a cause-and-effect relationship. Does the type and level of education lead to supporting one model of politics versus the other? Does reading exhaustive information about the efficacy of a skincare product lead to building a positive attitude towards that product? Who is more credible as an influencer of a new diet: a clinical dietician or a celebrity with a history of weight loss? These questions refer to establishing causal relationships and require quantitative techniques. Humans are not good at judging causality, so asking audience members why they made a particular choice will most likely not reveal the cause of their actions. It can tell us about their *perceived* causes of behaviour, but not the actual ones. Qualitative methodologies may reveal the contents of the thoughts of audience members, but quantitative techniques are used to determine causality.

If a researcher wants to understand a causal mechanism in principle, experimentation should be used. In experimentation, a researcher aims to recreate the conditions that influence an audience member's judgement or decision. To distil a specific factor that is seen as a source of variation in responses, different versions of experimental stimuli are created that resemble real-life contexts. Social psychologists design experiments to mirror real-life contexts and ascertain that findings are generalisable. For PR, it means that they can be applied in everyday practice. In the context of social media or internet technology-mediated communication, today's experiments are typically conducted in laboratory settings to increase external and face validity. Those who participate in the experiments should not perceive the experimental scenarios as entirely fictitious, and the problems tested should be as close as possible to real-world settings. To compare two groups on a single dimension (e.g. the exact text of an endorsement from experts who differ only in their type of education), a statistical procedure called a t-test can be used. When samples from two similar populations of audience members are available, they are known to differ in their exposure to campaign messages, and their attitudes towards the brand, product, and purchase intentions can be compared. A statistical technique called analysis of variance, which is a special type of regression, can then be employed to analyse responses from participants and compare them across two or more conditions, taking into account additional, potentially influencing factors (covariates).

Social psychology, like other social sciences, does not directly address physical or bodily states and processes. Meaning that it investigates observable phenomena and their outcomes rather than any physical processes itself.[2] By employing various scientific methods of analysis and statistical procedures, psychology attempts to understand the mechanisms that govern human cognition, decision-making, judgement, and motivation. In a sense, a considerable degree of approximation and abstraction is required in a scientific psychological study of human behaviour. For example, to explain why a person relies more on information produced by an expert compared to their peers when making a judgement about a mobile phone brand, a psychologist would aim to establish on what dimensions an expert and a family member differ. First, the characteristics (dimensions) of both persons can be compared. There could be several dimensions that both would share: age, gender, country of origin, language spoken, etc. However, to compare all characteristics and identify the one that explains the attribution of expertise by an audience member, information about these characteristics needs to be collected using a consistent measurement method. The selection of information to be collected and compared is dictated by two general sources: theory and observation. First, existing theories or scientific evidence need to be evaluated in search of personal characteristics that relate to the perceived expertise. Often, this may not be enough, especially when attribution of expertise is prone to change due to contextual factors (consider if 15 years ago, a person without a degree, scientific background, or practical experience related to the production of cosmetics could become a trusted expert advising on the use of parabens in beauty products?). Therefore, previous evidence and context must be taken into account to analyse the influence of expertise on judgement. Physical characteristics of a person or testable knowledge level are insufficient to describe the mechanism of producing a psychological judgement. Thanks to a technique called regression analysis, which is used when one continuous variable (e.g. the amount of information remembered about a new product) leads to a causal change in a different continuous variable, a linear relationship can be identified. For example, it can be used to see if the age of participants is associated with more positive or negative views about a brand and higher intentions to purchase. If, however, a researcher wants to build a more complex model, which would analyse several additional sources of influence (e.g. age of participants, gender, and channel of communication), regression-based models that include mediators and moderators can be tested. As it often happens, age alone does not explain differences in judgements; other age-related factors can also play a part. A regression-based design is used when data is collected rather than manipulated (like in an experiment).

The experimental method does not contest the complexity or bidirectionality of influences between factors affecting behaviour. Positivist quantitative methods enable one to appreciate the complexity or multilevel nature of influences, but in a systematic and carefully planned approach, allowing for the step-by-step identification or disconfirmation of effects. Although in media and audience research, experimentation is the object of criticism, arguments brought by, for example, Ruddock (2001) seem to come from authors who have a somewhat distorted or incomplete view of experimental methodology. For example, Lewis says that 'experimenters see the world is driven by forces that can be separated' and 'assume that people can be cleansed of their social background' (Lewis, 1991 in Ruddock, 2001, p. 39). None of these statements is remotely accurate, and they are based on a rather superficial understanding of psychological methodology and principles. Firstly, experimenters believe that these forces can be identified, not separated. The process of identification is based on two principles: constructing precise definitions of the tested constructs and controlling (or monitoring) potentially confounding factors. This is to say that when an experimenter wants to understand the effect of media on a specific group of individuals, they first need to define a specific behaviour or attitude they would be looking for. Secondly, about the supposed cleansing, all major psychological theories, including Bandura (Bandura, 1977, 1991) but also cognitive psychologists like Festinger (Festinger, 1954, 1957), and all social psychologists nowadays, assume that in the process of socialisation – social learning – we acquire (1991) knowledge about ways of behaving that is accepted and followed by other people. What Lewis may refer to as cleansing can mean controlling for Psychologists gather additional characteristics of research participants to understand if there are regularities in their impact on behaviour and monitor them, even though they are not the central focus of an investigation. When data about these additional, potentially important characteristics are collected, they are included in statistical models to identify patterns of potentially meaningful confounding effects – nothing further from cleansing.

Public relations scholars may occasionally fall victim to misconstrued narratives about quantitative methodologies. Related to the *social* aspect of PR research, which is now primarily associated with sociological thinking, qualitative methodology is firmly attached to the social strand of research. It could be argued that the preference for qualitative methodologies results from a series of ontological and epistemological misinterpretations of quantitative methods. Although there should be no preference for one group of methods because the choice of methodology is related to the type of research question, anecdotal evidence suggests that the use of experimentation to produce evidence-based decisions by PR practitioners is very limited. University PR education may be partly at fault because a handful of PR degrees offer training in quantitative methods and statistics. Related to that, PR scholarship mentions criticism of quantitative, empirical science. In the introduction to their book Qualitative Research Techniques in Public Relations and Marketing Communication, Daymon and Holloway (2002) refer to the division formulated by Deacon and his colleagues between interpretive and objective ways of perceiving the world. The former refers to the process of constructing meanings of the surrounding social reality and expressing them through language, sounds, personal style, and social rituals (Deacon et al., 2021). The authors go on to argue that researchers who hold this view believe that social reality is not objective and is not perceived identically by all people. They are less interested in studying external factors that may influence behaviour and, instead, they focus on 'intentions, motivations and subjective experiences' (Daymon & Holloway, 2010, p. 4). Qualitative research is also usually associated with the subjective nature of social reality. However, the authors also make several incorrect claims. The first refers to the units of analysis and measurement in quantitative and qualitative research.

Firstly, the distinction between quantitative and qualitative research methods, which supposes a difference in the unit of analysis, the former being numbers, the latter being words, does not seem right. In quantitative psychological research, units of analysis are not numbers. Psychology research is interested in capturing different entities: attitudes, evaluations, opinions, judgements, behaviours, etc. The way they are measured, however, involves numbers. Social psychological research, driven by the need to measure the content of thoughts objectively, cannot alter reality merely by changing the nature of mental processes; it has its roots in empiricism. Michell (1997) explains that psychology is underpinned by a scientific philosophy, as it rests on empirical realism, which assumes that an independent world exists and that methods of learning about this objective reality can be found through quantifiable means. One of the central concepts of modern psychology is that of quantity, and 'if an object is quantitative, then it is, in principle, measurable' (p. 358). So, although the unit of measurement could be a number (although this is not always the case), this does not imply that quantitative psychologists are ultimately interested in analysing numbers. Statistical analyses involving numbers are performed to understand how mental processes and mental constructs change or behave in order to introduce objectivity and understand the regularities of human behaviour. In such cases, the measurement of quantitative units involves assigning numerals to objects or events according to established rules (Stevens, 1946). It is possible when an additive structure between attributes is presumed (Michell, 1997, p. 375). Numbers are used only insofar to represent units of change within a process or intensity of a state.

It is undoubtedly correct that modern psychology is an empirical science in the sense that it necessitates evidence to arrive at conclusions. However, psychology remains interested in the subjective nature of human experience, and people also construct their reality – different people have different schemata, stereotypes, and attitudes towards seemingly similar objects. Quantitative methods in psychology do not stand in opposition to the nature of subjective individual experience. The objective element in psychological, quantitative investigations is represented as the pursuit of universal processes and their structure, which all people share. How does age influence the speed of information processing and the quality of decisions? How are the processes of stereotyping different across the lifespan? Every person constructs their own meanings uniquely, and no two individuals on the planet share identical thoughts. It does, however, contest the fact that the process of stereotyping would not formally look similar in different persons. This is why psychology distinguishes between formal and content characteristics of processes. The formal aspect refers to identifying regularities that govern human behaviour. At the same time, the contents of thoughts explain the direction of behaviour, which involves various biases discussed earlier in the chapter when the concept of human rationality was introduced.

The commitment of psychology to science does not come without drawbacks, and the discipline itself is not free of ideological bias. When psychological research is conducted on issues of societal importance, criticism is often inevitable, especially as the line between objective, expert judgement and normative judgement is rarely clear. As Howitt (1991) put it: 'rarely, if ever, could psychologists let their data stand without interpretation' but further adds that 'psychology should seek to have something to offer society on the significant problems facing it' (Howitt, 1991, p. 148). We can take the example of Blue Monday to illustrate this point. The elements of the equation, and depending on their definition, are fairly objective. We can learn about the average annual temperature to identify the coldest day. The margins or error for calculating the distance from New Year's Eve can also be calculated. Averaging the monthly salary and average debt can also be achieved. It is, however, a task of a different magnitude to come up with a formula in which these factors are factored in and weighted to locate the most depressing day of the year. In science, this refers to the process of developing a theoretical model. As such, several steps need to be completed first, and all of them require scientific expertise.

Formal Nature of Quantitative Evidence: On the Generalisability of Qualitative and Quantitative Findings

The famous PR campaign 'Best Job in the World' involved creating a real position – an island caretaker – with a compensation of 150,000 Australian dollars for a six-month contract. The goal of this publicity stunt was to change the perception of the Great Barrier Reef islands as an attractive tourist destination (Seitel & Doorley, 2012). The success of the campaign was related to a combination of context analysis, understanding the initial perception of the location, and inquiring into the knowledge of audiences about holiday destinations. However, it would be an abuse to say that an insight into this campaign provides knowledge characterised by generalisability. It would therefore not be advisable to create more 'Best job in the world' campaigns for any client who wants to increase awareness of their holiday offer. The above argument is not a criticism of practical experience. Knowledge and skills gained from everyday work in the industry provide important insights into the current social, cultural, and market context, as well as the needs of audiences, and offer opportunities to generate hypotheses that can later become the starting point for designing research plans. However, the specific nature of PR, combined with the highly dynamic nature of the consumer environment, the growing importance of some stakeholders, and the loss of power and legitimacy of others, makes it difficult to generalise and suggest lessons for other campaigns. A formal approach is necessary to identify the mechanism behind the success of any campaign.

In the psychological tradition, the term *formal* means: 'relating to form or abstracting from content' (Nęcka, 2000, p. 9). If mental processes are analysed from the formal side, we are not interested in the content of the cognitive process. A related term – model, is 'a deliberately simplified and usually idealised and imaginary representation of a phenomenon, with fundamental properties that are explicitly defined (or physically built) and from which other properties can be deduced by logical reasoning (or by empirical observation if the model is a physical object' (Colman, 2013, p. 404). The main 'elements' of the human mental architecture – constructs and processes that provide mental scaffolding that are relevant to the practice of PR are: memory, attention, knowledge, schemas, schemata, stereotypes, and goals. Understanding the formal aspects of processes governing judgement formation and decision-making, the behaviours of audiences can be examined more systematically. For example, memory capacity is limited and depends on internal factors: physiological arousal, body temperature, and heart rate (see Chapter 6). Secondly, the content of communication can be appreciated as demonstrating that audiences may reach different conclusions on contentious issues depending on the activation and proximity of goals they implicitly pursue (see Chapter 7). The identification of formal characteristics of processes is important because it can also help in producing generalisable findings.

While internal validity refers to the internal, formal properties of a concept, external validity describes the degree to which an investigated concept corresponds to the real world and can be generalised in different contexts (Calder et al., 1982; Cook & Campbell, 1979). If the researcher's interest is mainly theoretical, the inference of external validity is of little concern (Cook & Campbell, 1979). Trafimow (2023) contends that the ongoing discussions about internal and external validity concerns lead to the belief that a type of trade-off is embedded in the process of designing research studies: maximising internal validity lowers external validity and vice versa. He further argues that in laboratory experiments, internal validity is increased, but this is due to the abstraction of content and the obscuring of social context. In other words, to identify causal relationships between mental processes, traits, or other internal phenomena, the role of external factors, such as language (that may lead to different biases) or aesthetic context (e.g. how information is presented visually), is limited to a bare minimum. As a result, participants in such experiments receive information that looks almost 'surgically' clean but could raise concerns of applied-focused scholars in PR, as well as advocates of qualitative methodologies. In public relations scholarship, external validity concerns are typically raised in the context of participant samples and their demographic characteristics in quantitative studies.

When conducting an experimental study in laboratory settings, researchers strive to have a reasonable degree of control over independent variables and attempt to minimise the impact of random and contextual factors on the experimental process. Let us consider a scenario in which a researcher is testing the recall level of a press release based on its different formal characteristics. A working hypothesis suggests that words written in capital letters are memorised better than noncapitalised ones. Two versions of the press release are created, whereby in version A, keywords are written in bold, while in version B, they are not. The experiment designed to test this hypothesis involves one independent variable with two levels (CAPITAL versus non-capital letters). In this scenario, no assumptions are made about the various factors influencing recall. Consequently, the scenario does not imply that these factors are unimportant (such as the number of words, timeliness of sending, or alignment with the editor's interests). To make the predictions externally valid, the sample of participants should reflect the characteristics of the population that would constitute the audience of the tested press release.

One particular area of concern in psychological research related to understanding the formal characteristics of processes and external validity is student sampling (Hovland, 1959). In a research project, a pivotal question is to what extent a student sample would exhibit different characteristics than a general sample of similar age or a random sample taken from any population. The answer to this question is nuanced. While some intellectual skills are prone to training (Żelechowska et al., 2017) and may be influenced, for example, by formal education, the variance of these skills within a sample of students can be similar to that in the general population. Not surprisingly, students can differ from the general population in several characteristics. Sears (1986), for example, listed variables that change over the lifespan, leading to the conclusion that overreliance on student samples in the US between the

1960s and 1980s resulted in an over-exaggeration of differences between variables, such as cognitive skills, sense of self, and compliance with authority. However, in the third decade of the 21st century, in the EU and the US, the percentage of people with a tertiary education is between 40 and 50% (Galan, 2025). For example, Hanel and Vione (2016) conducted an extensive study comparing a student sample with a general population sample from 59 countries and 86,272 participants, concluding that students may differ from the general population, primarily in terms of personal and attitudinal variables. Calder's opinion that 'sophisticated arguments for external validity accept the universal nature of theoretical research and reject common sense conceptions such as the automatic superiority of random samples' (Calder et al., 1982, p. 241) holds. When a formal model is tested, students can be used to test it, primarily because the goal of formal quantitative research is to establish how a mechanism works rather than what the outcome of this process is.

Today, psychological methods of gathering and evaluating evidence present an intriguing possibility for PR practitioners. However, when content creation is fully outsourced to AI tools, the ability to evaluate evidence and separate fact from fiction could become a necessity and a core competence of the PR industry. For this to occur, practitioners and academics must engage in dialogue and knowledge exchange. Otherwise, the scientist–practitioner gap will continue to grow even larger than it is today.

Theory Versus Practice Gap and the Cumulative Nature of Psychological Evidence

In psychology, the scientist-practitioner gap 'refers to the division between psychologists who believe that clinical practice should be heavily informed by empirical studies and those who believe clinical judgment and intuition should be paramount' (Cautin, 2011, p. 197). It is defined as 'a mismatch between what the scientific literature demonstrates to be effective versus ineffective treatments and what clinicians often do in practice' (Cautin, 2011, p. 198). Questions asked by Tavris (2003) apply to the practice versus theory of PR conundrum with sound accuracy: How do we know what is true? What kind of evidence is required to support a hypothesis? (Tavris, 2003, p. xiv). Practitioners would probably be divided as well when asked to what extent scientific evidence applies to their work. Historically, Bernays seems to have a somewhat divided view on that subject as he saw that psychology could never become an exact science. However, when asked by Howard Penn Hudson what he thought about PR practitioners who prefer practice over theory, Bernays's response categorised such objections as 'poppycock' (Bernays, 1986, p. 11). In a sense, for Bernays, PR was neither purely theoretical nor purely practical; as much as practitioners should have understood the basics of science, academics needed to comprehend the intricacies of practice. In an ideal situation, the relationship between science and the practice of PR should be circular and symmetrical. The science of PR should legitimise, inform, and inspire the practice, and the practice should reciprocally inspire, inform, and legitimise its science.

Tavris (2003) explains the gap between the science and the practice of psychology as underpinned by natural tensions resulting from different goals and training. The differences between the science and practice of PR are also evident and deserve to be uncovered, as both sides of the argument may hold idealised impressions about each other. However, building relationships between an organisation and its stakeholders is often a goal, and everyday practice is frequently subjected to the expectations of clients and other organisational departments, which may differ or even contradict the standards of the profession. For example, despite the efforts of professional associations, outputs are the most commonly used measurement of PR rather than outcomes (see Chapter 5). The gap between the practice and science of PR may be wider than that in psychology due to the complexity of public relations practice.

Not only are the goals and training of PR practitioners and academics different, but the level of acceptance of scientific evidence among PR practitioners is also lower. As Cornelissen (2000) suggests, 'scientific knowledge is seldom used in an unaltered form in practice' (p. 315). This could be true for at least two groups of reasons. First, I argue that public relations operates on three levels: the micro, mezzo, and macro levels of processes. Physiological processes, such as heart rate and bodily arousal, interact with mental processes, including memory, attention, and information processing. These, in turn, produce behavioural manifestations: group thinking, stereotyping, and normative group influence. Moving one level upward, behaviours explain the expressed organisational values and aims. However, they can also influence macro-level phenomena that are the area of interest for sociologists, for example, national identities, class, or gender. Ultimately, for a practitioner, any PR scenario involves a constellation of factors (variables) that can be monitored only to a moderate extent, with the majority of them changing dynamically and left only partly observable. The multiplicity of forces shaping PR contexts leads some practitioners to consider the discipline of PR as an art form rather than a science. However, comparing PR to art could implicitly limit the potential to develop relevant theories and apply them in the practice of PR. The uncontrollability of complex scenarios that PR deals with daily can result in taking limited responsibility for explaining all factors, especially unintended consequences of PR activity (Dozier & Lauzen, 2000).

Although PR could be seen as a form of art, the field still requires the science of psychology. However, the way psychological terms are used in popular discourse may prevent practitioners from viewing psychology as an exact science that produces legitimate evidence. One reason for this is offered by John (1998), who explains that the nature of the knowledge psychology produces means that psychologists lack epistemic authority. Unlike many scientific disciplines, which an average person may perceive as less immediately relevant to everyday life and whose vocabulary is only used by a narrow group of experts, psychology and its lexicon are omnipresent. People increasingly talk about their feelings and try to find 'hacks' to manage their lives efficiently. They are often – mistakenly – led to believe that by changing the content of their thoughts and 'affirm' – for example, wealth or beauty – they can change their material possessions and physical appearance. Indeed, words like attitudes, personality, emotions, feelings, extro- and introvert, or even psychological disorders like narcissism, passive-aggression, or bi-polar are often used by non-psychologists.

Psychology, as a discipline that seeks to explain human behaviour, is particularly well-positioned to inspire everyday conversations but also, worryingly, to serve as the playground for tools to be borrowed by other disciplines that often claim their interest and assume epidemic authority as experts in understanding human behaviour. Social media are full of naturally born psychologists and life coaches. While sometimes there is nothing wrong in saying that someone is a good 'psychologist' because they are good with people, a clear distinction between the science of psychology and the lay use of the word must be maintained. Otherwise, people will become victims of pseudo-psychologists, who promise 'to cure you in 5 days, 5 minutes, or 5 orgasms' (Tavris, 2003, p. xiv). Tavris refers to the upsurge of pseudoscientific psychological theories, especially notable during the countercultural revolution, as a 'benign nuisance' to psychological scientists. However, today, the internet and social media have blown the pseudo-promise of lay psychology out of manageable proportions. Psychological claims can be 'put to the test' almost instantly, and everyone feels entitled to 'verify them' against the existing body of psychological knowledge. This can explain why Blue Monday has become a widespread cultural phenomenon. If psychology is not exactly a science, it does not need exact evidence.

One important lesson that scientific psychology has learned exceptionally well is the approach to producing evidence, which tames enthusiasm for novelties (such as claims that five orgasms can cure you). This concept involves cumulatively building knowledge, not only by introducing new ideas but also by testing older predictions in new contexts, critically examining outcomes, and suggesting new iterations. 'Modern science is not based on the achievements of extraordinary individuals but on the epistemic force of disciplinary communities' (Stichweh, 2015, p. 13728). Unlike psychology, which appears as a field with a more precise focus, better-defined traditions, and shared definitions of methods, in PR, standing on the shoulders of giants is possible, but psychological examples can be inspiring. For example, nudge theory has received considerable attention and gained widespread praise, as well as found applications in several disciplines, including behavioural science, economics, and politics. Practitioners in the fields of public communication, advertising, and public relations have also used it effectively. The UK government had its Nudge Unit established in the Cabinet Office in 2010 to 'apply behavioural science to public policy'.[3] The development of the choice architecture introduced by Thaler and Sunstein (2008) would not have been possible without the previous advances in psychology. For example, Tversky and Kahneman (1974) and Gilovich et al. (2002) had previously explained systematic biases in human judgement. They identified heuristics of availability (overestimating the probability of an event based on how easily a similar event is recalled), anchoring (overreliance on the first piece of information received), and representativeness (overestimating the probability of an event based on comparing it to an existing prototype). Different outcomes of hot, intuitive judgements and systematic elaboration during decision-making were comprehensively tackled by postulating the dual processes theory, which recognises that automatic, intuitive decisions are made based on available schemas and memories when motivation or ability is limited (Chaiken & Trope, 1999; Strack & Deutsch, 2004). The concept of hot cognition was proposed in 1963 by Abelson, and the concept of scripts was most prominently introduced by Schank and Abelson in 1977. The idea of nudging is also based on the psychological concept of priming, a notion with a long and established tradition of research among psychologists. Thaler and Sunstein's (2008) excellent contribution to understanding human choice does not purport to be completely novel. Instead, it is an example of skilful exploration of existing psychological and behavioural evidence, the identification of – and critically – the demonstration of how the evidence can be comprehensively applied to improve action for the benefit of individuals and society. Additionally, pseudoscientific psychological ideas appear to play a role in the pursuit of understanding human behaviour. Neurolinguistic programming – which now has the status of pseudoscience – is just one example of presenting existing psychological theories under the disguise of a new 'answer-all' phenomenon. One contribution of NLP to psychology is positive: it strengthens the interest in the role of content in thoughts and language in shaping the outcome of basic psychological processes. It can be partly attributed to NLP that the original research by Mehrabian on non-verbal components of communication (Mehrabian & Ferris, 1967; Mehrabian & Wiener, 1967) has been re-examined to understand that the infamous formula, placing just 7% weight on verbal communication, has been found to have no evidential support.

Taken together, the picture should not remain grim. Public relations is a field that has appreciated its multiparadigmatic character and has experience in listening to different voices, as well as being open to various methodologies. For me, this is due to its focus on relationships. Chapter 5 focuses on the psychology of the object of PR and suggests that with some updating, several aspects of relationships could be researched more objectively and decrease the gap between the theory and practice of PR. Psychology could serve as a source of epistemic authority for PR scholarship, and revisiting the object of PR from a psychological perspective could help achieve this goal.

Notes

1 Explorations conducted by Curtin (2022) did not confirm any existing copy of Ivy Lee's declaration, and its existence is now only based on indirect sources.
2 In psychology, psychophysiology investigates the impact of heart rate, skin conductance, etc, on other processes.
3 In 2014, the unit, officially known as the Behavioural Insights Team, expanded into a limited company and is now owned by an NGO.

References

Abelson, R. (1963). Computer simulation of "hot cognition". In S. S. Tomkins & S. Messick (Eds.), *Computer Simulation of Personality* (pp. 277–298). Wiley.
Andre, P., Boneva, T., Chopra, F., & Falk, A. (2024). Globally representative evidence on the actual and perceived support for climate action. *Nature Climate Change*, *14*(3), 253–259. https://doi.org/10.1038/s41558-024-01925-3
Bandura, A. (1977). *Social Learning Theory*. Prentice-Hall.
Bandura, A. (1991). Social cognitive theory of self-regulation. *Organizational Behavior and Human Decision Processes*, *50*(2), 247–287.
Bentele, G., & Seidenglanz, R. (2008). Trust and credibility—Prerequisites for communication management. In A. Zerfass, B. van Ruler, & K. Sriramesh (Eds.), *Public Relations Research: European and International Perspectives and Innovations* (pp. 49–62). VS Verlag für Sozialwissenschaften.
Bernays, E. L. (1986). *The later years: public relations insights 1956-1986*. Howard Penn Hudson Assc Inc.
Burnett, D. (2012, January 16). Blue Monday: A depressing day of pseudoscience and humiliation | Psychology | The Guardian. *The Guardian*. https://www.theguardian.com/science/blog/2012/jan/16/blue-monday-depressing-day-pseudoscience
Calder, B. J., Phillips, L. W., & Tybout, A. M. (1982). The concept of external validity. *Journal of Consumer Research*, *9*, 240–244.
Cautin, R. L. (2011). Invoking history to teach about the scientist-practitioner gap. *History of Psychology*, *14*(2), 197–203. https://doi.org/10.1037/A0022897
Chaiken, S., & Trope, Y. (Eds.). (1999). *Dual-Process Theories in Social Psychology*. Guilford Press.
Chase, V. M., Hertwig, R., & Gigerenzer, G. (1998). Visions of rationality. *Trends in Cognitive Sciences*, *2*(6), 206–214. https://psycnet.apa.org/record/2001-11516-001
Colman, A. M. (2013). *Oxford Dictionary of Psychology*. Oxford University Press.
Cook, T. D., & Campbell, D. T. (1979). *Quasi-Experimentation: Design and Analysis Issues for Field Settings*. Rand McNally. https://www.scholars.northwestern.edu/en/publications/quasi-experimentation-design-and-analysis-issues-for-field-settin
Cornelissen, J. P. (2000). Toward an understanding of the use of academic theories in public relations practice. *Public Relations Review*, *26*(3), 315–326.
Curtin, P. (2022, July, 6-8). *Revisiting a U.S. public relations origin myth from a labor perspective: The 1902 and 1906 Anthracite Coal Strike/Stoppage. International History of Public Relations Conference, Bournemouth, United Kingdom.*
Daymon, C., & Holloway, I. (2002). *Qualitative Research Methods in Public Relations and Marketing Communications*. Routledge.

Daymon, C., & Holloway, I. (2010). *Qualitative Research Methods in Public Relations and Marketing Communications*. 2nd ed. (Vol. 9780203846544). https://doi.org/10.4324/9780203846544

Deacon, D., Murdock, G., Pickering, M., & Golding, P. (2021). Researching Communications: A Practical Guide to Methods in Media and Cultural Analysis. *Bloomsbury Academic*. https://doi.org/10.5040/9781501316951

Dozier, D. M., & Lauzen, M. M. (2000). Liberating the intellectual domain from the practice: Public relations, activism, and the role of the scholar. *Journal of Public Relations Research*, *12*(1), 3–22.

Drug Overdose Deaths: Facts and Figures | National Institute on Drug Abuse (NIDA). (n.d.). Retrieved March11, 2025, from https://nida.nih.gov/research-topics/trends-statistics/overdose-death-rates

Etcof, N., Orbach, S., Scott, J., & D'Agostino, H. (2004). "The real truth about beauty: A Global Report" Findings of the Global Study on Women, Beauty and Well-Being. https://www.clubofamsterdam.com/contentarticles/52%20Beauty/dove_white_paper_final.pdf

Festinger, L. (1954). A Theory of Social Comparison Processes. *Human Relations*, *7*(2). https://doi.org/10.1177/001872675400700202

Festinger, L. (1957). *A Theory of Cognitive Dissonance*. Stanford University Press. https://psycnet.apa.org/record/1993-97948-000

Forgas, J. P., Fiedler, K., & Crano, W. D. (2020). Applications of social psychology: History, issues and prospects. In J. P. Forgas, W. D. Crano, & K. Fiedler (Eds.), *Applications of Social Psychology: How Social Psychology Can Contribute to the Solution of Real-World Problems* (pp. 1–19). Routledge/Taylor & Francis Group. https://doi.org/10.4324/9780367816407-1

Foucault, M. (2000). Truth and power. In P. Rainbow (Ed.), *Essential Works of Foucault, 1954-1984* (Vol. 3, pp. 111–133). New Press Essential.

Galan, S. (2025, April 15). *Population with Higher Education by Country 2022*. Statista. https://www.statista.com/statistics/232951/university-degree-attainment-by-country/

Gigerenzer, G., & Todd, P. M. (1999). Fast and frugal heuristics: The adaptive toolbox. In G. Gigerenzer, P. M. Todd, & The ABC Research Group (Eds.), *Simple Heuristics that Make Us Smart* (pp. 3–34). Oxford University Press. https://psycnet.apa.org/record/1999-04366-001

Gigerenzer, G., Todd, P. M., & The ABC Research Group. (1999). *Simple Heuristics that Make us Smart*. Oxford University.

Gilovich, T., Griffin, D., & Kahneman, D. (Eds.) (2002*). Heuristics and Biases: The Psychology of Intuitive Judgment*. Cambridge University Press. https://doi.org/10.1017/CBO9780511808098

Hanel, P. H. P., & Vione, K. C. (2016). Do student samples provide an accurate estimate of the general public? *PLoS ONE*, *11*(12). https://doi.org/10.1371/journal.pone.0168354

Hiebert, R. E. (2003). Public relations and propaganda in framing the Iraq war: A preliminary review. *Public Relations Review*, *29*(3), 243–255. https://doi.org/10.1016/S0363-8111(03)00047-X

Hovland, C. I. (1959). Reconciling conflicting results derived from experimental and survey studies of attitude change. *American Psychologist*, *14*(1), 8–17. https://doi.org/10.1037/h0042210

Howitt, D. (1991). *Concerning Psychology: Psychology Applied to Social Issues*. Open University Press.

John, I. (1998). The scientist—practitioner model: A critical examination. *Australian Psychologist*, *33*(1), 24–30.

Kruglanski, A. W. (1989). Lay epistemics and human knowledge: Cognitive and motivational bases. In *Lay Epistemics and Human Knowledge*. Springer US. https://doi.org/10.1007/978-1-4899-0924-4

L'Etang, J. (2008). Public relations, persuasion and propaganda: Truth, knowledge, spirituality and mystique. In A. Zerfass, B. van Ruler, & K. Sriramesh (Eds.), *Public Relations Research* (pp. 251–269). VS Verlag für Sozialwissenschaften. https://doi.org/10.1007/978-3-531-90918-9_16

Lewandowsky, S., Ecker, U. K. H., & Cook, J. (2017). Beyond misinformation: Understanding and coping with the "post-truth" era. *Journal of Applied Research in Memory and Cognition*, *6*(4), 353–369. https://doi.org/10.1016/j.jarmac.2017.07.008

Lewis, J. (1991). *The Ideological Octopus: An Exploration of Television and its Audience* (*Routledge Library Editions: Television, Vol. 9*). Routledge. https://doi.org/10.4324/9780203379899

Lyotard, J.-F. (1984). *The Postmodern Condition*. University of Minnesota Press.

Mehrabian, A., & Ferris, S. R. (1967). Inference of attitudes from nonverbal communication in two channels. *Journal of Consulting Psychology*, *31*(3), 248–252. https://doi.org/10.1037/h0024648

Mehrabian, A., & Wiener, M. (1967). Decoding of inconsistent communications. *Journal of Personality and Social Psychology*, *6*(1), 109–114. https://doi.org/10.1037/h0024532

Michell, J. (1997). Quantitative science and the definition of measurement in psychology. *British Journal of Psychology*, *88*(3), 355–383. https://doi.org/10.1111/j.2044-8295.1997.tb02641.x

Morse, S. (1906, September). An awakening in Wall Street. *The American Magazine*, *62*, 457–463.

Nęcka, E. (2000). *Pobudzenie intelektu: zarys formalnej teorii inteligencji*. [in polish: Arousal of the intellect: an outline of the formal theory of intelligence]. Universitas.

Nichols, T. M. (2017). *The Death of Expertise: The Campaign Against Established Knowledge and Why It Matters*. Oxford University Press.

Payne, J. W., Bettman, J. R., & Johnson, E. J. (1993). *The Adaptive Decision Maker*. Cambridge University Press. https://doi.org/10.1017/CBO9781139173933

Pluckrose, H., & Lindsay, J. (2020). *Cynical Theories: How Activist Scholarship Made Everything about Race, Gender, and Identity—and Why This Harms Everybody*. Pitchstone Publishing.

Postmodernism | Definition, Doctrines, & Facts | Britannica. (n.d.). Retrieved March25, 2025, from https://www.britannica.com/topic/postmodernism-philosophy

Rampton, S., & Stauber, J. C.. (2003). *Weapons of Mass Deception: The Uses of Propaganda in Bush's War on Iraq*. Robinson.

Ruddock, A. (2001). *Understanding audiences: Theory and Method*. SAGE Publications Ltd.

Russell, J. H., & Patterson, D. M. (2025). *The Weaponization of Expertise: How Elites Fuel Populism*. MIT Press.

Russell, K., & Myers, C. (2019). The misunderstood nineteenth century U.S. press agent. *Public Relations Review*, *45*(2), 246–257. https://doi.org/10.1016/J.PUBREV.2018.12.010

Russell, K. M., & Bishop, C. O. (2009). Understanding Ivy Lee's declaration of principles: U.S. newspaper and magazine coverage of publicity and press agentry, 1865–1904. *Public Relations Review*, *35*(2), 91–101. https://doi.org/10.1016/J.PUBREV.2009.01.004

Schank, R. C., & Abelson, R. P. (1977). *Scripts, Plans, Goals, and Understanding: An Inquiry into Human Knowledge Structures*. Psychology Press.

Scott, R., & Whitwam, R. (2025, February 11). The 4 Best Android Phones of 2025 | Reviews by Wirecutter. *The New York Times*. https://www.nytimes.com/wirecutter/reviews/best-android-phone/

Sears, D. O. (1986). College sophomores in the laboratory. Influences of a narrow data base on social psychology's view of human nature. *Journal of Personality and Social Psychology*, *51*(3), 515–530. https://doi.org/10.1037/0022-3514.51.3.515

Seitel, F. P., & Doorley, J. (2012). *Rethinking Reputation, How PR Trumps Marketing and Advertising in the New Media World*. Pallgrave Macmillan. https://us.macmillan.com/books/9781137092229/rethinkingreputation/

Simon, H. A. (1955). A behavioral model of rational choice. *Source: The Quarterly Journal of Economics*, *69*(1), 99–118. https://about.jstor.org/terms

Sloman, S., & Fernbach, P. (2017). *The Knowledge Illusion: Why We Never Think Alone*. Riverhead Books.

Stacks, D. W. (2010). *Primer of Public Relations Research*. Guilford Publications.

Stevens, S. S. (1946). On the theory of scales of measurement. *Science*, *103*(2684). https://doi.org/10.1126/science.103.2684.677

Stichweh, R. (2015). Scientific disciplines, history of. In *International Encyclopedia of the Social & Behavioral Sciences*. 2nd ed. https://doi.org/10.1016/B978-0-08-097086-8.03048-8

Stone, A. A., Hedges, S. M., Neale, J. M., & Satin, M. S. (1985). Prospective and cross-sectional mood reports offer no evidence of a "blue Monday" phenomenon. *Journal of Personality and Social Psychology*, *49*(1), 129–134. https://doi.org/10.1037/0022-3514.49.1.129

Stone, A. A., Schneider, S., & Harter, J. K. (2012). Day-of-week mood patterns in the United States: On the existence of 'Blue Monday', 'Thank God it's Friday' and weekend effects. *The Journal of Positive Psychology*, *7*(4), 306–314. https://doi.org/10.1080/17439760.2012.691980

Strack, F., & Deutsch, R. (2004). Reflective and impulsive determinants of social behavior. *Personality and Social Psychology Review*, *8*(3). https://doi.org/10.1207/s15327957pspr0803_1

Sunstein, C. R. (2017). *#republic: Divided Democracy in the Age of Social Media*. Princeton University Press. https://doi.org/10.1111/jcom.12344

Tavris, C. (2003). The widening scientist-practitioner gap: A view from the bridge. In S. O. Lilienfeld, S. J. Lynn, & J. M. Lohr (Eds.), *Science and Pseudoscience in Clinical Psychology* (pp. ix–xvii). Guilford Press.

Thaler, R. H., & Sunstein, C. R. (2008). *Nudge: Improving Decisions about Health, Wealth, and Happiness*. Penguin Books.

Trafimow, D. (2023). A new way to think about internal and external validity. *Perspectives on Psychological Science*, *18*(5), 1028–1046. https://doi.org/10.1177/17456916221136117

Tversky, A., & Kahneman, D. (1974). Judgment under uncertainty: Heuristics and biases. *Science*, *185*(4157). https://doi.org/10.1126/science.185.4157.1124

Webster, D. M., & Kruglanski, A. W. (1994). Individual differences in need for cognitive closure. *Journal of Personality and Social Psychology*, *67*(6), 1049–1062. https://doi.org/10.1037/0022-3514.67.6.1049

Żelechowska, D., Sarzyńska, J., & Nęcka, E. (2017). Working memory training for schoolchildren improves working memory, with no transfer effects on intelligence. *JournalofIntelligence*,*5*(4),1–20.https://doi.org/10.3390/JINTELLIGENCE5040036

5

THE OBJECT

PR from the Perspective of Psychology

Interdisciplinarity and the Condition of the Field PR

Hutton (1999) observes that the identity crisis affecting Public Relations since the beginning of the 20th century is one of its own making. PR has not developed a majority-accepted definition of the field; there is no clear purpose, and no dominant metaphor exists. It is difficult to disagree with this diagnosis. Some authors suggest that PR could have developed between 500 and 2,000 different definitions (Harlow, 1976; Wojcik, 2005). The need for a new definition is, at the very least, debatable, and in most cases, those definitions do not introduce anything new. Definitions of PR may differ in focus (on organisational goals versus on individuals), accentuate one or two-way aspects of PR (building relationships versus changing opinions), or have a different temporal orientation (e.g. the responsibility is only for immediate actions versus also including nonimmediate consequences of PR activity). Let us consider the following perspectives, which could be seen as different:

> Propagandist, press agent, public information officer, public relations or public affairs official, political campaign specialist, lobbyist – whatever their title, their aim is the same: to influence public behavior.
>
> *(Cutlip, 1994, p. xi)*

> PR is the flow of purposive communication produced on behalf of individuals, formally constituted and informally constituted groups, through their continuous transactions with other social entities. It has social, cultural, political and economic effects at local, national and global levels.
>
> *(Edwards, 2012, p. 21)*

DOI: 10.4324/9781003610403-5

Academic PR has several disciplinary homes: in business schools, management, journalism, and media, and the multitude of definitions could be a consequence of the lack of interdisciplinary training, as well as personal formative experience of practitioners who can enter the profession with different disciplinary and professional backgrounds (St. John III et al., 2014). Each of the schools of thought has created its own histories of PR, occasionally claiming the origins of PR in their respective disciplines. However, the multiplicity of definitions and perspectives should not lead to the conclusion that the definitions are mutually contradictory.

Hutton also accurately argues that it is astonishing to be unable to build a definition at a seemingly basic level by focusing on the nature of the relationships contained in the discipline's name. This apparent gap has been filled, according to Hutton, by critics, as it can lead to PR being hijacked by other disciplines. That is all too clear. The terms spin and spin doctors have emerged in public discourse (Miller & Dinan, 2007), and the negative perception of the discipline has been reinforced by the perspective of journalistic science, which has for a long time constructed what some theorists of the phenomenon have described as a discourse of denial (Macnamara, 2014). Symptomatically, PR degrees are being subsumed by other disciplines, partly due to market demands but also partly because of the postulated and ill-defined convergence of the advertising, media, and communication industries (Hardy, 2022). Consequently, differences in the definition of PR exist between academics and practitioners, vary between practitioners, and often collide within academia. This state of internal and external inconsistency is not conducive to achieving agreement on what is the object of PR and how to evaluate it. According to White, (2000), PR Practitioners seem to have an implicit grasp of understanding what they do and consider the effort to define it a waste of time. Anecdotal evidence suggests that White's observation remains valid: practitioners know what PR is, and verbalising it is fruitless and only amusing to academics.

From a scholarly standpoint, the two visions of the object of PR, as explained by Cutlip's (1994) and Edwards's (2012) definitions, are not contradictory. From a practical perspective, the question of whether PR has individual, social, cultural, and economic effects is somewhat different. Practical PR is primarily concerned with the meso level and interaction between organisations (or groups) and their publics. Psychology plays a role here as members of publics possess individual mental characteristics – an area of psychological expertise. The practical concern for practitioners, however, is whether they should be responsible for the unintended and long-term effects of their activity on a macro level.

The multi-paradigmatic character of public relations scholarship (Cutlip, 1994; Grunig & Hunt, 1984; Grunig, 1992; Heath & Toth, 1992; Kent et al., 2002; L'Etang & Pieczka, 1996; Olins, 1990; Pearson, 1989; Toth, 1992) is an expected consequence of the interdisciplinary roots and everyday practice of PR. Consequently, the dominance of one paradigm in scholarship is not viewed as beneficial to the discipline. Edwards warns that the dominance of one paradigm may lead to the marginalisation of those who challenge the dominant perspective (Edwards, 2012). While it seems the multi-paradigmatic character of PR has been appreciated in academia, as well as it is valuable from a scholarly perspective, for practitioners, at least at times, it can lead to confusion. Aa a field born out of practice, when relevant practical problems arise, the answers to them should not (massively) vary depending on a theoretical orientation of the person required to provide an evidence-based response (consider again: how to find out what is the most depressing day of the year?). Although several paradigms are prominently pursued in academic PR, none of them appears to fully leverage the individual level of analysis. One explanation for the missing skillset could be related to the lack of a theoretical element. More precisely, what appears to be lacking in PR scholarship is the individual-level analysis, most commonly associated with psychology.

Developing psychology-inspired scholarly strand research in PR may appear somewhat challenging. On the one hand, in the American Grunig-inspired normative functional paradigm, the cognitive psychological element seems to provide an important source of inspiration. However, social cognitive psychology has ceased to inform PR theory. This means that a considerable repertoire of modern social cognitive approaches, attitude research, and attitude–behaviour links has not been effectively introduced to PR scholarship. In addition, the derailment from the psychological tradition that occurred partly as a consequence of the critique of the 1950s definition of rationality meant that the 1970 understanding of heuristics as an adaptation to the environment is missing. On the other hand, for different reasons, in the European school of public relations, a scepticism exists, whereby 'simplistic, extreme positivist views and normative principles, regarding for example, [what] professionals should do' (Valentini & Luoma-Aho, 2023).

Practitioners may perceive the poorly defined object of PR as a nuisance. In the European PR scholarship, the scope appears to have expanded, which practitioners may view as making their job more challenging and adding even more responsibilities. Valentini and Luoma-Aho (2023) mention the following four traits, which they consider characterising the European school of PR: (1) a deep connection to society at large, (2) strong emphasis on responsibility, (3) broad understanding of stakes and stakeholders, and (4) theoretical and methodological diversity. The psychological potential of the latter two seems intuitive. It can increase understanding of stakeholders and shed light on the principles of cognitive mechanisms that underlie attitude formation and decision-making. The normative postulate of methodological diversity should also play a role here, as psychological and quantitative methodologies are essential to understanding the mechanisms of social behaviour of stakeholders and individual members of the public, in particular. In essence, positioning psychology as the basis of higher-level inquiries, as envisioned by McDougall (1919), seems intuitively attractive, especially for a psychologist.

Somewhat alleviating practitioners being overburdened with tasks was the distinction between the practice of PR and scholarly activity made by Dozier and Lauzen (2000). They suggested that public relations, understood as a (1) professional activity and (2) intellectual domain, understood as an area of knowledge developed by the scientific community, should be treated differently. Public relations as a profession involves managing communication to build two-way, symmetrical (i.e. balanced and mutually beneficial) relationships between an organisation and its publics. In the intellectual domain, public relations involves the study of activities, communications, and relationships between an organisation and its environment, as well as the examination of the intended and unintended consequences of these relationships, both for the individual and for society as a whole. Developing a consistent, psychological level of analysis of PR as a practical activity, consistent with Dozier and Lauzen (2000), would cause several problems. From an ethical standpoint, psychologists are expected not to ignore nonimmediate outcomes of their actions and have developed methodological expertise in identifying complex mechanisms that involve indirect influences on behaviour. Additionally, wellbeing is a central concern in psychology.

PR as an intellectual domain gives more leeway for psychology. Dozier and Lauzen (2000) place academic PR in the field of behavioural and social sciences and note that, unlike PR as a professional activity, the intellectual domain admits to different levels of analysis. The following sections aim to provide a comprehensive rationale for involving psychology in the practice and theory of PR.

Rationale Behind the Identification of Psychological Perspective in PR

In his review of psychological thought in the practice and scholarly tradition of public relations, (White, 2000) asked the following question, the importance of which seems critical when looking at the present challenges of the politics-public relations-media-audiences interaction: 'why are [psychological] theories of social interaction, group dynamics, attitude and opinion formation not included?' (White, 2000, p. 151). Part of the problem seems to stem from a misunderstanding of what psychology is and how it investigates its research problems. Chapters 1–4 attempted to clarify these areas. In the following section, I will argue that the neglect observed by White could be a consequence of different disciplinary traditions associated with the concepts of public opinion and attitudes. I will attempt to demonstrate that the identification of a psychological perspective within Public Relations scholarship is not only scientifically appealing but also crucial for the discipline's overall development.

An illustrative account of the approaches adopted by the discipline's theorists is provided by Brown (2014), who, in describing the qualitative perspective of humanists and the quantitative approach of social science representatives, draws attention to the diversity and acceptance of many, even contradictory perspectives of the former, and the subordination to the pursuit of defining universal principles, of the latter. The purpose of this comparison, reminiscent of Greek poetry, is essentially to present the two main research schools of PR, which, Brown argues, define the discipline's internal orientations differently. Brown includes critical analysis, rhetoric, ethnography, philosophy, literary theory, and history among the qualitative methodologies of humanities. He argues that the qualitative approach of the humanities takes complete account of the interdisciplinarity of PR, whereas the dominant social science viewpoint represented for many years by Grunig (Grunig & Hunt, 1984; Grunig, 1992), although commendable for its objectivity, leads to too much ambiguity and inconsistency by seeking to propose a one-size-fits-all theory of PR. Brown refers to his idea as the Public Relations of Everything, arguing that contemporary PR cannot be reduced to communication management or the communication of organisations. He also blames Grunig's approach for its low explanatory power. He argues for a more complex and normative nature of the discipline, further raising that the narrow focus of Grunig's model is also not very exploratory.

At first glance, it is difficult to disagree with some of Brown's diagnoses; PR in the 21st century is increasingly complex to distinguish from marketing and advertising at a strategic level, despite earlier efforts to treat the disciplines relatively independently. If one were to stop the presentation of Brown's arguments at this point, one would have to agree with him. It seems impossible to construct a single, coherent theory of public relations that explains the entire spectrum of phenomena and processes associated with the discipline. Moreover, defining PR narrowly as the management of an organisation's communication not only simplifies the problem by omitting cultural factors and the active role of the media in the communication process with the publics, but also overlooks the psychological perspective. Additionally, it downplays the issues of ethics and influence on human wellbeing, implying that these processes are secondary and of lesser importance for immediate consideration. There is just one problem with this line of argumentation: by not explicitly including culture or psychology in the functional perspective (ideally, every time this perspective is discussed), a lack of those influences should not be claimed. Against this backdrop, however, the theoretical stance developed in the present volume meets Brown's (2014) perceived criteria of social science objectivity. Furthermore, the objectivity of the social sciences approach and the use of quantitative methods in conducting research do not preclude seeing the interdisciplinary nature of public relations as a field of knowledge. Nevertheless, while the Grunig school has developed PR theory from the perspective of the organisation, as the management of communication with the organisation's publics, the psychological perspective begins with a different viewpoint: that of an audience member.

Three Levels of Analysis: Micro, Meso, and Macro

In 2024, a PR agency from London sent a creative mailer to journalists containing a dermatological cosmetic aimed at improving the dryness of atopic skin. It accompanied it with a bag of crisps and a slogan, 'Don't get salty about your skin'. This was intended as a play on words, but the PR team missed an important point: eating crisps can exacerbate skin conditions. How truthful was the evidence (the bag of crisps) provided in support of the product's functional benefits? PR has been most associated with words (versus visuals), but its expertise should go beyond phonetic proximity or grammatical correctness. In the field of Public Relations, truthful communication is widely regarded as a fundamental principle and cornerstone of ethical practice (Black, 1995). Nevertheless, the evidence derived from the practice of PR is reminiscent of the question raised in Chapter 1 (see Ihlen & Verhoeven, 2012). The practice of Public Relations should also be about its impact on individuals. Will eating crisps help alleviate the atopic skin condition, or will it worsen it? Indirectly, the fact that the psychological perspective is currently missing can explain why the wellbeing of audience members and their needs are not adequately addressed in PR practice.

As explained in the introduction, evidence points to the shift towards the sociological perspective in PR (the macro level): 'complex fields such as journalism, public relations, and business constitute intellectual domains that focus on a specific social context—often a social institution or cluster of institutions' (Dozier & Lauzen, 2000). Dozier and Lauzen (2000) created a two-dimensional figure, an adaptation of Paisley's (1972) work in the field of communication. Their goal was to position public relations in relation to level fields of science (e.g. physiology, psychology, and sociology), fundamental focal variable fields (e.g. communication and cybernetics), and complex focal variable fields. In the interpretation of Dozier and Lauzen (2000), several implicit assumptions are made, and their relevance for the need to properly define the discipline of psychology and its role in PR will now be explained. As rationalised by the authors, higher-level fields subsume lower-level fields. The idea behind this conceptualisation is sound in principle: the authors list several subfields, that is, physiological psychology, social psychology, and social anthropology, and position them as subfields of psychology, sociology, and anthropology (respectively). However, in light of the evidence from Chapter 2, the figure could also be a potential source of confusion with regard to the definition and scope of social psychology. While a few sociologists would still argue for identifying social psychology as a subfield of sociology, the rich tradition and flourishing scholarship of psychological social psychology instead convincingly consider social psychology as a branch of psychology.[1] Somewhat automatically, a form of consensus has formed around the idea that the social component in PR is satisfied only by sociological theory and methods. This could have led to the conclusion that social effects should be expected and investigated on a societal level. Existing criticism of the meso level of the functional paradigm also did not help. Unfounded claims that organisational–public relationships are not 'social' enough might have shifted the discussion towards higher-level fields, giving sociological and critical perspectives the torch of righteousness. Ultimately, the role of psychology in explaining the social aspect of PR has been missed. Partly because the discipline had been viewed through the prism of psychoanalysis and the early works of Bernays, and later as a laboratory science in context-free settings. To make matters worse, later, when psychology observed considerable progress and evolution, much of its social psychological contributions were hijacked by other disciplines – unbeknownst to social psychologists.

Based on the disambiguation of the definition and the scope of social psychology presented in Chapter 2, a revised version of Dozier and Lauzen's (2000) diagram has been created to illustrate my argument. Figure 5.1 aims to accurately represent the position of social psychology as a subdiscipline of psychology. The correction is not merely figurative, as it opens the possibility of studying individual-level processes and their role in higher-level phenomena. The three-dimensional figure is helpful in demonstrating that complex focal variable fields can utilise theories developed across all levels, as well as explaining the shared status of research questions that are addressed by different levels of analysis. While both sociology and psychology are interested in understanding human behaviour in a real-life context, it is psychology that introduces knowledge about the areas that White, (2000) expected to see in PR scholarship.

Although there should be neither contradiction nor competition in how psychology and sociology respond to practical problems of public relations, relocating social psychology as a subdiscipline of psychology offers one additional benefit. The starting point of inquiry in psychology is the individual. In contrast with Mead's definition (1934), psychology views the group from the perspective of the individuals that constitute it. Psychologists begin by examining the internal mental architecture and observing how it interacts with the external environment. Following observations made by communication and public opinion scientists, this calls for a better micro-macro link to be established in order to understand how individuals interact with other individuals, groups, organisations, society, and the system (Pan & McLeod, 1991). The following perspective is applied here to study public relations phenomena:

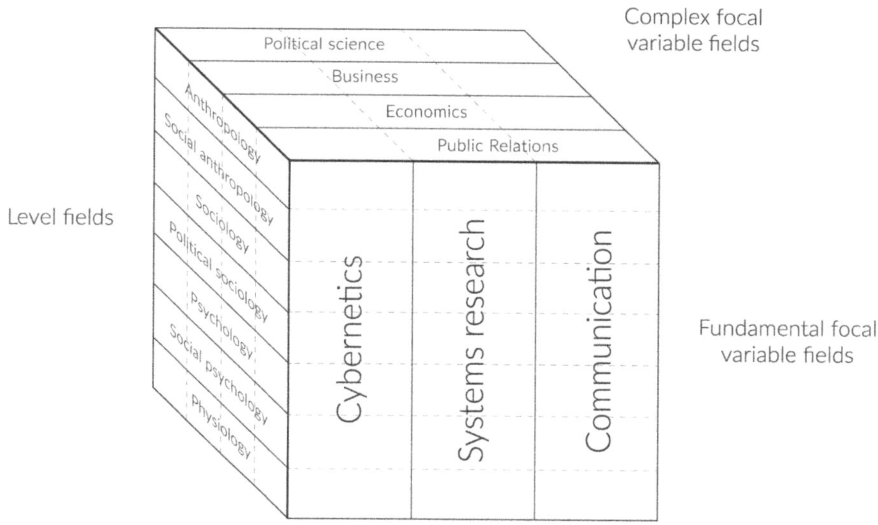

FIGURE 5.1 Position of the discipline of public relations in relation to other fields of science.

> [...] micro individual relationships describe the cognitive, affective, motivational, and personality bases of individuals' attitude development and change, as well as opinion formation and expression. The processes at this level, [...], may be categorized by three types of related activities: media exposure and processing behavior, cognitive processing and inference making, and opinion expression.
>
> *(McLeaod et al., 1995, p. 61)*

The study of public opinion and the study of mass communication 'grew up in the context of social psychology and political science' but 'were separated not only from each other but also from their shared theoretical parentage' (Katz, 1995, p. xxii). The concepts of attitudes and public opinion, which share several similarities, provide a bridge for studying public relations phenomena from a psychological perspective.

Attitudes and Public Opinion

Opinion is commonly understood as a judgement or belief which should be made about matters that do not require scientific evidence. Public opinion is a related concept, but when applied to political communication, it is not a simple aggregation of individual opinions and should be considered an element of a larger system that also includes mass communication (E. Katz, 1995). Historical analysis of Minar (1960) viewed public opinion as a primarily political concept, and it appears that public opinion in the 1960s transcended the realms of political science and other disciplines, including psychology. In Minar's (1960) typology, Machiavellian public opinion was a force that the mass of men could impact politics and should be managed by the state. Minar also demonstrated the progressive individualism of the ideas of Hobbes, Locke, and the Utilitarians, for whom individuals – and not a mass of people – played a role in shaping their relationship with the state. Although public opinion has roots in ancient political theory, the modern meaning of public – a body of reasoning citizens – was introduced by the Enlightenment, and public opinion became 'thinkable in the modern sense' (Peters, 1995). Although many definitions of the concept of public opinion function today (Childs, 1965), Noelle-Neumann (1995) suggests that they can be categorised either as relating to a rational instrument of opinion formation and decision-making in democracy or as a function of social control promoting consensus.

Gruning's foundational work on the development of a comprehensive PR theory was inspired by Dewey's (1927) concept of opinions that emerge and are voiced around political issues, leading to the formation of the public. Grunig began his research programme in the 1960s and 1970s, focusing on the study of communication between individuals, whom he later approached collectively as publics (Grunig & Kim, 2021). The goal of the research programme has been ambitiously comprehensive, as it aimed to analyse the communication behaviour of members as a function of individual responses towards issues. To achieve this, he incorporated psychological theories, as explained in greater detail in Chapter 3. Grunig's inclusion and subsequent use of psychological evidence could also be seen as symptomatic of the divergence of paths between psychology and mass communication in public opinion research observed since the 1960s.

Although 'many of the pioneers of public opinion and communication research were themselves social psychologists' and 'symbiotic relationships among social psychology and public opinion, communication and survey research persisted from the 1920s to the mid-1950s' (Beniger & Gusek, 1995, p. 219), neglect of interest in individual-level processes and a decline in the importance of psychological processes in explaining media and mass communication started in the 1960s. The individual-level analysis in political research on public opinion is said to be somewhat forgotten, whereas a separate line of psychological inquiry has developed around theories of attitudes, which address the individual level by describing attitudes as cognitive and affective activities of individuals (McLeod et al., 1995). The cognitive psychology and social cognition revolution is said to mark a new era of collaborations between communication and psychology scholars (Beniger & Gusek, 1995), and 'today's students of public opinion and human interaction believe, almost as an article of faith, that human communication and behavior are socially derived and motivated' (Glynn et al., 1995, p. 249). However, in Public Relations scholarship, interdisciplinary collaborations involving the social cognitive school of psychological thinking seem rare. A question could be asked: to what extent are PR students aware that relationships that are the object of public relations are socially derived and motivated, and what is the potential of psychology to inform the practice of PR?

Katz (1995) notes that public opinion cannot be seen simply understood as the aggregation of private opinions. This makes perfect sense when the concept of public opinion is approached as a multifaceted political phenomenon. However, although PR has been inspired by early conceptualisation of the publics and the role of public opinion in democracy and society (Dewey, 1927), from the pragmatic, practical perspective, public relations is more concerned with the process and outcomes of individual opinions of the members of the public. PR examines the overt manifestations of opinions that members of the public express and is interested in whether these manifestations lead to behavioural outcomes. A shift in public opinion research, instigated by the cognitive revolution in psychology, led to a change in the studied dependent variables: from attitudes to information processing (Beniger, 1987). However, although the scholarly object of the research has shifted from focusing on outcomes (attitudes) to the process (information processing), this should not alter the fact that, for practitioners, practice-focused public relations research remains more concerned with the outcome of the activity. There is also a benefit of the social cognitive revolution, which involves a better understanding of the mechanisms of judgement formation and decision-making. Similarly to Public Relations, the field of public opinion research lacks a unifying theory (Glasser & Salmon, 1995). Investigating the psychological components of information collection and processing makes public opinion research a branch of political psychology (Zaller, 1992).

The definition of PR supported by CIPR views it as a discipline and field of professional practice that aims to achieve understanding between an organisation and its publics, using communication to achieve this goal. The 'understanding' aspect can be equated with the opinions, members of publics express. What could be the difference between following the political tradition of investigating public opinion as opposed to choosing the path of the psychological concept of attitudes? On the one hand, public opinion is, in a sense, a psychological concept: 'Every opinion is a marriage of information and predisposition: information to form a mental picture of the given issue, and predisposition to motivate some conclusion about it' (Zaller, 1992, p. 7). This observation is consistent with the psychological perspective. It can be said that each belief or attitude is an outcome of the knowledge formation process, which entails testing various hypotheses, and its credibility partly rests upon the ability to postpone making judgements and collecting more evidence.

The psychological character of public opinion suggests that it would seem helpful to rely on psychological terminology when examining phenomena related to public opinion. However, public opinion scholars favour media and political terminology over psychological language, considering it too technical. Choices made by public opinion scholars are often dictated by the linguistic preferences of media pundits (Zaller, 1992). Insofar as PR is concerned with the communicative actions of publics, one distinction that could be proposed between attitudes and opinions is that for PR, opinions are overt and become of interest only if they are voiced. Otherwise, as pointed out by Ajzen (1989), the conceptual distinction between opinions and attitudes is pointless, as no differences have been found in how they influence behaviour. In fact, the distinction between opinions and attitudes can be a matter of disciplinary tradition only.

> Overall, there is far too little discussion between the different conceptual traditions, which frequently leads to re-formulations of the same ideas – often dressed up in newer and more fancy terminology – or an unnecessary and unconstructive competition over the hegemony of one concept over another.
>
> *(Bergman, 1998, p. 82)*

'An attitude is an individual's disposition to respond favourably or unfavourably to an object, person, institution, or event, or to any other discriminable aspect of the individual's world' (Ajzen, 1989, p. 241). In Ajzen's multicomponent view, attitudes consist of cognition, affect, and conation (behaviour). The measurement of attitudes involves inferring the contents from responses belonging to the above categories. Content-wise, although it has long been debated whether the basis of attitudes is purely affective (Petty & Cacioppo, 2012; M. J. Rosenberg & Hovland, 1960; Zajonc & Markus, 1982), it can be argued that affective (versus cognitive) persuasive communication simply triggers qualitatively different attitude-change processes (Rosselli et al., 1995). A cognitive element of attitude has been overwhelmingly acknowledged and put as central for the understating regularities in attitude change and their influence in shaping behaviour (Ajzen & Fishbein, 1980).

A three-faceted structure of attitudes – that is, affective, cognitive, and behavioural – now seems a universally accepted idea in social psychology (Bagozzi, 1978; Breckler, 1984) To give an example, an attitude of a person (e.g. employee) towards an object (e.g. an organisation) involves associated feelings and emotions (e.g. pride from being a member of the community of employees) and judgement or belief about it (e.g. the organisation is a good social citizen), as well behavioural intent (e.g. willingness not to search for employment elsewhere and come to work with enthusiasm). The behavioural dimension of the underlying attitude could manifest itself in attending every event organised by the organisation and being at work on time. Notably, while congruence between the three elements provides more stability by reducing dissonance, a conflict between elements or within an element is plausible and, in fact, not uncommon (Maio et al., 2000). A consumer can appreciate the long-range battery of an electric car brand but may dislike the company's political involvement, particularly through its CEO's questionable actions.

From a functional standpoint, 'attitudes serve to simplify reasoning and behavior by providing guides for how to interact with (e.g., approach or avoid) an attitude object' (Maio & Haddock, 2007, p. 568) and despite the fact that not all human behaviour is attitude-driven and a large part of it could be seen as automatic (Bargh, 1994), the role of attitudes in predicting behaviour should not be overlooked. Not only does the content of attitudes imply the importance of past behaviours, which may serve as an indicator of future actions, but also beliefs and emotions have their supporting function in understating what the upcoming behaviour would look like. Seen in this light, the theory of attitudes can be easily applied to the practice of PR, helping to refocus the attention of communicators on the outcomes of their actions.

Most normative models of planning and evaluation for Public Relations campaigns appear to rely on the assumption that changes in attitudes are desired outcomes of professional PR activity (Gregory, 2016; Stacks & Michaelson, 2017; Watson & Noble, 2009). On the most basic level of outcomes, *awareness* should be considered as a property of audience members having knowledge related to a PR programme. The second category of outcomes fully overlaps with – *attitudes* – and three types of evaluation by audience members should be investigated: *emotional*, *cognitive*, and *behavioural intentions*. Although occasionally attitudes have been fully equated with emotion in relevant PR scholarship (Gregory, 2022), extant psychological evidence suggests that attitudes are also cognitive evaluations and, in addition, consist of behavioural intentions. The structure of attitudes encompasses both emotional and cognitive components; that is, attitudes are not solely emotions, and equating attitudes with emotional evaluation of objects is a mistake. The last type of outcome is behaviour. Although evaluating a change in behaviours could be considered the priciest element of evaluation research, the behavioural component of attitudes could enable practitioners to probe into the intentions of audience members and form predictions about their behaviour. Another benefit of the proposed stronger integration of attitudinal research with PR scholarship and practice could lead to bringing a long tradition and vast repertoire of techniques of measuring attitudes: their emotional and cognitive components, as well as behavioural intentions. These include surveying audience members using different types of questions, from Likert-type scales to semantics differentials, employing the technique of measuring reaction times and measuring implicit associations. In addition, the methodology of attitude measurement can help identify active publics more efficiently (Grunig, 1997; Kim & Grunig, 2011) by measuring their behavioural intentions. This is not to suggest that the suggested benefits of the psychological perspective would come at no cost. First, PR university curricula should be modified to include training in relevant areas. Secondly, practitioners would also be expected to receive basic training in quantitative methods of attitude measurement, as well as relevant statistical knowledge necessary to analyse or at least interpret obtained results. It can be seen as one of the most pressing needs, as PR appears to suffer from a lack of evaluation.

Evaluating the Outcome

What do PR practitioners evaluate, if anything? Evaluation takes place scarcely, and my personal experience suggests that budget constraints and time limitations are named the biggest culprits. Negotiating an additional 10% of the budget for evaluation can become a double-edged sword as clients and agencies often differ in their definition of what PR is and how to measure it. In my view, the ambiguity of the real object of PR practice is the biggest flaw. The problem is very practical: What can be expected from PR? Despite 'relationships' being the definitional component of the profession, they are evaluated rarely, and instead, a short-cut, widely criticised and misleading measure is used: outputs. Next is the issue of commitment to objectives, and the first related obstacle is the discrepancy between what a client wants and what (typically) an agency is accustomed to being held accountable for, more specifically, outcomes versus outputs. This problem is not new and has been a persistent issue in the PR industry for decades. Macnamara's excellent model and rationale behind it are as valid as ever here and should continue to serve as a gold standard (Macnamara, 2015, 2023, 2018). To understand the current shortcomings in measuring PR effectively, a brief examination of the most popular – and arguably the most misleading – measure of PR is necessary.

The need for media monitoring arose as a result of the growing number of newspaper titles and editions in the late 20th century. Historically, newspaper monitoring involved scanning the content, cutting out relevant articles, and holding them together with a clip (Sterling, 2009). The first world press media monitoring service was established in London by Henry Romeike in 1881 and in New York in 1884. Romeike was born in Riga (present-day Latvia – then Russia) in 1855 and received his education in Prussia due to the nationality of his father. Looking for excitement and job opportunities around Europe, Romeike landed in Paris, where he learnt about artists paying for back issues of magazines that featured their names and comments about their work (Baylen, 2000). He subsequently formed a partnership with a newsdealer, which has grown into a profitable business – Romeike and Curtice – that has survived to modern times. The success of his enterprise can be partly attributed to identifying a psychological need for attention sought by politicians and businessmen of the era, which led to coining the phrase 'romeiked' which meant 'compiled in scrapbooks' (The Press: Clipping Business | TIME, n.d.).

Whereas in the 19th and early 20th centuries, newspaper clippings could reveal journalists' opinions of artists' work and satisfy the vanity of the nouveau riche, today, they are of limited value in evaluating PR. Academic consensus exists about how PR should be monitored and measured, and one of the outputs of PR – media mentions – is considered only intermediate evidence in the pursuit of the actual outcome of PR: a change in awareness, attitude, and behaviour of members of publics. Although professional associations support this view and advocate for a change in how PR is measured, media mentions are still used to calculate how much money a media mention would cost if it were paid advertising. This is despite the fact that, according to the Barcelona Principles, a set of guidelines endorsed by leading professional PR bodies (including AMEC, CIPR, PRSA, PRCA, IPR, the Global Alliance, and ICCO), Advertising Value Equivalency (AVE) is a flawed measure of PR. AVEs mistake cost with value, functionally confuse advertising and PR, and, critically, do not account for target audiences. AMEC has produced a helpful guide for practitioners that includes 21 reasons for not including AVE in PR evaluation (AMEC, n.d.). However, despite a sound argument against it, companies continue to use it under different names, such as Estimated Media Value (EMV).

The consequences of the lack of agreement about the object and outcome of PR are very tangible. A lack of clarity about goals and objectives leads to poor planning and confusion regarding measurement. For Bagnall (2024), the solution to all mentioned problems is joint work by agencies and organisations on outcome-focused objectives and developing more realistic expectations. He explains that the poor quality of PR agency's work is a common reason for the frustration of senior in-house practitioners. PR Week's research, cited by Bagnall (Harrington, 2024), shows that the disgruntlement is reciprocated by public relations agencies, which rate the quality of the majority of PR briefs they receive from in-house communication teams as very poor, or – at best – average. When both PR agencies and in-house departments have different definitions of what a PR plan should involve, what are (and what are not) PR tactics and how to evaluate success. Clearly, there is a lack of agreement regarding this element. Anecdotal evidence from 2024's London is about one PR agency that did not consider that creating and sending a creative mailer to media was a PR task and outsourced it to another, more *specialist* agency.

It would seem that public relations practitioners have inadvertently led themselves to this paradoxical situation, whereby their work is subject to scrutiny through the lens of 18th-century entertainment media. Today, the choice of this approach is driven by marketing-oriented practitioners, who seek to compare the effects of PR and advertising but mistakenly focus on the outputs rather than the outcomes. Although the amalgamation of the approaches is consistent with the interdisciplinary character of the profession, the resulting situation describes the worst possible choice of interdisciplinary borrowing. Despite numerous calls for a revision of the methods and standards of evaluation (e.g. Macnamara, 2015, 2023), the industry seems to resiliently resist the temptation to professionalise the evaluation of their work, possibly in an attempt to preserve established practices and avoid confusing clients. The validity of this latter point is not without foundation, however. Typically, PR, whether functioning as an agency or an in-house partner, occupies a subordinate role to marketing. If the marketing department adheres to a single method of measurement – in this case, output of PR – the argument that the evaluation method would, at best, be informative of a relationship between a PR department and journalists would have a slight chance of succeeding. Although several factors, including a lack of skills, a lack of knowledge of evaluation models, and organisational inertia, can be listed as factors responsible for using AVE as a measure of PR, its continued use could have negative consequences for PR practitioners. The absence of consensus on the definition of Public Relations, the prioritisation of content production as a core PR function, and the rapid adoption of generative AI tools in everyday PR practice have put the future of the profession in question.

The Object: Relationships in Context

The discussion so far has focused on the general principles of integrating psychology with the practice of PR, suggesting that attitudes can serve as a source of knowledge about the outcome of PR activities. However, attitudes are not the single object of PR. If this were the case, public relations would become a branch of psychology. PR is a multilevel, multi-paradigmatic field of practical activity that has emerged in the context of political, economic, and psychological progress. Its object remains the same: *public relations*.

This object can be investigated, with some limitations, from at least several vantage points, and attitudes are just one of them. Neither of these investigations would be complete; however, each of them will be informative about an aspect of a relationship, depending on the specific questions asked. Three critical aspects of such investigations come into focus: the actors of the relationship, the process that involves the mechanism, and the components of exchange between the actors (e.g. information or goods) and the outcome of the relationship (i.e. awareness, attitudes, and behaviours). The nature of the said investigations is constrained, like the problem that can be explained – using a distant parallel – to Schrödinger's Cat. In practice, only one aspect of a relationship can be adequately investigated with a single method of measurement; this is partly due to the multifaceted character of practical PR problems and the complexity of the field, as previously discussed by Dozier and Lauzen (2000). For example, psychological methodology can be employed to understand the mechanism (process) by which PR activity's outcome affects individual audience members, but to comprehensively tackle the societal impact and its consequences at institutional or class levels, a sociological lens should be used in the next step.

Related to attitudes, one other psychological concept seems to be at play when discussing the object of PR. The free-will aspect of an individual can be psychologically related to the concept of trust, which is explored in Public Relations as an important precursor to building effective relationships (Bentele & Seidenglanz, 2008; Ledingham & Bruning, 1998; Moloney, 2005; Valentini, 2020). Definitions of trust vary in their focus, but most of them include psychological elements. In PR, trust is defined as 'one party's level of confidence in and willingness to open oneself to the other party' (Hon & Grunig, 1999, p. 3). A more general view has been explored in a business context. For Botsman (2018), trust is a confident relationship with the unknown. The 'unknown' seems to only exist when decisions of an individual are unconstrained and undetermined. If such decisions were predictable, for example, determined by some external power, the concept of trust would become irrelevant (the consequences of adopting the perspective of an individual who is capable of making their decisions and internal mental processes taking part in them are elaborated in Chapter 6). Consequently, the expectations of PR audience members could become an area of psychological investigation in PR. This is particularly necessary, given that remarkably little has been discussed in PR regarding the mechanism of building relationships. So far, there seem to be more questions than answers: What are the consequences of a relationship based on trust for organisations? What are the differences between trust in relationships built by human actors in comparison to organisation-publics trust? Can trust be formed with AI-created actors? Do members of publics have different expectations towards AI or AI-mediated relationships? The social cognitive perspective advanced in this monograph goes beyond the knowledge aspects of understanding that are at the core of PR. Emotions, morality, and identity could be seen as the next big players to enter the game, and PR should be ready.

The main argument I present in this chapter is fundamentally simple. The relationships formed between organisations and publics are psychological because they involve individual human beings, rather than inanimate objects or physical entities, who possess mental characteristics necessary for establishing those relationships. While various metaphors may exist to portray a connection between a brand, an organisation, or a political party and the publics, on both sides of the equation, there exist individual members of the publics and individual representatives of a brand or organisation (as well as individual members of the press/media that mediate the relationship). On the audience side, individuals engage with the mental representations of organisations and the presumed human beings associated with those representations. Not only should the practice of PR involve goals that include measurable outcomes, but also the impact of PR programmes should be considered (even when explicit intentions of action-takers are not formulated on the macro level or indirect effects are not immediately realised).

Lastly, relationships happen in context. Following Schrödinger's Cat metaphor, the communication environment of audience members should be monitored, but it must not be considered a sole outcome of PR activity. When PR agencies measure the number of media mentions or AVE, they do precisely that: they evaluate the communication context of their publics. While it is helpful to be aware of it, the connection between this context (the output of PR activity) and changing attitudes may or may not exist. Although Hutton (1999) argues that definitions of PR tend to focus more on the nature of the task rather than the purpose of Public Relations, the inclusion of a psychological perspective that builds on social cognitive and situated cognition theories to manage everyday relationships in context seems profitable. In summary, Public Relations should be concerned with relationships and their context rather than focusing solely on the production of content or analysis of context (see Figure 5.2).

The ambiguity around the object of PR reminds me of one of Love Actually's scenes, where a character, portrayed by Rowan Atkinson, puts a lot of effort and distinction (not to mention time) into gift-wrapping a necklace bought by Alan Rickman's character. The dialogue follows like this:

> - I don't need a bag, I'll put it in my pocket.
> - Oh, this isn't a bag, sir.
> - Really?
> - This is so much more than a bag.
> - Ooh!
> - Could we be quite quick, please?
> - Prontissimo.
>
> (Curtis, 2003)

The definitions that both characters had for the Christmas gift and its recipient, along with the implications of their actions, differed and were influenced by many preconceptions. Bringing the argument back to the discussion of this chapter, at the most obvious level of relevance, when a client and PR agency have different definitions of the object of PR, at least one party will not be satisfied with the service. A similar situation, where parties start with

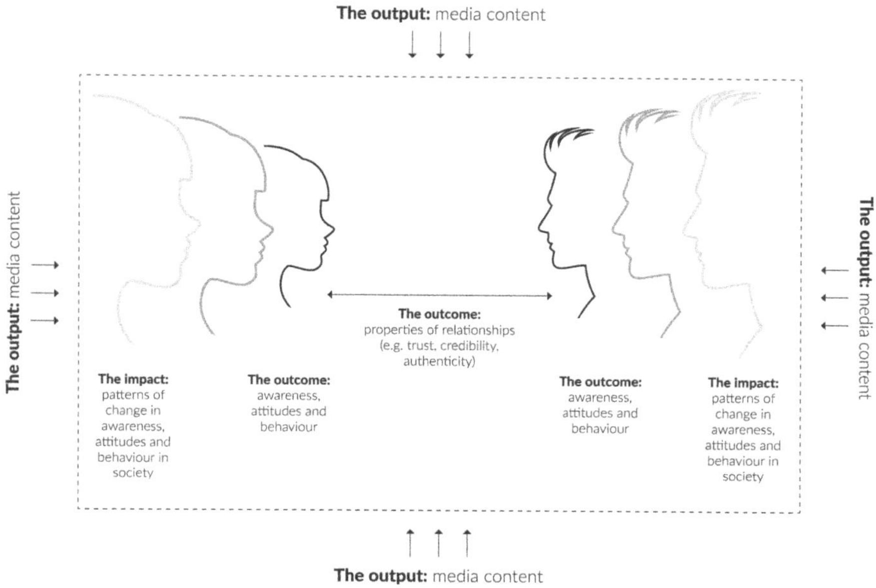

FIGURE 5.2 The object of public relations.

numerous and often hidden assumptions, can be imagined regarding the object of public relations in practice. The decision of whether public relations should be evaluated based on the content it produces versus the relationships it fosters is not trivial, and the choice to be made consciously by practitioners is strategic. In my view, this decision the profession must make has never been more critical for the very existence of PR. Here is a summary of the consequences. If public relations continues to be evaluated as a function responsible only for creating content (albeit with limited control over it), the entire industry risks cannibalisation by advertising and integrated marketing agencies and/or, and – or concurrently – full outsourcing to generative AI. The following chapters will talk about what this perspective means, highlighting how the psychology of PR can provide valuable insights into what audience members and publics members need, as well as exploring how content plays a role in building relationships and the challenges posed by a communication environment filled with too much content.

When Katz (1960) expanded his theory of attitudes, he included the following functions: adaptation, ego defence, expression of values, and knowledge. This last function is associated with one of the basic human needs: the need to understand and the need to know. In formulating his claims, Katz relied on observations of the human social environment. To understand the process of attitude formation and change, he thought it would be necessary to examine the mechanism of opinion formation and analyse in detail the channels of communication, the social structure, and the relationship between the individual and the media, as well as the role of opinion leaders. Drawing on his earlier work (Sarnoff & Katz, 1954), he concluded that contemporary explanatory models, which sought to define people as either unambiguously rational or irrational, were hardly universal, and their predictive power was limited to specific situations. It was impossible to explain the issue of attitudes without considering the motivational basis, which can vary depending on the function that the attitude serves. The arousal of the conformity motive is thought to be related to the activation of important human needs, leading to an increased sense of external gratification and the avoidance of punishment. A perceived threat can arouse attitudes that protect the ego. The availability of information related to a person's cherished values would lead to the arousal of value-expression attitudes. Most relevant for this monograph is the knowledge function of attitudes. People are constantly seeking to acquire knowledge that will make the surrounding reality meaningful and prevent it from being perceived as chaotic and disorganised. Further, people seek referent information to help them understand their environment. As much as Bernays did not like the concept of attitudes, he also derogated the role of motivation in explaining human behaviour (Bernays, 1986). He persisted that motivation, as well as attitudes, obscure the big picture of human behaviour with all its complexities. It is quite the opposite. Motivation and attitudes are the necessary elements that connect, rather than distort, the understanding. Chapter 6, discusses in detail the history and practical implications of one particular motivation: the epistemic need and its implications for manoeuvring through a communication environment overloaded with information.

Note

1 Standards for the accreditation of undergraduate, conversion, and integrated Master's programmes in psychology by the British Psychological Society also recognise social psychology as a branch of psychology.

References

Ajzen, I. (1989). Attitude structure and behavior. In A. R. Pratkanis, S. J. Breckler, & A. G. Greenwald (Eds.), *Attitude Structure and Function* (pp. 241–274). Lawrence Erlbaum Associates, Inc.

Ajzen, I., & Fishbein, M. (1980). *Understanding Attitudes and Predicting Social Behaviour*. Prentice-Hall.

AMEC. (n.d.). The definitive guide: why AVEs are invalid. Retrieved May2, 2025, from https://amecorg.com/wp-content/uploads/2019/11/22-reasons-to-say-no-to-AVEs-by-Richard-Bagnall-11-June-2017.pdf

Bagnall, R. (2024). According to PRWeek UK research, over 65% of #publicrelations agencies rate the quality of briefs that they receive from in house comms teams as either 'very poor', 'poor' or just 'average' [Linkedin Post]. https://www.linkedin.com/posts/richardbagnall_publicrelations-pr-planning-activity-7224767877772443648-xSfl/

Bagozzi, R. P. (1978). The construct validity of the affective, behavioral, and cognitive components of attitude by analysis of covariance structures. *Multivariate Behavioral Research*, *13*(1). https://doi.org/10.1207/s15327906mbr1301_2
Bargh, J. A. (1994). The four horsemen of automaticity: Awareness, efficiency, intention, and control in social cognition. In R. S. Wyer & T. K. Srull (Eds.), *Handbook of Social Cognition* (2nd ed., Vol. 1, pp. 1–40). Lawrence Erlbaum Associates, Inc.
Baylen, J. O. (2000, February). *Romeike, Henry (1855-1903), Originator of a Press-clipping Service*. https://doi.org/10.1093/anb/9780198606697.article.1601406
Beniger, J. R. (1987). Toward an old new paradigm the half-century flirtation with mass society. *Public Opinion Quarterly*, *51*(4 PART 2), S46–S66. https://doi.org/10.1093/poq/51.4_PART_2.S46
Beniger, J. R., & Gusek, J. A. (1995). The cognitive revolution in public opinion and communication research. In T. L. Glasser & C. T. Salmon (Eds.), *Public Opinion and the Communication of Consent* (pp. 217–248). The Guilford Press.
Bentele, G., Seidenglanz, R. (2008). Trust and credibility: Prerequisites for communication management. In: Zerfass, A., van Ruler, B., Sriramesh, K. (eds), *Public Relations Research: European and International Perspectives and Innovations* (pp. 49–62). Wiesbaden: VS Verlag für Sozialwissenschaften https://doi.org/10.1007/978-3-531-90918-9_4
Bergman, M. M. (1998). A Theoretical note on the differences between attitudes, opinions, and values. *Swiss Political Science Review*, *4*(2). https://doi.org/10.1002/j.1662-6370.1998.tb00239.x
Bernays, E. L. (1986). *The Later Years: Public Relations Insights 1956-1986*. Howard Penn Hudson Assc Inc.
Black, S. (1995). *The Practice of Public Relations*. Routledge.
Botsman, R. (2018). *Who Can You Trust? How Technology Brought us Together and Why it Might Drive Us Apart*. Penguin.
Breckler, S. J. (1984). Empirical validation of affect, behavior, and cognition as distinct components of attitude. *Journal of Personality and Social Psychology*, *47*(6). https://doi.org/10.1037/0022-3514.47.6.1191
Brown, R. E. (2014). *The Public Relations of Everything: The Ancient, Modern and Postmodern Dramatic History of An Idea*. Routledge.
Childs, H. L. (1965). *Public Opinion: Nature, Formation and Role*. Van Nostrand Reinhold Inc.
Curtis, R. (2003). *Love Actually [Video recording]*. Studio Canal, Working Title Films, DNA Films.
Cutlip, S. M. (1994). *The Unseen Power: Public Relations: A History (Routledge Communication Series)*. Routledge. https://www.routledge.com/The-Unseen-Power-Public-Relations-A-History/Cutlip/p/book/9780805814651
Dewey, J. (1927). *The Public and Its Problems*. Swallow.
Dozier, D. M., & Lauzen, M. M. (2000). Liberating the intellectual domain from the practice: Public relations, activism, and the role of the scholar. *Journal of Public Relations Research*, *12*(1), 3–22.
Edwards, L. (2012). Defining the 'object' of public relations research: A new starting point. *Public Relations Inquiry*, *1*(1), 7–30. https://doi.org/10.1177/2046147x11422149
Glasser, T. L., & Salmon, C. T. (Eds.). (1995). *Public Opinion and the Communication of Consent*. Guilford Press.
Glynn, C. J., Ostman, R. E., & McDonald, D. G. (1995). Opinions, perception, and social reality. In T. L. Glasser & C. T. Salmon (Eds.), *Public Opinion and the Communication of Consent* (pp. 249–277). The Guilford Press.
Gregory, A. (2016). *Planning and Managing Public Relations Campaigns: A Strategic Approach*. Kogan Page Publishers.

Gregory, A. (2022). Artificial intelligence, big data and all change. In J. Falkheimer & M. Heide (Eds.), *Research Handbook on Strategic Communication* (pp. 209–220). Edward Elgar Publishing.

Grunig, J. E. (1992). The development of public relations research in the United States and its status in communication science. In H. Avenarius and W. Armbrecht (Eds.), *Ist Public RelationsEine Wissenschaft?* (pp. 103–132). Westdeutscher Verlag.

Grunig, J. E. (1997). A situational theory of publics: Conceptual history, recent challenges and new research. In D. Moss, T. MacManus, & D. Vercic (Eds.), *Public Relations Research: An International Perspective.* (pp. 3–48). International Thomson Business Press.

Grunig, J. E., & Hunt, T. (1984). *Managing public relations.* Holt, Rinehart and Winston.

Grunig, J. E., & Kim, J.-N. (2021). The four models of public relations and their research legacy. In C. Valentini (Ed.), *Public Relations* (pp. 277–311). De Gruyter. https://doi.org/10.1515/9783110554250-015

Hardy, J. (2022). *Branded Content: The Fateful Merging of Media and Marketing.* Routledge.

Harlow, R. F. (1976). Building a public relations definition. *Public Relations Review*, 2(4), 34–42. https://doi.org/10.1016/S0363-8111(76)80022-7

Harrington, J. (2024, July 31). *Client Briefs Dissected – 'We've Had Some Over 50 Pages Long'.* PR Week UK. https://www.prweek.co.uk/article/1882531/client-briefs-dissected-%E2%80%93-weve-50-pages-long

Heath, D. R. L., & Toth, E. L. (1992). Rhetorical and critical approaches to public relations II. Routledge. https://doi.org/10.4324/9781315045474

Hon, L. C., & Grunig, J. E. (1999). Guidelines for measuring relationships in public relations. Institute for Public Relations. https://instituteforpr.org/wp-content/uploads/Guidelines_Measuring_Relationships.pdf

Hutton, J. G. (1999). The definition, dimensions, and domain of public relations. *Public Relations Review*, *25*(2), 199–214. https://doi.org/10.1016/S0363-8111(99)80162-3

Ihlen, Ø., & Verhoeven, P. (2012). A public relations identity for the 2010s. *Public Relations Inquiry*, *1*(2), 159–176. https://doi.org/10.1177/2046147x11435083

Katz, D. (1960). The functional approach to the study of attitudes. *Public Opinion Quarterly*, *24*(2). https://doi.org/10.1086/266945

Katz, E. (1995). Introduction: The state of the art. In T. L. Glasser & C. T. Salmon (Eds.), *Public Opinion and the Communication of Consent* (pp. xxi–xxxiv). The Guilford Press.

Kent, M. L., & Taylor, M. (2002). Toward a dialogic theory of public relations. *Public relations review*, *28*(1), 21–37.

Kim, J. N., & Grunig, J. E. (2011). Problem solving and communicative action: A situational theory of problem solving. *Journal of Communication*, *61*(1). https://doi.org/10.1111/j.1460-2466.2010.01529.x

L'Etang, J., & Pieczka, M. (Eds.) (1996). *Critical Perspectives in Public Relations.* International Thomson Business Press.

Ledingham, J. A., & Bruning, S. D. (1998). Relationship management in public relations: dimensions of an organization-public relationship. *Public Relations Review*, *24*(1), 55–65. https://doi.org/10.1016/S0363-8111(98)80020-9

Macnamara, J. (2014). *Journalism and PR: Unpacking 'Spin', Stereotypes, and Media Myths.* Peter Lang Publishing Inc.

Macnamara, J. (2015). Breaking the measurement and evaluation deadlock: A new approach and model. *Journal of Communication Management*, *19*(4), 371–387. https://doi.org/10.1108/JCOM-04-2014-0020

Macnamara, J. (2023). A call for reconfiguring evaluation models, pedagogy, and practice: Beyond reporting media-centric outputs and fake impact scores. *Public Relations Review*, *49*(2), 102311. https://doi.org/10.1016/J.PUBREV.2023.102311

Macnamara, Jim. (2018). *Evaluating Public Communication: Exploring New Models, Standards, and Best Practice*. Routledge.
Maio, G. R., Esses, V. M., & Bell, D. W. (2000). Examining conflict between components of attitudes: Ambivalence and inconsistency are distinct constructs. *Canadian Journal of Behavioural Science*, *32*(2), 71–83. https://doi.org/10.1037/H0087102
Maio, G. R., & Haddock, G. (2007). Attitude change. In A. W. Kruglanski & E. T. Higgins (Eds.), *Social Psychology: Handbook of Basic Principles* (2nd ed., pp. 565–586). The Guilford Press.
McDougall, W. (1919). *An Introduction to Social Psychology* (14th ed.). Methuen & Co. Ltd.
McLeaod, J., Pan, Z., & Rucinski, D. (1995). Levels of analysis in public opinion research. In T. L. Glasser & C. T. Salmon (Eds.), *Public Opinion and the Communication of Consent* (pp. 55–85). The Guilford Press.
Mead, G. H. (1934). *Mind, Self and Society*. University of Chicago Press.
Michaelson, D., & Stacks, D. W. (2017). *A Professional and Practitioner's Guide to Public Relations Research, Measurement, and Evaluation*. Business Expert Press.
Miller, D., & Dinan, W. (2007). *A Century of Spin: How Public Relations Became the Cutting Edge of Corporate Power*. Pluto Press.
Minar, D. W. (1960). Public opinion in the perspective of political theory. *Political Research Quarterly*, *13*(1). https://doi.org/10.1177/106591296001300103
Moloney, K. (2005). Trust and public relations: Center and edge. *Public Relations Review*, *31*(4), 550–555. https://doi.org/10.1016/j.pubrev.2005.08.015
Noelle-Neumann, E. (1995). Public opinion and rationality. In T. L. Glasser & C. T. Salmon (Eds.), *Public Opinion and the Communication of Consent* (pp. 33–54). The Guilford Press.
Olins, Wally. (1990). *Corporate Identity: Making Business Strategy Visible Through Design*. Harvard Business School Press.
Paisley, W. (1972). *Communication Research As a Behavioral Discipline*. Stanford University, Institute for Communication Research.
Pan, Z., & Mcleod, J. M. (1991). Multilevel analysis in mass communication research. *Communication Research*, *18*(2), 140–173. https://doi.org/10.1177/009365091018002002
Pearson, R. (1989). Beyond ethical relativism in public relations: Coorientation, rules, and the idea of communication symmetry. *Public Relations Research Annual*, *1*(1–4), 67–86. https://doi.org/10.1207/S1532754XJPRR0101-4_3
Peters, J. D. (1995). Historical tensions in the concept of public opinion. In T. L. Glasser & C. T. Salmon (Eds.), *Public Opinion and the Communication of Consent* (pp. 3–32). The Guilford Press.
Petty, R. E., & Cacioppo, J. T. (2012). *Communication and Persuasion: Central and Peripheral Routes to attitude change*. Springer Science & Business Media.
Rosenberg, M. J., & Hovland, C. I. (1960). Cognitive, affective and behavioral components of attitudes. In M. Rosenberg, C. Hovland, W. McGuire, R. Abelson, & J. Brehm (Eds.), *Attitude Organization and Change: An Analysis of Consistency among Attitude Components* (pp. 1–14). Yale University Press.
Rosselli, F., Skelly, J. J., & Mackie, D. M. (1995). Processing rational and emotional messages: The cognitive and affective mediation of persuasion. *Journal of Experimental Social Psychology*, *31*(2), 163–190. https://doi.org/10.1006/JESP.1995.1008
Sarnoff, I., & Katz, D. (1954). The motivational bases of attitude change. *Journal of Abnormal and Social Psychology*, *49*(1), 115–124. https://doi.org/10.1037/H0057453
St. John III, B., Lamme, M. O., & L'Etang, J. (2014). Pathways to public relations: Histories of practice and professio. In B. St. John III, M. O. Lamme, & J. L'Etang (Eds.), *Pathways to Public Relations*. Routledge. https://doi.org/10.4324/9780203074183
Sterling, C. H. (2009). Clipping services. In *Encyclopedia of Journalism* (pp. 315–316). SAGE Publications, Inc. https://doi.org/10.4135/9781412972048

The Press: Clipping Business | TIME. (n.d.). Retrieved January15, 2025, from https://time.com/archive/6767050/the-press-clipping-business/
Toth, E. L. (1992). The case for pluralistic studies of public relations: rhetorical, critical and systemperspectives. In E. L. Toth, & R. L. Heath (Eds.), *Rhetorical and Critical Approaches to Publicrelations* (pp. 3–16). Lawrence Erlbaum Associates.
Valentini, C. (2020). Trust research in public relations: an assessment of its conceptual, theoretical and methodological foundations. *Corporate Communications: An International Journal*, *26*(1), 84–106. https://doi.org/10.1108/CCIJ-01-2020-0030
Valentini, C., & Luoma-aho, V. (2023). The European School of Public Relations: Origins, Main Traits, and Theoretical Contributions. In C. H. Botan, & E. J. Sommerfeldt (Eds.), *Public Relations Theory III: In the Age of Publics* (pp. 338–356). Routledge.
Watson, Tom., & Noble, Paul. (2009). *Evaluating Public Relations: A Best Practice Guide to Public Relations Planning, Research & Evaluation*. Kogan Page.
White, J. (2000). Psychology and public relations. In D. Moss, D. Verčič & G. Warnaby (Eds.), *Perspectives on Public Relations Research*. (pp 161–172). Routledge. https://doi.org/10.4324/9780203192924-13
Wojcik, K. (2005). *Public Relations: Wiarygodny Dialog z Otoczeniem*. Placet.
Zajonc, R. B., & Markus, H. (1982). Affective and cognitive factors in preferences. *Journal of Consumer Research*, *9*(2), 123. https://doi.org/10.1086/208905
Zaller, J. R. (1992). The nature and origins of mass opinion. Cambridge University Press. https://doi.org/10.1017/cbo9780511818691

6

THE INDIVIDUAL

Members of Audiences and Publics

The Age of Members of Publics in Public Relations Practice

Sommerfeldt and Iannacone (2023) consider publics as the christening term of PR and, at the same time, a primitive one – although everyone seems to know what it is, the definition of it is ambiguous and vague. The psychological perspective of PR that I am advancing in this volume focuses on the individual level of analysis, so the question arises: how to connect this level with research that focuses on audiences or publics? It can be seen that the distinction between audiences or publics as bodies consisting of individuals and constituting the respective terms would be irrelevant to psychological investigations. After all, the object of analysis in psychology is human behaviour, and the optics of psychology differ from Mead's sociology, where the starting point of inquiry is a group or society. However, in the attempt to integrate psychology with PR, such a view would not only be incorrect but also lead to simply building another version of psychology in public relations, as opposed to the psychology of PR. The view of publics in PR appears to follow Mead's sociological tradition, which first examines a group or community. Then it recognises that it comprises individuals with thoughts and feelings that constitute it. The vast majority of PR scholarship that investigates the public in the social context is steered towards sociological and critical analyses of 'the capacity for public relations in making communities and societies a better place in which to live' (Botan & Sommerfeldt, 2023, p. 1).

Although from a quantitative point of view, audiences and publics can be seen as simply aggregations of individuals, the differences between them are not trivial. Different criteria lead to identifying a collective of individuals that is an audience or publics. In this chapter, I will offer a psychological

DOI: 10.4324/9781003610403-6

explanation of the process of identification and organisation of publics. Warner refers to: 'a public is never just a congeries of people, never just the sum of persons who happen to exist. It must, first of all, have some way of organising itself as a body and of being addressed in discourse. And not just any way of defining the totality will do. It must be organised by something other than the state' (Warner, 2002, p. 414). Although Warner believes that public exists by the 'virtue of being addressed' (p. 413), I think that this problem is even more complex from a psychological perspective. A member of publics emerges when they subjectively experience the act of being addressed, but in fact, it is a piece of divisive content that is processed qualitatively that leads to the emergence of publics. It is the content that leads to the identification of publics and its members.

The argument will be organised around the process depicted in Figure 6.1. In this illustration, I summarise the impact of content, first received only quantitatively and without deliberating how information that an individual receives is informative for them personally and significant for their group identity. In psychology, Allport offered the following, now classical definition of the public 'defined as the number of people holding a certain opinion,

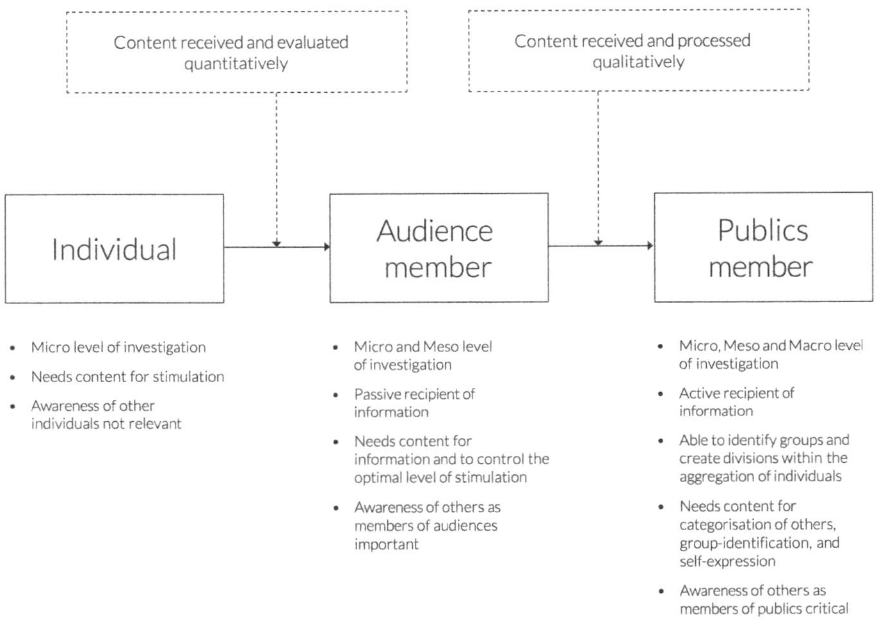

FIGURE 6.1 Conceptual diagram of simplified influence of content and its apprehension driven by external realisation of others that informs how the concept of an individual evolves into a member of audiences and a member of publics.

and the people holding that opinion would be identified as those belonging to that public' (Allport, 1937, p. 9). Historically, in PR and mass communication scholarship, publics arise around an issue (Dewey, 1927; Lippmann, 1922). The act of forming an opinion (attitude) was critical for identifying publics. However, for individual-level analysis, the term 'content' is more useful as it captures meanings and context rather than the formal characteristics of communication. Content can also be looked at quantitatively versus qualitatively. Consequently, the concept of content will be used to demonstrate that there are differences between its qualitative and quantitative processing by individuals, and it has a 'creational' capacity to identify audience and publics members. The idea that content is a mediator between communicators and audiences in the context of propaganda and mass communication is not new. Most prominently, it has been acknowledged by Lasswell (1946), who considered its impact on building relationships with audiences, appreciating individual dignity, and strengthening democracy. This part of the book should be read in conjunction with Chapter 7, which explicitly addresses the context- and content-related phenomena which make the distinction between audience members and public members meaningful.

Although this is not entirely accurate, the terms *audiences* and *publics* have been used in communication studies interchangeably. What is the nature of audiences, and how do they differ from publics? What are the limits of social psychological inquiry into individual minds? How independent are they in making judgements and decisions? When content is received and processed quantitatively, we can refer to the audience members. The quantitative consideration of content will enable us to see its abundance, which can also be problematic for humans. When content is processed qualitatively, comparisons and divisions that lead to the identification of publics occur.

Already 20 years ago, Ruddock (2001) mentioned media saturation as a phenomenon, the existence of which was widely noticed and accepted. But then, to discuss media effects, he investigated the macro level of analysis and concluded that assessing the effects of this saturation requires acts of interpretation and evaluation in an ideological sense. This is not necessarily correct. As discussed in Chapter 4, quantitative, formal investigations of the effects of media and communication on individuals are enabled by psychology. In other words, psychology enables the discovery of causal relationships between different variables without qualifying them as good or bad and formulating moral guidelines. Ruddock does not discuss this aspect of the psychological, micro-level perspective. The qualitative approach of Ruddock can be seen in how he refers to the 'erosion of conservative sexual mores' (Ruddock, 2001, p. 20), which assumes the existence of certain political stances (liberal versus conservative) and ideological preferences of viewers (recipients) of the content. So, his observation was not formal but qualitative; one ideology is better than the other. In other words, Ruddock suggested problems caused by a particular type of content (quality) and its quantity. Both dimensions – quantity and quality – have been successfully studied in psychology and can be applied to the practice of PR. Let me first define the audience and illustrate the differences and similarities in approaching the concept from a psychological versus a higher-level field perspective.

An audience can be defined simply as a group of individuals who receive a message. This is a meso-level definition that looks primarily at a group, an entity that is homogeneous and passive. Postmodern thinkers propose a reconsideration of the audience in PR research as decentred rather than autonomous beings and allude to the positivist stance as failing to grasp the influence of social factors, such as religion or education, on the individual's subjectivity (Zompetti & Moffitt, 2008). It is challenging to ascertain the origins of this misguided perspective. However, it should be noted that the psychological comprehension of human behaviour, which is firmly anchored in the principles of positivist social science, has effectively addressed inquiries concerning how humans acquire the capacity to think and act in response to external influences. For instance, the seminal theory of Bandura (1977) comprehensively and morally-neutrally delineated the joint influences of internal and external factors on an individual's actions.

It can also be argued that part of the problem with 'discovering' new perspectives on topics of pivotal role is the lack of communication between disciplines, hermetic language, or discipline identity issues that motivate scholars to conceive level-specific theories instead of focusing on phenomena and being driven by evidence. The following passage from Zompetti and Moffitt (2008) is offered to illustrate the argument under discussion:

> any person possesses multiple meanings/images toward any organization, social issue or other person. Further, these images are the result of the intersection of any number of social, gender, political, family, or business factors. Given that an image is a product of an intersection of factors, any person holding a particular image is, in fact, always open to change her/his image(s) given a change in any one of the intersecting factors.
>
> *(Zompetti & Moffitt, 2008, p. 280)*

Next, let us look at William James' (1890) excerpt from his first Psychology book:

> Properly speaking, a man has as many social selves as there are individuals who recognize him and carry an image of him in their mind. To wound any one of these his images is to wound him. But as the individuals who carry the images fall naturally into classes, we may practically say that he has as many different social selves as there are distinct groups of persons about whose opinion he cares. He generally shows a different

> side of himself to each of these different groups. Many a youth who is demure enough before his parents and teachers, swears and swaggers like a pirate among his 'tough' young friends. We do not show ourselves to our children as to our club-companions, to our customers as to the laborers we employ, to our own masters and employers as to our intimate friends.
>
> *(James, 1890, p. 258)*

We can see that already in the 19th century, psychology was interested in questions now asked by critical theory. However, the language used in psychology differs from that of critical theory, and this might be one reason, besides the influence of disciplinary traditions, that the micro-level focus of psychology and the macro-level focus of critical thought have been more effective in PR. To illustrate my point in detail, I have rewritten the original passage from Zompetti and Moffitt (2008) using psychological terminology.

> Any person's attitude towards an organisation consists of multiple cognitions (cognitive representations). These knowledge structures, effectively acting as social evaluations, have been formed by a person's experience through the process of social learning that informs a person's (self) perception of gender and own identity and is shaped by an environment that includes family, politics, and business.
>
> *(promotional) communication*

The objective of this demonstration was twofold. Primarily, it was to highlight the psychological level of analysis that employs the theoretical expertise of social psychology. Moreover, the fundamental purpose of this approach was to demonstrate the existence of a psychological understanding of an audience as primarily consisting of individuals. The examination of individuals in relation to their attitudes, cognitive representations, social evaluations, and perceptions of family and societal roles is advantageous due to the extensive scholarly tradition of probing into the effects of relationships between these phenomena (intraindividual research) and knowledge of the interaction between individuals and groups (interindividual research). To align the argument with the central focus of the chapter, I note that all of the psychological concepts discussed here (i.e. attitudes, social evaluations, etc.) involve the processing of content at some stage. In other words, they are outcomes or reflections of the process of receiving and processing information. The underlying mechanisms of information and knowledge acquisition are crucial for individuals to function effectively. These factors are also important because analysing how individuals process new information is a key area of interest in audience studies.

Audience Members: Searching for News

The purpose of the next section is to demonstrate the centrality of motivational processes that provide an explanatory basis for human decisions, attitude formation, and behaviour. Understanding the news and information landscape requires addressing whether audience members like new information, need it, and how they use it, as they are a crucial element within this context. From a psychological perspective, the history of different views on what is commonly referred to as epistemic motivation is also fascinating, as it reveals the development of various schools of thought and the gradual integration of behaviourist, developmental, information processing, and social cognitive approaches. Epistemic motivation should also be relevant for the practice of PR as, in psychology, it is considered to be the essential link between 'I think' and 'I act', connecting the cognitive stage of information processing with the effects of a behavioural nature. Motivation, as a hypothetical explanatory construct, describes differences in the direction and intensity of human behaviour.

The desire to understand reality is commonly considered one of the most important tendencies that explain human behaviour. Initially, this group of epistemic motives was associated with curiosity. However, curiosity itself had been discussed much earlier than modern psychological thought was developed. It was already mentioned by Aristotle, who pointed to the intrinsic motivation to study science as an end rather than a means to other ends. In contrast, St. Augustine criticised curiosity itself, treating it as a vain pursuit of knowledge and lust unless the goal of the activity was progress towards what is immortal and unchanging: God. William James (1890) considered curiosity an emotion similar to fear. The function of such an emotion was to motivate the organism to explore the environment; the function of fear was to limit the risks associated with this exploration. McDougall (1919) enriched James' argument by defining curiosity as one of the basic human instincts aroused by a vague perception or identification of a stimulus. In McDougall's view, curiosity, although basic, depended on other instincts, which served as a mediator of stimulus identification. Although Maslow (1943) is recognised as a precursor of modern humanistic psychology, who was instrumental in drawing attention to the concept of needs, he began his research as a behaviourist. Given the great popularity of his theory, it is worth mentioning here the references it contains to the issues at hand. Maslow saw the acquisition of knowledge and systematising information about the surrounding reality as a means of achieving other needs, such as safety and self-actualisation. In Maslow's view, cognitive needs should not be considered different from more basic needs and a desire (need) for knowledge (a desire to know). This need was equivalent to the desire to be aware of the surrounding reality and satisfy one's curiosity about facts. In addition to the desire to know, he also noted the need to structure and systematise knowledge in order to make sense of and understand the relationships between meanings, which is said to be motivated by the desire to comprehend. According to Maslow, the need for knowledge should be included in the general hierarchy of human needs and treated as a component of personality, as the drive for knowledge is fundamental.

Several common assumptions also characterise contemporary accounts of motivation. Drawing on Heider's (1958) notion of intention, behaviour is defined as motivated if it is aimed at achieving a desired outcome or goal. The development of knowledge about human behaviour's motives could be seen as a discussion of the explanatory power of concepts like motive, drive, need, and goal. This corresponds to the evolution of distinctive psychological schools of thought and their increasing popularity in the discipline of psychology (Thrash & Elliot, 2003). Motivation research has traditionally focused on questions related to the processes that precede the decision to (1) choose a goal, (2) persist in the pursuit of the chosen goal, and (3) the intensity of the level of performance of specific instrumental activities that lead to the achievement of a particular goal. Most contemporary theories of motivation also assume that human behaviour is goal-directed. The psychology of motivation distinguishes several enduring dispositions that correspond to the most common sets of goals. These include (a) motives for maintaining stability within the human organism, (b) motives related to human social functioning, and (c) dispositions related to competent response to the environment. In the overview that follows, I will focus on epistemic motives and their influence on human behaviour.

Early approaches to curiosity, developed primarily by behaviourists and emphasising its drive mechanism, pointed to an internal, and therefore bodily, source of stimulation. Although behaviourists differed in seeing curiosity either as a primary or secondary role in regulating behaviour, all accounts suggested that curiosity led to negative tensions that could be reduced through exploratory behaviour. An interesting view of curiosity, one which is closer to a personality perspective, was proposed by Freud, who treated curiosity as a derivative of the sexual drive and sought its roots in the sublimation of early childhood exploratory behaviour. In that sense, any curiosity was, in a way, sexually driven. However, the most important behaviourist researcher who influenced the way we think about human exploratory behaviour was Berlyne (1954), who introduced the concept of the epistemic motive into psychology. Berlyne leaned towards the drive nature of curiosity, but also included a cognitive aspect. The cognitive properties of external stimuli, among which he included novelty, complexity, and surprisingness (uniqueness), were thought to have the effect of increasing the organism's overall arousal level and increasing curiosity. Berlyne not only developed the concept of curiosity and its underlying mechanisms but also proposed a systematisation and categorisation of information about the concept. He suggested that the construct has a two-dimensional nature, consisting of perceptual and epistemic curiosity on one dimension and specificity and diversity on the other. Perceptual curiosity, which was said to be aroused by novel stimuli and satisfied by their exposure, was thought to explain several regularities observed in animal experiments (Dember, 1956; Fowler, 1965). Epistemic curiosity, defined as the pursuit of knowledge, was previously thought to be a primarily human trait. The second dimension was concerned with the nature of the information sought. For example, the search for specific information was thought to be related to solving a specific problem, while seeking diverse information was thought to be the organism's response to boredom in the environment. Berlyne was also among the few early investigators of the phenomenon of curiosity who attempted to address the problem of situational determinants that increase the organism's level of arousal and induce exploratory behaviour. He conducted a series of experiments aimed at identifying stimulus features that were thought to lead to cognitive conflict, thereby stimulating curiosity. Berlyne (1954) showed that information arousing greater curiosity was later better remembered. Fowler (1965), who postulated the existence of a homeostatic source of curiosity stimulation, also strongly disagreed with Berlyne's account. He believed that exploratory behaviour could emerge much earlier than the external stimulus that leads to it.

Contemporary analyses of the development of the concept of curiosity and the motivation to explore reality often argue that it is impossible and unnecessary to determine conclusively whether a motive of an epistemic nature is a form of drive. Post-behaviourist accounts of the drive to explore the human environment place much more emphasis on understanding the process of acquiring new information and the influence of external factors on the initiation of exploration.

Searching for Information as Adaptation and Response to Inconsistency

It seems a little debatable that the modern view of motivation has evolved since Murphy (1947). In his work on the biopsychosocial basis of personality, motivation was viewed as a form of energy akin to Bergson's *élan vital* (Bergson, 1911), which denied the possibility that it possessed any tools for dealing with reality. In contrast to the views of behaviourists, who saw curiosity as a form of drive, proponents of cognitive incongruence theories suggested that curiosity is triggered by perceived incongruence with expectations. Two assumptions were shared. Incongruence was said to trigger the human desire to understand the world, and the relationship between the level of curiosity and the degree of incongruence with expectations took the form of an inverted U.

In a modified version of his theory, presented in Drives and the C.N.S., Hebb (1955) presented the view that the human nervous system is constantly at work and, therefore, must be active. He argued that curiosity is a manifestation of the natural human tendency to process information. He postulated the existence of a natural, expected level of inconsistency, which he described as a state of pleasurable stimulation. His ideas were supported by research into the development of children conducted by Piaget (1926), who observed a motivational force in children resulting from a cognitive imbalance between existing and incoming information. Leuba (1955) reached similar conclusions based on research findings on cognitive and perceptual curiosity. His idea – the theory of optimal stimulation – was an attempt to explain some of the behaviours of living organisms in which the drive was observed to be intensified. The researcher acknowledged that living organisms, including humans, do not always tend to reduce drives but rather to increase their intensity. Leuba, referring to the experimental results of K.C. Montgomery (1955), described the behaviour of rats in a maze. The animals first explored their environment and then moved to the food location. The more basic drive (hunger reduction) gave way to curiosity. Leuba's line of argument was based on the specificity of the environment that was unique to humans. To explain the range of human activities, it would not be sufficient to consider simple drives – he explained – because the motives of human behaviour appeared to be more complex. People learn how to engage in activities that lead to an optimal level of stimulation. According to Leuba (1955), humans perceive a state of optimal stimulation as a state of pleasure, while a lack of adequate stimulation produces negative emotions.

One of the pioneers of modern motivation theory was Hunt (1963), who proposed an information-processing perspective tied to human motivation. This was one of the first accounts that established a link between the cognitive and motivational systems. According to Hunt, the processing of information is the source of human motivation. It involves comparing incoming information with standards, which are defined as organisations of previously encoded information in the brain. The effect of the comparison process was either confirmation of a standard or detection of a discrepancy. Hunt predicted the existence of the optimal level of discrepancy; a discrepancy more minor than optimal caused boredom, while a discrepancy larger than expected led to fear and panic. The identification of discrepancies had motivational functions. The first was to stimulate, and the second was to control the direction of activity. The reduction of the discrepancy was said to lead to the disappearance of motivation and was equivalent to achieving the goal. Haber (1958) also postulated the existence of an optimal level of adaptation to the environment and stimulation. The optimal level of adaptation was equivalent to the expectation of a certain level of stimulation coming from the external environment. Levels lower or higher than expected led to different affective states: boredom in the case of suboptimal stimulation and fear in the case of stimulation that exceeds expectations. The optimal discrepancy was expected to produce a positive motivational state: interest. Driver and Streufert (1965) also addressed the problem of optimal incongruence as adaptation. The theory assumes that a person learns to expect a certain level of incongruence. If this level was higher or lower than the optimum, they could either try to reduce (or increase – respectively) its level or adapt by setting a new optimum.

Unlike previously discussed theories, according to Nuttin (1964), humans were not motivated by the desire to adapt to their environment, but by the possibility of changing it. Nuttin believed that men adopted a temporal perspective (they were future-oriented) and, within this perspective, they could defer immediate gratification. Human activity was said to be motivated by the discrepancy between plans and intended results. This view not only emphasises that an adequate level of discrepancy is a state that positively motivates action, but also defines the nature of the relationship between individuals and the environment. Humans are not cognitive conformists who merely want to adapt to the environment and achieve a pleasurable state of stimulation. The natural consequence of striving to eliminate perceived discrepancies is constant intervention in the environment, disturbing the state of equilibrium. Kagan (1972), who examined the mechanism of reducing discrepancy as a type of motive, also focused on what happens when attempts to remove inconsistency are unsuccessful. These failures to process information in a way that aligns with our systems of beliefs may result in embarrassment, anxiety, fear, shame, or guilt.

Epistemic Need and Attitude Change

Although Maslow first introduced the term 'need for knowledge' as a fundamental human need and element of psychology, Cohen's research likely popularised the concept of the need for cognition. Cohen et al. (1955) defined the need for cognition as the desire to understand and find meaning in the surrounding world (or situation) in order to experience reality better. The degree of integration and meaning, in this perspective, was considered to be subjective and interindividually variable (different people need different amounts of information). The researchers further suggested that the unmet need for cognition could lead to tension and frustration, for example, when one finds oneself in a situation that is not sufficiently clear and lacks sufficient cues for interpretation and structure. Failures to satisfy the need for cognition would lead to negative emotions and increase the effort required to structure and understand the environment.

The development of research in the psychology of attitude formation and change has led to a greater focus on questions concerning the role of motivation, understood as a state that varies in its characteristics but is always present for individuals. Sarnoff and Katz (1954) attempted to show that an individual is influenced by one of three motivational processes at any given time. Motivation can be an ego defence mechanism, provide rewards and punishments, or be aimed at testing reality. Testing reality was said to be related to the need for exploration, understood as the desire to gain knowledge about the world around us. The exploration of reality understood in this way influenced the form and content of attitudes, which were a function of the information currently available to the individual. It was further assumed that all three motives interacted with each other. An important practical implication of Sarnoff and Katz's (1954) theory is the assumption that changing an attitude requires knowledge of the motivational basis that constitutes it, as well as the necessity of choosing an appropriate method that is consistent with that basis.

Although Cohen and his colleagues are the authors of the concept of the need for cognition, Cacioppo and Petty (1982) are responsible for its contemporary, most popularised conceptualisation in academia. Cacioppo and Petty defined the need for cognition as a stable dimension of individual differences in the tendency to engage in and derive pleasure from cognitively taxing activities. The need was associated with an intrinsic motivation that reflected a focus on the cognitive process itself rather than its outcome. Petty et al. (2009) also emphasised that the need for cognition is only moderately correlated with cognitive ability, which means that an individual may need to derive pleasure from learning about the world and receiving information, but may fail to arrive at correct conclusions. Thus, in terms of its influence on decision-making, the need for cognition is said to primarily affect the amount of information processed (e.g. Levin et al., 2000; Yang & Lee, 1998). The construct has also been used to explain the halo effect (Perlini & Hansen, 2001), the anchoring effect (Epley & Gilovich, 2006), priming (Petty et al., 2008), or stereotyping (Crawford & Skowronski, 1998). Caccioppo and Petty's idea is perhaps closest to what Murphy described as the joy of thinking (Murphy, 1947, p. 405). However, while Cacioppo and Petty (1982) were not interested in the outcome of the process (its goal), Murphy had already asked what the engagement in the thinking process was aimed at. While his answer would not satisfy contemporary social-cognitive psychologists, it pointed in an inspiring direction shared by many researchers – connectedness to reality. Other researchers have also highlighted the competence aspect of the tendency to seek coherence and the desire to understand the world around us. For example, Bar-Tal et al. (1999) distinguish between the search for specific and unambiguous information and the ability to construct knowledge structures based on environmental cues. In doing so, they pointed out that not all people are equally capable of the level and type of information processing they expect.

The theories cited in this section point to an important aspect of human activity. Learning about the surrounding reality is a crucial aspect of everyday existence. The search for new and stimulating information is often found in news searches. Historically, researchers have differed in their positioning of this type of behaviour in relation to other basic needs. Berlyne's introduction of the notion of epistemic motivation and his distinction of it as a specifically human process is an important point that drew attention to the issue of knowledge: information that is valued should help people understand reality in a meaningful and coherent way. The adoption of the approach to information processing that is guided by motivation and subject to the satisfaction of different goals also led to the identification of two categories of information discrepancies responsible for triggering the motivational process: formal (related to the quantity of information) and content-related (content-related problems seem to have elicited more interest in media and communication scholars inquiring into media effects on audiences, see e.g. Ruddock, 2001). From a formal perspective, the central notion is that of resources and their availability.

The Age of Information Overload and Comparisons

In 1973, Kahneman introduced the concept of resources and assumed the existence of a non-specific *mental energy* available in the human cognitive system. To deal with any cognitive task (receiving and processing information is one of them), individuals need mental resources, for example, working memory and attention. One way motivation and information processing can be examined jointly involves arousal and its impact on resource allocation across two tasks performed simultaneously (Humphreys & Revelle, 1984). In psychology, arousal describes the quantitative dimension of motivation. Arousal is commonly understood to be a general increase in bodily activity. Anderson (1990) defined it as a hypothetical construct used to explain the effects that physical exercise, time of day, stimulant drugs, or sleep deprivation have on the human body. Thayer (1989) further identified two types of arousal: tense and energetic. Several factors, including physical exercise, the time of day, and the prospect of a reward, influence energetic arousal. Conversely, tense arousal has been linked to stressful situations and noise. According to Thayer, both tense and energic arousal have been demonstrated to influence the level of performance in cognitive tasks.

There exists a plethora of everyday situations in which an individual appears to be immobilised and incapable of acting effectively, not only in the eyes of a psychologist but also in the eyes of the individual. For instance, the average person who has just witnessed a car accident and been forced to observe scenes that evoke unpleasant emotions would not be able to solve analogy test tasks at a level close to their actual ability immediately following a negative experience. This is, naturally, a deliberate exaggeration intended to emphasise the impact that stress can have on the human cognitive system. However, information found in social media, and media in general, has arousing potential, too. Abundant data suggest that, as a society, we have developed an incredible capacity to remain divided on many different issues (Goldsworthy et al., 2022). The question, therefore, arises as to whether the knowledge about the psychology of human arousal can be translated into the work of a PR professional.

An individual can be considered an audience member when they receive content from a media source. If the audience member is involved with, for example, two or more social media posts, they can be said to perform two cognitive tasks simultaneously, and for that, they need mental resources. Those resources can be allocated to separate activities depending on their subjectively perceived importance. However, an increase in arousal levels would lead to focusing on one of the posts at the expense of the attention paid to the other. That would happen as a consequence of the arousal limiting available resources. However, a different scenario is also plausible, and the reallocation of resources (scarce as a consequence of heightened arousal) could also occur between different aspects of the same task. This may be the case when several components can be identified within a single task, such as multiple topics within a single piece of content.

Additionally, an individual audience member may increase the speed of task execution while simultaneously sacrificing precision, which means reading more information but not fully understanding everything with the same level of accuracy. A resulting trade-off between accuracy and the quantity of information processed will lead to a reduction in the amount of information remembered. Epistemic motivation can also play a positive role. For instance, simple instructions highlighting the topic's relevance can elicit it. We do that automatically every day. Despite the fatigue and being overburdened with data, if a topic touches on an important subject, such as our family or decisions of considerable financial impact, we can overcome limitations and release additional mental energy to engage in processing information carefully. This mental energy release is managed by epistemic motivation.

Trade-Offs

Increasingly, there is not enough mental energy available to audience members, despite their willingness to deal with incoming communication efficiently. The consumption of social media content has been demonstrated to engender a wide range of psychological effects, encompassing cognitive, emotional, and physiological responses (Clayton, 2023; Nesi et al., 2022; O'Day & Heimberg, 2021). The abundance of communication is directly linked with the problem of arousal, as psychological research has established a link between the use of social media and arousal. The key concept that has been shown to play a role is dopamine. The dopamine hypothesis is related to the theory that proposes a biological basis for certain psychological phenomena, particularly those related to reward-seeking behaviour and the motivation to pursue goals. While Isen (1999) demonstrated that positive affect is associated with increased dopamine secretion, the occurrence of negative affect does not necessarily entail a decrease in dopamine secretion. Consequently, the effects on the cognitive system may be disparate. In practice, this may mean that an individual confronted with a variety of information, both positive and negative, will be exposed to the effects related to the secretion of dopamine. Research suggests that audience members seek socially valuable information on social media (Fareri & Delgado, 2014), and receiving positive comments or likes serves this function. This has the potential to render the act of searching for news a rewarding endeavour in itself, irrespective of whether the information obtained is positive or negative. A dopamine rush has been observed to occur in response to learning about issues with which audience members agree, as well as those with which they disagree, through social media, which may explain how social media turned some audience members into 'dopamine addicts' (Lembke, 2021).

The influence of the quantitative characteristics of information found in social media, specifically the requirement to present content with a limited character count, is interesting for another reason related to information processing. According to Easterbrook's hypothesis (1959), attention acts as a mediator between arousal and performance. As the body's arousal level increases, the amount of information that can be processed decreases. Easterbrook (1959) hypothesised that, up to a certain point, the range of peripheral cues – that is, those that are partially or temporarily relevant to the task – decreases, while the level of use of central cues – that is, those that are directly relevant to the task – remains the same. These changes have been observed to be associated with an improvement in the performance of the primary task or with maintaining a high level of performance in a stressful situation. As learning progresses (e.g. reading information on social media), the optimal high level of performance shifts higher towards greater use of cues (Easterbrook, 1959). A progressive reduction in the range of cues used initially leads to an increase in performance, followed by a subsequent decline, as shown in the performance curve commonly referred to as the 'inverted U'. In any given task, the reduction of extraneous cues simultaneously improves task performance by reducing the number of peripheral, that is, irrelevant, cues. The finding that the total range of information transfer decreases with increasing arousal is consistent with Hull's Law (1943), which states that the probability of a dominant response increases with increased arousal. Consequently, the likelihood of other responses to these cues decreases simultaneously. Increased arousal has been shown to affect the generalisation of stimuli, with the result that some cues become less salient as arousal increases (Hull, 1943). As noted by Kahneman (1973), the human cognitive system is limited, and as the difficulty of a task increases, so does the discrepancy between expected and actual levels of attention. In situations where task performance is suboptimal and associated arousal levels are low, individuals often demonstrate a lack of sufficient effort. Conversely, when individuals experience excessive arousal, their field of attention becomes more restricted, and their ability to discriminate between stimuli decreases. This phenomenon can also occur in the context of social media use. In circumstances where information processing is limited by arousal, two different scenarios can arise. First, there is a possibility that the number of sources a person uses will decrease. Second, and more generally, the average length of a message may be reduced. In a state of arousal, a trade-off must be made. In light of these findings, the question of the responsibility of PR communicators and the potential for a shift in tactics comes to mind. Given how much information (content) is produced as a part of PR activities, communicators should be aware that although they contribute to positive experiences associated with releases of dopamine, they also contribute to overloading audience members with information, fatigue and – indirectly – participate in the depletion of cognitive resources of audience members (this aspect is explored in relation to AI-generated content in Chapter 7).

In the context of producing content that elicits both positive and negative emotions, the well-known phrase coined by P.T. Barnum, 'there is no such thing as negative publicity', can be re-examined. Regardless of whether publicity consists of negative or positive information, it could trigger the rewarding mechanism of dopamine release. An audience member will experience a rewarding feeling of learning about something socially relevant and valuable. However, we should not limit the psychological interpretation of negative publicity to the psychophysiological level. Such an analysis would be superficial and of limited practical use for PR practice.

Nevertheless, it must be acknowledged that the practice of evaluating PR that involves AVEs indirectly reaches this type of conclusion. For instance, certain media outlets employ the number of mentions in print media, the number of views on the Internet, or the number of likes on social media as a metric to ascertain their degree of opinion-forming power. Indeed, psychological research suggests a relationship between dopamine and the number of likes or comments on social media. In summary, AVE could be indirectly related to the quantitative responses of audience members, and content can attract attention and influence the reward system. However, AVE does not refer to a qualitative change in opinion in a particular direction (positive or negative) in line with the organisation's intentions and objectives.

Publics: Loneliness, Need to Have an Opinion, and Technology-Induced Vulnerability

Analyses of PR output that scrutinise media mentions, likes or comments, while informative of the communication context in which media members exist, do not reveal anything about their attitudes, feelings, or behavioural intentions. It is the process of qualitative evaluation of content by audience members that allows them to reconsider them as members of the public. Members of publics receive content, process it, and evaluate it against existing beliefs, as well as existing beliefs of groups they belong to. This is when complex affective states can be produced, for example, condemnation or moral outrage, which has been linked to the spread of fake news (McLoughlin et al., 2024). The qualitative aspect of content evaluation appears to be critical to understanding the outcome of PR activities. The evaluation of content determines whether publics members find it novel and interesting and whether it has the potential to change their feelings, cognitive evaluations, and the decision to act. In conjunction with the general characteristics of the communication landscape, we can identify several trends in the responses of publics to commonly emerging thematic issues.

It can be hypothesised that the characteristics of the communication and societal landscape that come to the fore are increased human interaction with social media, frequent usage of technology in everyday life (Hoehe & Thibaut, 2020), and important political and social events that significantly change the nature of relationships between individuals, groups, and even nations (Witt et al., 2023). Evidence suggests that episodes evoking intense, often extreme emotions are triggered by information encountered in the media. This phenomenon appears to occur more frequently than in real-life interactions, as research on progressive isolation and loneliness, such as Cacioppo's, would suggest (Cacioppo & Patrick, 2008). Notwithstanding the accelerated access to information and incessant, even addictive, utilisation of social media, there is increasing recognition of the adverse impact on mental wellbeing, manifesting in feelings of profound loneliness. Concurrently, in the context of events such as the SARS-CoV-2 pandemic and the concurrent restrictions on physical interaction, there appears to be a decline in social abilities, including emotional expression, reading, monitoring, and self-regulation (Twenge, 2023). The prevailing symptom characterising post-pandemic audience members is loneliness (Bu et al., 2020), which has not only affected the mental health of audience members (Fancourt et al., 2021) but also their relationships with brands, for example, by decreasing brand engagement (Wang et al., 2022) or changing consumers' shopping habits (Kannan & Kulkarni, 2022).

The quest for knowledge, facilitated by epistemic motivation, can be restricted not only by situational factors but also by major societal-level phenomena. In such instances, we can observe systematic generational trends in how people approach information differently. Similar to the individual- and group-level phenomena, different patterns of information processing emerge among groups of diverse members of the public, leading to the creation of new social issues. The evolution of internet information technologies and social media has most obviously led to better access to information. However, a host of problems are now associated with it, including the low credibility of information and the audience's inability to process information both qualitatively and quantitatively (Bermes, 2021). During the COVID-19 pandemic, historical events and technology collided, and these factors appear to have played a role in driving generational differences in attitude and behaviour, which publics belonging to Gen Z are mostly affected by (Twenge, 2023). Members of Gen Z publics also said to be characterised by high levels of narcissism (Twenge & Campbell, 2010). A combination of factors may have led to the emergence of a pattern of behaviours, which are underpinned by feelings of grandiosity, uniqueness, and a need for admiration, mixed with a desire for external validation (Foster et al., 2003; Raskin & Terry, 1988). In individuals diagnosed with narcissistic personality disorder, the utilisation of social media platforms has been observed to result in a decline in psychological distress and arousal levels. This phenomenon can be attributed to the validation derived from self-promotion through the act of receiving positive feedback in the form of likes on self-presentation content, such as selfies (Boursier et al., 2020; Nash et al., 2019; Shane-Simpson et al., 2020). In a related vein, Chmiel and Thompson (2024) analysed members of Gen Z publics and their propensity to share content that is low in facticity to discover that they seem to be engaged in a constant balancing act between fighting the experience of loneliness and the need for recognition and admiration on social media. Chmiel and Thompson proposed the term *digital peacocks* to describe why, when detached from others and lacking the opportunity to communicate, Gen Z peacocks share fake news to be admired and to regain control over their epistemic environment.

The quest for epistemic control of the environment may be regarded as an attempt by members of the publics to gain power following prolonged periods of social alienation and engagement in social relationships, a phenomenon which a lack of social skills may further exacerbate. The following hypothesis is put forward: members of publics, formed around topical issues, undergo group-level psychological phenomena. In doing so, said members strive for cohesiveness, thereby building a strong identity around divisive issues. However, in the event of experiencing a sense of powerlessness, they may engage in behaviours that appear to defy rationality, such as the propagation of fake news. A further piece of evidence suggests that individuals experiencing a sense of powerlessness may be more likely to subscribe to conspiracy theories (Abalakina-Paap et al., 1999). However, the dissemination of false information by digital peacocks can be regarded as a strategic manoeuvre. The act of disseminating false information by members of the publics, who perceive themselves to be in command of adverse circumstances, may constitute an affirmation of authority and power. This finding aligns with the conclusions of van Prooijen and Acker (2015), who demonstrated that individuals' belief in conspiracies can be mitigated when they perceive a sense of environmental control. A well-established line of inquiry into collective narcissism supports the view that publics are formed around issues. This process is characterised by an exaggerated perception of one's group superiority, which is underlined by implicit feelings of group vulnerability (de Zavala et al., 2009). The subject matter of these issues has the potential to be divisive, to the extent that placing one's trust in beliefs that have been propagated by one's group, even if these beliefs are erroneous, can result in the perception of those who do not subscribe to the same beliefs as being dehumanised (Marchlewska et al., 2025). Consequently, it has been argued that the prevailing climate of somewhat 'moderated' thought exchange is not conducive to the acceptance of alternative perspectives and the challenging of divergent views. This situation hinders the facilitation of productive discussions. It is particularly evident that American culture is characterised by a preoccupation with epistemic safety, a phenomenon that Lukianoff and Haidt (2018) term the *coddling of the American mind*. American culture should not be seen as unique, and Justice Oliver Wendell Holmes Jr's ideal of the marketplace of ideas, which would enable discussions and achieve consensus, seems globally more and more elusive. When Bernays considered what was needed for citizens to avoid divisions after World War II ended, he said that 'science has helped to make this the century of the common man' (Bernays, 1945, p. 3). Well into the third decade of the 21st century, it can be seen that although technology gave immense power to members of publics, the related overproduction of content has divided common men and made them vulnerable. One aspect of the self has remained unchanged. The individual narcissism that today leads to digital peacockery:

> A man's Social Self is the recognition which he gets from his mates. We are not only gregarious animals, liking to be in sight of our fellows, but we have an innate propensity to get ourselves noticed, and noticed favorably, by our kind. No more fiendish punishment could be devised, were such a thing physically possible, than that one should be turned loose in society and remain absolutely unnoticed by all the members thereof. If no one turned round when we entered, answered when we spoke, or minded what we did, but if every person we met 'cut us dead,' and acted as if we were non-existing things, a kind of rage and impotent despair would ere long well up in us, from which the cruellest bodily tortures would be a relief; for these would make us feel that, however bad might be our plight, we had not sunk to such a depth as to be unworthy of attention at all.
>
> *(James, 1890, p. 294)*

In this chapter, I attempted to explain some of the formal characteristics of the processes of gathering information as underpinned by human epistemic needs. The human need to know, combined with the need to engage in relationships and avoid loneliness, leads to constant trade-offs. Especially when there is too much content, members of publics could be left overloaded and divided. Chapter 7 focuses on what members of publics process and how the content of communication can further divide them. I will argue that the social cognitive approach in psychology explains the phenomenon of sharing content low in facticity – fake news – more effectively, and concepts of misinformation and disinformation, while technically correct, obscure the mechanism of building relationships. I will demonstrate the limited applicability of the latter two concepts to PR because they imply a mechanistic production of communication and transmission of information in decontextualised settings. I will analyse in detail the content of communication and its language, which is considered to be the main context of human behaviour (Mischel & Shoda, 2010). I will use psychological evidence to demonstrate how content can unite, divide, or override the search for truth and contextualise the argument around the current challenges of the practice of public relations.

References

Abalakina-Paap, M., Stephan, W. G., Craig, T., & Gregory, W. L. (1999). Beliefs in conspiracies. *Political Psychology*, *20*(3), 637–647. https://doi.org/10.1111/0162-895X.00160

Allport, F. H. (1937). Toward a science of public opinion. *The Public Opinion Quarterly*, *1*(1), 7–23.

Anderson, K. J. (1990). Arousal and the inverted-U hypothesis: A critique of Neiss's "reconceptualizing arousal". *Psychological Bulletin*, *107*(1), 96–100. https://doi.org/10.1037/0033-2909.107.1.96

Bandura, A. (1977). *Social Learning Theory*. Prentice-Hall.

Bar-Tal, Y., Raviv, A., & Spitzer, A. (1999). The need and ability to achieve cognitive structuring: Individual differences that moderate the effect of stress on information processing. *Journal of Personality and Social Psychology*, *77*(1), 33–51. https://doi.org/10.1037/0022-3514.77.1.33

Bergson, H. (1911). *Creative Evolution*. Henry Holt and Company.

Berlyne, D. E. (1954). A theory of human curiosity. *British Journal of Psychology*, *45*, 180–191.

Bermes, A. (2021). Information overload and fake news sharing: A transactional stress perspective exploring the mitigating role of consumers' resilience during COVID-19. *Journal of Retailing and Consumer Services*, *61*, 102555. https://doi.org/10.1016/J.JRETCONSER.2021.102555

Bernays, E. L. (1945). *Take Your Place at the Peace Table*. Gerent Press. https://web.english.upenn.edu/~cavitch/pdf-library/Bernays_Take_Your_Place_at_the_Peace_Table.pdf

Botan, C. H., & Sommerfeldt, E. J. (2023). Introduction. In C. H. Botan, & E. J. Sommerfeldt, *Public Relations Theory III: In the Age of Publics* (pp. 1–8). Taylor & Francis Group. https://doi.org/10.4324/9781003141396-1

Boursier, V., Gioia, F., & Griffiths, M. D. (2020). Selfie-engagement on social media: Pathological narcissism, positive expectation, and body objectification – Which is more influential? *Addictive Behaviors Reports*, *11*, 100263. https://doi.org/10.1016/J.ABREP.2020.100263

Bu, F., Steptoe, A., & Fancourt, D. (2020). Loneliness during a strict lockdown: Trajectories and predictors during the COVID-19 pandemic in 38,217 United Kingdom adults. *Social Science & Medicine* (1982), 265, 113521. https://doi.org/10.1016/j.socscimed.2020.113521

Cacioppo, J. T., & Patrick, W. (2008). *Loneliness: Human Nature and the Need for Social Connection*. W. W. Norton & Company.

Cacioppo, J. T., & Petty, R. E. (1982). The need for cognition. *Journal of Personality and Social Psychology*, *42*(1), 116–131. https://doi.org/10.1037/0022-3514.42.1.116

Chmiel, M., & Thompson, G. (2024). Gen Zs seeking companionship. Loneliness, individual and collective narcissism as predictors of sharing fake news. In D. Verčič, A. Tkalac Verčič, & K. Sriramesh (Eds.), *Public Relations and Human Well-being: Book of Abstracts of the 31st International Public Relations Research Symposium BledCom* (pp. 52–53). University of Ljubljana.

Clayton, R. B. (2023). Psychophysiological responses to using digital media. In R. L. Nabi & J. Gall Myrick (Eds.), *Emotions in the Digital World: Exploring Affective Experience and Expression in Online Interactions* (pp. 55–75). Oxford University Press. https://doi.org/10.1093/oso/9780197520536.003.0004

Cohen, A. R., Stotland, E., & Wolfe, D. M. (1955). An experimental investigation of need for cognition. *The Journal of Abnormal and Social Psychology*, *51*(2), 291–294.

Crawford, M. T., & Skowronski, J. J. (1998). When motivated thought leads to heightened bias: High need for cognition can enhance the impact of stereotypes on memory. *Personality and Social Psychology Bulletin*, *24*(10), 1075–1088. https://doi.org/10.1177/01461672982410005

de Zavala, A. G., Cichocka, A., Eidelson, R., & Jayawickreme, N. (2009). Collective narcissism and its social consequences. *Journal of Personality and Social Psychology*, *97*(6), 1074–1096. https://doi.org/10.1037/A0016904

Dember, W. N. (1956). Response by the rat to environmental change. *Journal of Comparative and Physiological Psychology*, *49*(1), 93–95. https://doi.org/10.1037/H0045411

Dewey, J. (1927). *The Public and Its Problems*. Swallow Press.

Driver, M. J., & Streufert, S. (1965). The General Incongruity Adaptation Level (GIAL) Hypothesis: An analysis and integration of cognitive approaches to motivation. Lafayette, Indiana: Institute for Research in the Behavioral, Economic and Management Sciences, Purdue University. Publication No. 114.

Easterbrook, J. A. (1959). The effect of emotion on cue utilization and the organization of behavior. *Psychological Review*, *66*(3), 183–201. https://doi.org/10.1037/H0047707

Epley, N., & Gilovich, T. (2006). The anchoring-and-adjustment heuristic: Why the adjustments are insufficient. *Psychological Science*, *17*(4), 311–318. https://doi.org/10.1111/J.1467-9280.2006.01704.X

Fancourt, D., Steptoe, A., & Bu, F. (2021). Trajectories of anxiety and depressive symptoms during enforced isolation due to COVID-19 in England: A longitudinal observational study. *The Lancet Psychiatry*, *8*(2), 141–149. https://doi.org/10.1016/S2215-0366(20)30482-X

Fareri, D. S., & Delgado, M. R. (2014). Social rewards and social networks in the human brain. *Neuroscientist*, *20*(4), 387–402. https://doi.org/10.1177/1073858414521869

Foster, J. D., Campbell, W. K., & Twenge, J. M. (2003). Individual differences in narcissism: Inflated self-views across the lifespan and around the world. *Journal of Research in Personality*, *37*(6), 469–486. https://doi.org/10.1016/S0092-6566(03)00026-6

Fowler, H. (1965). *Curiosity and Exploratory Behavior*. Macmillan.

Goldsworthy, A., Osborne, L., & Chesterfield, A. (2022). *Poles Apart: Why People Turn Against Each Other, and How to Bring Them Together*. Random House Business.

Haber, R. N. (1958). *Discrepancy from Adaptation Level as a Source of Affect.* Bobbs-Merrill.
Hebb, D. O. (1955). Drives and the C. N. S. (conceptual nervous system). *Psychological Review*, *62*(4), 243–254. https://doi.org/10.1037/h0041823
Heider, F. (1958). The psychology of interpersonal relations. John Wiley & Sons Inc. https://doi.org/10.1037/10628-000
Hoehe, M. R., & Thibaut, F. (2020). Going digital: how technology use may influence human brains and behavior. *Dialogues in Clinical Neuroscience*, *22*(2), 93. https://doi.org/10.31887/DCNS.2020.22.2/MHOEHE
Hull, C. L. (1943). *Principles of Behavior An Introduction to Behavior Theory.* Appleton-Century-Crofts.
Humphreys, M. S., & Revelle, W. (1984). Personality, motivation, and performance: A theory of the relationship between individual differences and information processing. *Psychological Review*, *91*(2), 153–184. https://doi.org/10.1037/0033-295X.91.2.153
Hunt, M. J. (1963). Motivation inherent in information processing and action. In O. J. Harvey (Ed.), *Motivation and Social Interaction: Cognitive Determinants* (pp. 35–94). Ronald Press.
Isen, A. M. (1999). Positive affect. In T. Dalgleish & M. J. Power (Eds.), *Handbook of Cognition and Emotion* (pp. 521–539). Wiley. https://doi.org/10.1002/0470013494
James, W. (1890). *The Principles of Psychology. Volume I.* Henry Holt and Company.
Kagan, J. (1972). Motives and development. *Journal of Personality and Social Psychology*, *22*(1), 51–66. https://doi.org/10.1037/h0032356
Kahneman, D. (1973). Attention and effort. Prentice Hall.
Kannan, P. K., & Kulkarni, G. (2022). The impact of Covid-19 on customer journeys: implications for interactive marketing. *Journal of Research in Interactive Marketing*, *16*(1), 22–36. https://doi.org/10.1108/JRIM-03-2021-0078
Lasswell, H. D. (1946). Describing the contents of communication. In B. L. Smith, H. D. Lasswell, & R. D. Casey (Eds.), *Propaganda, Communication, and Public Opinion* (pp. 74–94). Princeton University Press.
Lembke, A. (2021). *Dopamine Nation.* Dutton.
Leuba, C. (1955). Toward some integration of learning theories: the concept of optimal stimulation. *Psychological Reports*, *1*, 27–33.
Levin, I. P., Huneke, M. E., & Jasper, J. D. (2000). Information processing at successive stages of decision making: Need for cognition and inclusion-exclusion effects. *Organizational Behavior and Human Decision Processes*, *82*(2), 171–193. https://doi.org/10.1006
Lippmann, W. (1922). Public opinion. Harcourt, Brace & Co.
Lukianoff, Greg., & Haidt, Jonathan. (2018). *The Coddling of the American Mind: How Good Intentions and Bad Ideas Are Setting Up a Generation for Failure.* Penguin Publishing Group.
Marchlewska, M., Górska, P., Podsiadłowski, W., Rogoza, M., & Szczepańska, D. (2025). So different yet so alike? Political collective narcissism predicts blatant dehumanization of political outgroups among conservatives and liberals. *British Journal of Social Psychology*, *64*(2), e12803. https://doi.org/10.1111/BJSO.12803
Maslow, A. H. (1943). A theory of human motivation. *Psychological Review*, *50*(4), 370–396. https://doi.org/10.1037/h0054346
McDougall, W. (1919). *An Introduction to Social Psychology* (14th ed.). Methuen & Co. Ltd.
McLoughlin, K. L., Brady, W. J., Goolsbee, A., Kaiser, B., Klonick, K., & Crockett, M. J. (2024). Misinformation exploits outrage to spread online. *Science*, *386*(6725), 991–996. https://doi.org/10.1126

Mischel, W., & Shoda, Y. (2010). The situated person. In B. Mesquita, L. F. Barrett, & E. R. Smith (Eds.), *The Mind in Context* (pp. 149–173). The Guilford Press.

Montgomery, K. C. (1955). The relation between fear induced by novel stimulation and exploratory drive. *Journal of Comparative and Physiological Psychology*, *48*(4), 254–260. https://doi.org/10.1037/H0043788

Murphy, G. (1947). Personality: A biosocial approach to origins and structure. Harper & Brothers. https://doi.org/10.1037/10759-000

Nash, K., Johansson, A., & Yogeeswaran, K. (2019). Social media approval reduces emotional arousal for people high in Narcissism: Electrophysiological evidence. *Frontiers in Human Neuroscience*, *13*, 462261. https://doi.org/10.3389

Nesi, J., Rothenberg, W. A., Bettis, A. H., Massing-Schaffer, M., Fox, K. A., Telzer, E. H., Lindquist, K. A., & Prinstein, M. J. (2022). Emotional Responses to Social Media Experiences Among Adolescents: Longitudinal Associations with Depressive Symptoms. *Journal of Clinical Child and Adolescent Psychology: The Official Journal for the Society of Clinical Child and Adolescent Psychology, American Psychological Association, Division 53*, *51*(6), 907–922. https://doi.org/10.1080/15374416.2021.1955370

Nuttin, J. (1964). The future time perspective in human motivation and learning. In *Proceedings, 17th International Congress of Psychology*.

O'Day, E. B., & Heimberg, R. G. (2021). Social media use, social anxiety, and loneliness: A systematic review. *Computers in Human Behavior Reports*, *3*, 100070. https://doi.org/10.1016/J.CHBR.2021.100070

Perlini, A. H., & Hansen, S. D. (2001). Moderating effects of need for cognition on attractiveness stereotyping. *Social Behavior and Personality*, *29*(4), 313–322. https://doi.org/10.2224/SBP.2001.29.4.313

Petty, R. E., Brinol, P., Loersch, C., & McCaslin, M. J. (2009). The need for cognition. In M. R. Leary & R. H. Hoyle (Eds.), *The Need for Cognition* (pp. 318–329). The Guilford Press.

Petty, R. E., DeMarree, K. G., Briol, P., Horcajo, J., & Strathman, A. J. (2008). Need for cognition can magnify or attenuate priming effects in social judgment. *Personality & Social Psychology Bulletin*, *34*(7), 900–912. https://doi.org/10.1177/0146167208316692

Piaget, Jean. (1926). *Language and thought of the Child*. Routledge.

Raskin, R., & Terry, H. (1988). A principal-components analysis of the Narcissistic Personality Inventory and further evidence of its construct validity. *Journal of Personality and Social Psychology*, *54*(5), 890–902. https://doi.org/10.1037/0022-3514.54.5.890

Ruddock, A. (2001). *Understanding Audiences: Theory and Method*. SAGE Publications Ltd.

Sarnoff, I., & Katz, D. (1954). The motivational bases of attitude change. *Journal of Abnormal and Social Psychology*, *49*(1), 115–124. https://doi.org/10.1037/H0057453

Shane-Simpson, C., Schwartz, A. M., Abi-Habib, R., Tohme, P., & Obeid, R. (2020). I love my selfie! An investigation of overt and covert narcissism to understand selfie-posting behaviors within three geographic communities. *Computers in Human Behavior*, *104*, 106158. https://doi.org/10.1016/J.CHB.2019.106158

Sommerfeldt, E. J., & Iannacone, J. (2023). A "Public" by any other name: Reclaiming publics theory, and liberating publics from "OPR". In *Public Relations Theory III: In the Age of Publics* (pp. 23–37). Taylor and Francis. https://doi.org/10.4324/9781003141396-4

Thayer, R. E. (1989). *The Biopsychology of Mood and Arousal*. Oxford University Press.

Thrash, T. M., & Elliot, A. J. (2003). Inspiration as a psychological construct. *Journal of Personality and Social Psychology*, *84*(4), 871–889. https://doi.org/10.1037/0022-3514.84.4.871

Twenge, J. M. (2023). *Generations: The Real Differences between Gen Z, Millennials, Gen X, Boomers, and Silents, and What They Mean for America's Future*. Atria Books.

Twenge, J. M., & Campbell, K. W. (2010). *The Narcissism Epidemic: Living in the Age of Entitlement*. Atria Books.

van Prooijen, J. W., & Acker, M. (2015). The influence of control on belief in conspiracy theories: Conceptual and applied extensions. *Applied Cognitive Psychology*, *29*(5), 753–761. https://doi.org/10.1002/ACP.3161

Wang, T., Limbu, Y. B., & Fang, X. (2022). Consumer brand engagement on social media in the COVID-19 pandemic: The roles of country-of-origin and consumer animosity. *Journal of Research in Interactive Marketing*, *16*(1), 45–63. https://doi.org/10.1108/JRIM-03-2021-0065

Warner, M. (2002). Publics and counterpublics (abbreviated version). *Quarterly Journal of Speech*, *88*(4), 413–425. https://doi.org/10.1080/00335630209384388

Witt, M. A., Lewin, A. Y., Li, P. P., & Gaur, A. (2023). Decoupling in international business: Evidence, drivers, impact, and implications for IB research. *Journal of World Business*, *58*(1). https://doi.org/10.1016/j.jwb.2022.101399

Yang, Y., & Lee, H. J. (1998). The effect of response mode, prior knowledge, and need for cognition on consumers' information acquisition process. *Korean Journal of Industrial and Organizational Psychology*, *11*, 85–103.

Zompetti, J. P., & Moffitt, M. A. (2008). Revisiting concepts of public relations audience through postmodern concepts of metanarrative, decentered subject, and reality/hyperreality. *Journal of Promotion Management*, *14*(3–4), 275–291. https://doi.org/10.1080/10496490802623762

7

THE CONTENT

Artificial Intelligence, Fake News, and Relationships

For Lasswell (1946), content played a pivotal intermediary role between governments, private groups, individuals, and audiences. Content was considered instrumental in facilitating understanding, providing knowledge, and building relationships. However, as Lasswell aptly predicted, problems could arise due to the qualitative properties of content: symbols can have multiple meanings, and facts can be interpreted in different ways. Lasswell sought answers to questions about the impact of content on audiences in systematic and quantitative methods. In psychology, however, at least until the early 1980s, content had been considered a qualitative phenomenon – a form of noise that did not bring us closer to understanding the formal nature of the mind's architecture.

In the popular mind, we are now in the in-between period of the continuum predicted by Lasswell (1946). Questions about the risks associated with the ease of producing content in large quantities are slowly being formulated, and AI is not universally seen only as an 'enormous promise'. However, we have not yet fully addressed the prospect of adverse outcomes and the 'crushing catastrophe' (Lasswell, 1946, p. 74) that can be caused by content that divides rather than unites.

PR Versus Advertising: Content in PR Scholarship

In public relations literature, content has predominantly been examined through the lens of persuasion and as a qualitative phenomenon. For example, the content of persuasive messages can be examined to identify various characteristics that enable effective communication and are supposed to have an effect on audience members: their motivation, ability, and opportunity (MAO) (Hallahan, 2000). The major premise of the MAO model seems to

DOI: 10.4324/9781003610403-7

have been underpinned by psychological thinking. Hallahan based the model on dual-mode theories of persuasion (Chaiken, 1980; Chaiken & Trope, 1999; Chen et al., 1999; Petty & Cacioppo, 1986) which posit that persuasion is effective when motivation and the ability to process information are present. In these psychological models, the qualitative dimension of content plays a role when an audience member is motivated and has the ability to process information. In contrast, without those elements, only superficial characteristics of content are taken into account (in a sense, motivation transforms an audience member into a member of publics).

A small but interesting line of inquiry in public relations scholarship involves studies comparing the content of public relations and advertising communication. The academic examination of public relations professionals' efforts to overcome the challenges posed by advertising clutter remains limited, thereby sustaining the prevailing assumption that PR activities exert a more significant impact than advertising. The scarcity of relevant research stands in contrast to the common practice of creating consumer-facing communication involving the collaboration of public relations and advertising specialists. For instance, in an attempt to address this lack of research, Pohl (2009) suggested the Public Relations Return Value (PRRV) measurement tool, which aimed to quantify the financial return of PR activities for organisations. The idea of evaluating the impact of PR on organisational performance is inspiring, and if substantiated by econometric data, should significantly contribute to enhancing the status of PR specialists within organisational decision-making processes. However, as discussed in Chapter 5, despite efforts to identify single measures of PR and advertising, these tools are often based on outdated models rooted in media and journalism.

Findings related to the apparent superiority of one PR content have been mixed. Tkalac Verčič et al. (2008) observed equal credibility assigned to advertising and editorials, but limited their findings to social issue campaigns. In contrast, Rosengren's (2008) study posited that advertising holds an advantage over editorial content in capturing the attention of consumers, and she further noted that once their attention had been secured, it was publicity that elicited higher brand recall compared to advertising messages. In a similar vein, Jo (2004) found that advertising with weak argumentation led to more favourable attitudes towards the brand. This finding suggests that the quality of the message is a pivotal factor in mediating attitudes towards a brand based on different types of messages. Another study by Eisend and Küster (2011) sought to differentiate between the effects of advertising and found that the credibility of publicity was three times as strong as that of advertising, but only when consumers had no prior knowledge of the product.

As demonstrated, a few researchers have shown that public relations – advertising interface content characteristics should not be intuitively taken for granted. When other variables are controlled for, apart from content type alone (Hallahan, 1999), it becomes evident that there is a significant overlap between public relations and advertising brand communication. One thing that PR and advertising professionals have in common is the attention they pay to content production, which is problematic in light of the individual-level findings discussed in Chapter 6.

Content Quantity and Artificial Intelligence

Bill Gates was among the first entrepreneurs to see the value of content for organisations, content creators, and businesses. However, it is perhaps without the proper scrutiny how his phrase 'Content is king' has become a mantra for content creators and businesses. While in his essay, Gates explained the need for high-quality content and advocated for content providers to be properly compensated for their work, the current focus on content is largely quantitative. Every minute, 25.1 million emails are sent, 3.47 million YouTube videos are watched, and 138.9 million reels are played on Facebook and Instagram (Dixon, 2025). Also, every minute, 16,000 videos are posted on TikTok. Intuitively, it would seem that the excessive interaction with content found on digital media will have some effect on audience members. Indeed, that is the case. The frequency of social media use is associated with attentional deficits, that is, symptoms of ADHD in adolescents (Ra et al., 2018), lower level of wellbeing in adolescents and adults (Twenge & Campbell, 2018), and has a negative impact on the mental health of children (Cardoso-Leite et al., 2021). Although AI itself is not a novel concept, recently, one of its functionalities – content generation capabilities – has become accessible to the general public. Generative artificial intelligence has been defined as 'computational techniques that are capable of generating seemingly new, meaningful content such as text, images, or audio from training data' (Feuerriegel et al., 2024). Content generated using AI tools is only seemingly new, and the recent revelation about how Meta used databases containing books and research papers to train its OpenAI (Reisner, 2025) demonstrates that answers provided by AI are, in fact, summaries of content that have already existed, and AI have been able to access. Truthfulness of AI-generated content also seems to be an issue as some AI tools seem to have been trained to avoid providing fact-based responses to politicised topics (Booth & Milmo, 2025). Generating content can also account for fake accounts on social media: only in the first quarter of 2024 TikTok removed 171 million fake accounts (Statista, 2025).

For a profession vested in communication, which uses content production as one of the means of achieving its goals, AI can be a blessing in disguise. AI-content generation tools have taken the PR industry by storm and seem to have further fuelled the necessity to create content for the sake of content creation only. Data from the UK shows that copywriting and editing are the top activities undertaken by PR professionals (Chartered Institute of Public

Relations, 2024) and are also ones that are performed most commonly by professionals regardless of their level of seniority. The same study mentions AI, fake news, and disinformation and expanding set of the skillset required of individual practitioners and loss of specialisation as the top three challenges facing the profession. More than 90% of surveyed professionals have used AI in their work, and some 50% use it either often or on a daily basis. Findings from the US present a similar pattern. Sixty-six percent of communicators admit to using AI frequently, and 54% see the input from AI in content creation-related tasks. One-third of emails are created with the help of AI, and 27% of social posts, 26% of articles, and 15% of press releases were said to have been created using AI. The impact of AI on American communicators' work is overwhelmingly positive: around 1/3 of practitioners expect AI to improve, add value, and help be creative, while only 10% anticipate some complications (WE Communications, 2024). However, the same report listed the areas of concern raised by communicators. Information security, factual errors, and misinformation, and data privacy are considered the most important.

Despite using AI every day, communication professionals report not being entirely ready for the challenges of digitalisation and experiencing pressure to adapt to a never-stopping information flow (Brockhaus et al., 2023). In a large, cross-national study of PR professionals, most professionals seem to have agreed that AI would change their profession and they would need to adapt, but as explained by Zerfass et al. (2020), PR professionals seemed to approach it passively, through the perspective of a 'third-person' observer. The AI task challenge is seen as a leadership issue, and the need for self-education is eminent, but specific guidelines and training advice have not been formulated.

The general direction of travel for the profession of PR, which has been widely agreed, involves, for example, causing no harm and taking responsibility that would mitigate threats to wellbeing (Verčič et al., 2025). In fact, experts in different domains have been weighing its advantages and risks. Dame Wendy Hall identified some challenges, including the need for ethical, responsible (and regulated) development, the potential impact on employment, gender and diversity issues, data security concerns, and its role in producing misinformation, as well as its role in warfare (Bagnall, 2024). In a vein related to PR, Gregory (2022) explored the implications of AI from an organisational and societal perspective.

In advertising and PR, content creation agencies have been mushrooming, and the trend does not seem to be slowing. Generative AI is further aggravating this trend by creating an illusion of creating new information, while in fact (so far), AI is only aggregating information it has access to. This is important because, although audience members might have the impression that the produced texts or images are novelty, they are not new and creative in the full sense of the term. They appear to be transformations of existing content sourced from existing web content, books, scholarly papers, and databases with restricted access.

When looking at the implications of AI on the practice of PR, the questions related to individual-level consequences of building dialogue in PR relationships have not been articulated in full. Although big-data approaches and new methodologies in PR research that would include machine learning and social networks are said to be conducive to developing new indicators of dialogic communication (Sommerfeldt & Yang, 2018), the micro-level of audience members or publics members is never mentioned. Psychological perspective, for me, is necessary to appreciate the symmetrical character of organisation–publics relationship. That means that two lines of research are necessary: the wellbeing of PR professionals, with a particular focus on the consequences of AI and the digital environment and accepting the unintended consequences of PR activities for members of publics. PR communicators should not expect that unscrutinised overproduction of content will not affect vulnerable audiences.

Content Processing

In the current information landscape, characterised by an abundance of content, audience members face an important challenge dictated by their psychological epistemic needs (Chapter 4). They search for content, seen by them as evidence, to make everyday decisions on matters ranging from minimal significance (e.g. what to eat for breakfast) to substantial weight, such as which political leader to support, which school or university to choose for education, or which country to live in safely. Although, from a formal perspective, the process of forming judgements about any topic is seemingly logical and involves gathering evidence to produce judgements, abundant data also suggests that the information produced and shared by individuals is rarely accurate, often biased, and resembles the lay nature of the human knowledge construction process (e.g. Kruglanski, 1989). Psychology has developed a more nuanced understanding of how people use content (information) when making judgements, and this can be seen through the evolution of dominant metaphors used to describe human cognition and the role of epistemic motivation in it: from Consistency Seeker, through a Naive Scientist and a Cognitive Miser, a Motivated Tactician, to an Activated Actor (Fiske & Taylor, 2020a, 2020b). In the latest version of the metaphor, Fiske proposed the term, which underscores the social, goal-oriented, and divisive character of people's judgements and behaviours: 'Inequality Enablers endorse stereotypes and other judgments that determine who is deserving and who is blameworthy' (Fiske & Taylor, 2020b, p. 295). Even when it comes to people who are tolerant and open, their tolerance is limited to situations when outgroup members are seen as sharing the norm of tolerance. Paradoxically, when this norm is violated, more prejudiced responses can result (Fairlamb & Cinnirella, 2021). In other words, the process of categorising others and evaluating to what extent they share 'our' norms, habits, and behaviours is an ongoing activity aimed at deciding whether 'them' deserve the same rights, status, and treatment. The metaphors used in psychology to explain the purpose and direction of the processes of gathering and processing social information also reflect the transformation of the concept of rationality. In social psychology, the evolution of how rational decisions are defined accentuates the strategic and adaptive nature of the processes of content selection. An audience member, on one hand, is driven by the need to explore the environment and gather relevant information, but on the other, is limited by their working memory capacity and attentional resources. Each piece of seemingly novel information rewards audience members with a burst of dopamine, but it potentially also leads to an increase in arousal, which limits the quantity of information that can be processed. The mechanism of content selection and processing is, at the same time, the manifestation of the need to identify oneself in relation to others – determine group membership, validate the ingroup, and derogate the outgroup. The building blocks of the argument, which involve initial content selection based on its accessibility and applicability and its subsequent use that satisfies the social goals of audience members, will be discussed in the following sections.

Kruglanski (1989) proposes two explanatory metaphors within the framework of his Theory of Lay Epistemics: the LEGO block and the searchlight. He distinguishes between the information that constitutes the totality of human knowledge, which he theorises as a construction of interdependent and interrelated elements, and that part of it that is available at any given moment, illuminated by the processes of attention (Kruglanski, 1989). These two metaphors facilitate the comprehension of the varying degrees of accessibility of the knowledge we possess. The totality of knowledge can be likened to a structure composed of LEGO blocks, representing a multitude of elements that are either directly or indirectly interconnected. The origins of information vary – there is book knowledge, but also all our private experiences. It is important to note that not all this information is necessarily available at any given moment, thus giving rise to the second metaphor: the searchlight. This metaphor illustrates that, at any given moment, only part of the total knowledge is involved in the process of forming a judgement. A more nuanced illustration of the LEGO blocks metaphor is found in Anderson (1983).

To facilitate a more detailed understanding of what happens next, it is useful to recall a simple scheme of information processing. The process can be subdivided into several phases. Initially, a stimulus is encoded. The subsequent phase involves the storage of this code in memory, where it can be retrieved and utilised in the formation of judgements, impressions, or attitudes (Kruglanski, 1996). Anderson's (1983) theory of spreading activation was developed based on Newell's model of the mind's architecture to explain the varying status of information in the mind (Newell, 1990, 1992). So, how is the information activated?

The terms *availability* and *accessibility* are used in cognitive psychology as metaphors to explain the differences in the status of information that an individual may possess. The term availability is used to denote the presence of a particular piece of knowledge, that is, a portion of information, in a person's memory store (=LEGO blocks). A given piece of information may be stored in memory, but for various reasons, it may not be reachable and thus not used in the process of interpretation or identification of an external stimulus. The second concept is that of accessibility (similar to searchlight), defined as 'the activation potential of available knowledge' (Higgins, 1996, p. 134). By introducing a definition based on the term potential, Higgins (1996) points to the essential properties of information in a state of readiness for use. Concurrently, he differentiates this potentially accessible portion of information from the entirety of human knowledge, a substantial proportion of which appears to reside in a latent state. In contrast, Tversky and Kahneman (1973) defines accessibility as the ease with which specific content comes to mind. This accessibility is influenced by both the characteristics of the cognitive system and the characteristics of the stimulus situation (Tversky & Kahneman, 1973). The final concept, applicability, refers to the status of content in the memory system. In an attempt to create an adequate definition of this term, its relational character becomes evident. The applicability of a piece of information is determined by the degree to which it resembles the stimulus that serves as a reference. The degree of appropriateness thus qualifies already available information as usable in the process of formulating a judgement. It is also noteworthy that information that appears to have a status of applicability does not necessarily speak of direct similarity (Higgins, 1996).

The model of memory organisation developed by Anderson (Anderson, 1983; Anderson et al., 2004) posits that motivation, particularly epistemic motivation as detailed in Chapter 5, exerts a significant influence on the processing of information, thereby affecting the degree of activation of elements within a content-related network. Motivation can also influence the extent to which active constructs influence the process of formulating judgements or opinions (Kunda, 1990). In sum, it is at the stage of information processing when the content is processed qualitatively and is recognised as applicable, members of the audiences see it as meaningful and become members of publics.

In addition to the intensity of epistemic motivation, which explains the level of engagement in content processing, the direction of motivation is also crucial to understanding how audience members engage with content. Psychology has identified several groups of major goals and motivations that are active in relation to other people or in the presence of groups. Firstly, people are egotistic in their social judgements: when they assign causes to behaviours, they want to preserve a favourable image of themselves (Snyder et al., 1976). They are also cognitively egocentric – they see themselves, as well as the groups they belong to, as more responsible for group actions and decisions, especially when the outcome is possible. This effect is related to higher cognitive availability of information consistent with those attributions (Ross & Sicoly, 1979). In addition, members of publics seem to be equipped with an astonishing ability to consider other individuals as ingroup (belonging to their own publics) or outgroup members (belonging to different publics). The process of deciding about group membership is efficient and instantaneous. In fact, very little information is needed to create divisions and groups, which involves using superficial, meaningless criteria (Tajfel, 1970).

Content Sharing and Group Decisions

Apart from the preference for novelty, which could be partly explained by the motive of curiosity discussed in Chapter 6, there are at least a few additional characteristics of content that can lead to processing them differently. People also seem to differ in how they value positive versus negative information. It had been previously thought that people were able to average the incoming information and weigh it 'democratically' (Anderson, 1981). However, further research has revealed that negative content is often more meaningful. The observed relationship has been explained in terms of the novelty of negative information (Fiske, 1980), its lesser ambiguity (Birnbaum, 1972), and its greater divergence (contrast) from the overall positive image of the typical person (Simpson & Ostrom, 1976). However, according to some psychologists, a more effective explanation is offered by Skowronski and Carlston (1987), who highlighted two content categories of information: morality and ability. A tendency towards negative evaluations was observed in relation to content related to a person's morality, whereas information related to ability levels was found to lead to more positive evaluations. The assumed correlations were presumed to be attributable to the enhanced diagnostic capacity of negative information concerning morality and positive information concerning ability level in character trait description. Wojciszke (Wojciszke et al., 1993) observed, however, that while the described mechanism was often confirmed with regard to negative evaluations, positive tendencies are observed much less frequently. This finding prompted psychologists to draw attention to the presence of an important moderator of the morality-performance model: the tendency to make evaluations of an extreme nature. The question that arose was about what caused this sought-after extremity. It was observed that the process of making inferences about the character traits of others can take two forms. The first is a descriptive process that aims to paint a comprehensive picture of another person and understand their intentions, and it will have a different meaning and function from a process of an evaluative nature. The latter will aim to decide between the tendency to pursue or avoid a relationship with the person being evaluated. Although these processes involve different content categories, they are interdependent and related to one another. Based on this distinction, Wojciszke and colleagues proposed a competing model to Anderson's (1981) model of evaluation averaging. According to their proposal, the evaluation of the other person depends on the intensity of positive and negative information. When extremes of both positive and negative characteristics are observed, a risk-avoidance strategy is triggered. This strategy may be adopted by an individual in order to avoid potential losses (expected on the basis of the observed high intensity of negative traits), which could threaten their wellbeing and survival. However, relying solely on this risk-avoidance strategy in new social situations may hinder the ability to form relationships with others. Wojciszke et al. (1993) propose that if a person who is the object of evaluation is characterised by a moderate intensity of negative and positive traits (so that the risk of danger in an adverse event scenario is also moderate), a positive evaluation will be produced. Wojciszke et al. (1993) suggested two categories of content that are present in the perception of self and others. The first category is agency, related to the realisation of goals, and the second is communion, related to the maintenance of social relationships. Both masculinity, task orientation, individualism, and agency relate to goals and interests relevant to the individual. In contrast, traditionally feminine characteristics, communion, collectivism, and morality place more emphasis on building relationships with others (Bakan, 1966; Bales & Slater, 1955; Bem, 2011; Hofstede, 1980; Wojciszke, 1994). A different set of factors is at play when judgements are made by groups seeking consensus. The direction of motivation, which explains how content is processed, partly accounts for that.

The fact that groups make errors is not a new phenomenon; however, for some time, a consensus had existed that groups produce better decisions than individuals (e.g. Steiner, 1972). This legacy manifests today, for example, in intuitive trust in free speech and the self-adjusting value of unlimited access to information. If everyone is given access to information and the opportunity to exchange ideas, good judgements should transpire. However, at least a few erroneous decisions in the recent history of mankind have been a result of groups who failed to produce – now, we would say – seemingly obvious judgements. This is perhaps one of the reasons psychologists paid much attention to analysing steps preceding the Bay of Pigs invasion of 1961, whereby a small group of CIA-trained Cuban exiles famously failed in overthrowing Castro's regime. Studies related to the phenomena behind the decision made by Kennedy's administration – groupthink – indicate that group decisions deviate from the initial decisions of group members towards more extreme outcomes. The phenomenon known as polarisation occurs especially when groups are characterised, among other factors, by a high level of cohesiveness and have a strong leader (Burnstein & Vinokur, 1977; Janis, 1972). When groups deliberate, instead of costly analysing all available alternatives in a systematic manner, they might be tempted to achieve unanimity and avoid a more nuanced and divisive judgement. A hidden group profile may emerge, where a pattern of unshared information exists, and when faced with a problem to solve, individuals in group settings choose to withhold vital data at the expense of decision quality (Stasser & Titus, 1985).

Aligned with the motives to preserve a group's consistency, a host of goals related to the preservation of one's own group position, image, as well as its wellbeing may come into play. Content that seems especially attractive is, firstly, consistent with existing stereotypes and knowledge shared by a group. Traditionally, two lines of argument were offered as an explanation for why stereotypical information is shared more easily: cognitive and motivational. Respective mechanisms often involve using language as a tool to protect ingroup members, their self-esteem, and ingroup identity. Several psychological phenomena serve as examples of people using language to satisfy group-related motives. One of them is the linguistic intergroup bias (LIB, Maass & Arcuri, 1992).

People use their language strategically, yet unknowingly, to enhance their own group's qualities, as well as to conceal weaknesses. Most notably, Maass and Arcuri (1992) analysed the relationship between language and cognition, suggesting that the transmission of stereotypes and organising information are among its main functions. The cognitive organisation function is particularly applicable to the relationship between the dictionary of a given language and its impact on the process of information systematisation and processing. For example, languages differ in polysemy, that is, a degree to which words, on average, are associated with multiple meanings, and this property can influence the organisation of the cognitive system, as well as the speed with which information is retrieved (Hunt & Agnoli, 1991). The fewer meanings are associated with a particular word, the quicker the correct meaning will be recognised. Other linguistic categories are more relevant to group-related phenomena. Maass et al. (1989) focused on the use of a specific versus abstract language to describe the behaviour of the ingroup versus outgroup to discover the intergroup linguistic bias (LIB) phenomenon. Researchers noticed that the positive behaviours of members of their own group and negative behaviours of outgroup members are described using abstract language, while concrete concepts are used to describe the negative behaviours of their own group and positive behaviours of the members of the outgroup. The use of abstract language to describe behaviour allows for drawing conclusions about the permanent predispositions of the described person or group (Jones & Nisbett, 1972). The use of a specific language, on the other hand, allows for narrowing the attribution of behaviour to a specific situation. Therefore, the observed mechanism allows one to maintain a positive image of one's own group and consider the friendly behaviours of outgroup members as an exception to the rule. Maass replicated the results by studying various contexts, including political parties (Maass et al., 1996), relations between representatives of different sexes (Fiedler et al., 1993), and competition between schools and sports teams (Arcuri et al., 1993). A partial example of this effect may be observed by President Trump's rationale behind the introduction of trade tariffs in April 2025. On April 7, he posted the following:

> The United States has a chance to do something that should have been done DECADES AGO. Don't be Weak! Don't be Stupid! Don't be a PANICAN (A new party based on Weak and Stupid people!). Be Strong, Courageous, and Patient, and GREATNESS will be the result!

In the post, Trump is using abstract categories (a 'panican', weak, stupid) to describe those who oppose the tariffs (presumed outgroup members), instead of more concrete words related to specific emotional reactions. Supporters are described as strong, patient, and courageous. Conversely, when Trump refers to his own group's reactions, he uses concrete language. He encourages them to stop whining or moaning, thus implying that those behaviours do not belong to the repertoire of stable characteristics of his supporters. On the one hand, the use of abstract language facilitates the description of behavioural acts in terms of permanent and stable characteristics (as opposed to a specific description of behaviour that is incompatible with expectations). On the other hand, it is associated with the expectation of desirable behaviour of the own group (versus outgroup). LIB can also be used to understand how language can be used deliberately to manipulate people into believing that the actions of their groups, even if controversial or openly negative, merely indicate momentarily behaviour and not stable character traits. LIB enhances ingroup identity and diminishes outgroup status by using more abstract language to describe positive ingroup behaviours and negative outgroup behaviours, and concrete words to describe negative ingroup behaviours and positive outgroup behaviours (Maass et al., 1989).

Information processing, as demonstrated, is not entirely independent of its content and impacts how groups share and use it. This effect is particularly evident in cases involving social information (information about other people). This apparent anomaly in the cognitive system is further evidence of the adaptive nature of human cognitive processes. Since the way we understand information reflects our ability to adapt, it might be useful to consider whether we can apply a similar method to a subject that interests both psychologists and PR professionals: fake news.

Misinformation, Disinformation, and Fake News

People lie. There is nothing new to that. If someone relied on the Enlightenment definition of rationality (see Chapter 4) to analyse why people lie in different contexts – political, economic, or personal – the predominant conclusions would indicate extreme irrationality and stupidity. However, such a view would be simplistic. Psychological explanations of the phenomenon of sharing fake news should not be considered superior, but can supply us with the missing, individual-level rationale.

Misinformation can be defined as 'any information that turns out to be false' (Ecker et al., 2022). A special type of misinformation is disinformation, which is simply intentionally communicated misinformation. A third category is also a type of misinformation, but it has some basis in reality or is taken out of context and with the intention to cause harm (Aïmeur et al., 2023; Carmi et al., 2020). For illustration, consider the following statement: '13 children dead because of a vaccine' (DeHovitz, 2014). While the statement is true, it refers to a 1901 case of contaminating diphtheria vaccine with tetanus that came from a horse that contracted it. Although the statement is true, when put in the context of the pseudoscientific debates about COVID-19 vaccines, it can be considered as misinformation (it does have a basis in reality and is taken out of the original historical context). The most problematic aspect of identifying disinformation and malinformation in real life is the criterion of intentions. It is often impossible to distinguish between the malicious intentions of the source and their lack of knowledge or skills. Disinformation also appears to be an old phenomenon. O'Shaughnessy (2020), for example, examines the Old Testament story of Joshua and the Battle of Jericho as an early example of manipulating information for military gain. As he explains, the Israelites' 'night attack with torches, drums and cymbals gives the impression of a mighty army and the inhabitants of Jericho surrender' (O'Shaughnessy, 2020, p. 56). Also, the concept of propaganda has its semantic roots in the institution of the catholic Church established in 1622 by Pope George XV, the Sacred Congregation for the Propagation of the Faith.

Fake news, too, to some authors, is an old phenomenon. In fact, it is such an attention-grabbing topic that the story about the most interesting piece of fake news from the 20th century is fake itself. On the 30th of October 1938, Mercury Theatre on WABC radio aired what later became a famous broadcast, 'War of the Worlds' by H.G. Welles. In this dramatisation, an announcer said the following:

> At twenty minutes before eight, central time, Professor Farrell of the Mount Jennings Observatory, Chicago, Illinois, reports observing several explosions of incandescent gas, occurring at regular intervals on the planet Mars. The spectroscope indicates the gas to be hydrogen and moving towards the earth with enormous velocity.
>
> (THE WAR OF THE WORLDS - SCRIPT - Orson Welles & the Mercury Theatre on the Air, *n.d.*)

The day following the broadcast, the New York Times proclaimed: 'Many Flee Homes to Escape "Gas Raid From Mars"—Phone Calls Swamp Police at Broadcast of Wells Fantasy' ('Radio Listeners in Panic, Taking War Drama as Fact', 1938). What has for decades existed in the collective memory as panic and chaos caused by a radio show should be considered an urban legend (Grimm, 2020b) and should simply be considered fake information itself. In fact, the panic was sporadic, and the public was tuned to a different station on the day (Pooley & Socolow, 2013). However, popular reviews of fake news in history typically include this largely exaggerated account of the impact of the War of the Worlds broadcast. The phenomenon of the War of the Worlds broadcast is illustrative of the need for a more precise definition of fake news and the dynamic and interactive properties of the phenomenon.

Several different definitions of fake news circulate. For example, Grimm (2020a) adopted Brody and Meier's view: Fake news is information that is inconsistent with factual reality. It is information that originates from the 'sender' of fake news, is transmitted through a communication channel, and is then received, typically, by the general public (Brody & Meier, 2021). Among many attempts to understand the phenomenon of the attractiveness of the content low in facticity (Ball, 2017; Bennett & Livingston, 2020; D'Ancona, 2017; Fuller, 2018; O'Connor & Weatherall, 2018), public relations scholarship has also contributed. Macnamara (2020) suggested that not only individuals but also organisational actors and the communication system as a whole are to be blamed for the spread of misinformation. Post-communication is argued to be a shift in public communication from the purpose of informing to disinformation, and humans have created this apparent failure in the context of information abundance ('perfect data storm'). One important factor in the post-communication landscape sketched out by Macnamara is the new Information and Communication Technologies (ICT) that have led to a disproportionate increase in the use of social media, which has not been accompanied by the adoption and creation of ethical guidelines. More fundamentally, he questioned the practices of content fabrication and disinformation by asking about the public interest and long-term consequences. One of the solutions suggested by Macnamara (2020), relevant from the perspective of my argument, is the call for better integration of social sciences and data science. Thompson (2020) appreciated the societal and political context of the post-truth environment and considered implications for the practice of PR. The role of communication and its content is now to divide and elicit emotional responses. When facts do not matter, and the definition of truth has become largely subjective, PR communicators are now seeking to develop almost theatrical performances. It would seem that in the condition painted by Thompson, PT Barnum would feel extremely comfortable.

Fake news is, to some extent, a concept similar to disinformation, and it relates to messages that are false and possess specific formal properties: they appear to be news or originate from a media outlet. In that sense, the motivation of the source of such content is not a particular area of concern. Common to all terms – misinformation, disinformation, malinformation, and fake news – is the implied violation of truth. In that sense, it would seem legitimate to analyse the reasons for sharing fake news as untruthful content that appears to be newsworthy. However, the focus on the content, structure, and formal characteristics of information may obscure the understanding of why fake news spreads so easily. In my view, more emphasis should be put on characteristics of members publics and the potential of fake news to satisfy their epistemic needs to cause divisions and enable the formation of new publics. It would make sense to look at fake news as something more than pieces of transmitted information, especially in light of the criticism the transmission communication models have received. The transmission model purported that communication exists in a decontextualised vacuum, 'outside social, cultural, and professional contexts' (Getchell et al., 2023). The transmission model of communication, seen as the mechanistic metaphor that focuses on identifiable elements of the process (source, information, channel, received) is also said to dehumanise the act of communicating (Krone et al., 1987). Despite its popularity, the transmission model was not the only model of communication, and other models – for example, psychological – appear to address the receiver's perspective more comprehensively. For example, models of perspective-taking (e.g. Clark & Carlson, 1982; Rommetveit, 1974) appreciate the value of context, observed reality, and the requirement of assuming the perspective of the other party to understand the meaning.

Fake news, understood as a relational concept, should focus on what sharing fake news would mean for a group that a member of publics belongs to. The easiest way of testing that would involve presenting members of publics with objectively false content and convincing them that it had been created by a person who was similar to them. Evidence supporting that line of thinking was obtained in an experimental study (Chmiel, 2018). Two different types of perceived similarity with an alleged and fictitious author of fake news (competence-related and opinion-related) were manipulated. In this study, participants who believed that the author of fake content was similar to them expressed a higher willingness to share fake news, and the effect was significant regardless of the perceived credibility of shared information. However, not only similarity was the driver of sharing fake news. In addition, political preferences and collective narcissism were controlled in this study, and a statistical model was built to explain that members of publics who support right-wing politics demonstrate a higher propensity to share fake news, but this relationship was moderated by collective narcissism. This finding was interesting as it shed light on a complex relationship between political preferences and fake content sharing. In many explorations of the topic, fake news is a politicised issue (Allcott & Gentzkow, 2017; Douglas et al., 2019). By considering collective narcissism as a moderator of spreading fake news, which explains why right-wing publics share false information, we can get a better insight into their needs. It could be suggested that the act of sharing fake content is related to removing the feelings of implicit inferiority with one's own group and further strengthens my point that publics members share divisive content to regain (or manifest) power.

To summarise, although the definitions of misinformation and related phenomena are succinct, they should be contextualised, as they only make sense when discussing wider media and communication environments rather than, for example, close relationships between individuals. Therefore, we should acknowledge that we identify misinformation and its variants within the context of large networks of individuals or communication environments. Consequently, relevant scholarship typically employs media and communication or social media perspectives to explain the spread of fake news. Indeed, the rapid development of information networks has made it a breeze to spread information (truthful or not). However, the prevailing response to the problem of fake news and the spread of misinformation has focused on the formal properties of the information being shared, following a communication model that overlooks the context and, more importantly, the psychological needs and characteristics of members of publics who often unintentionally help spread false content.

The final caveat to using the concepts of misinformation and disinformation to understand PR phenomena and inform PR practice relates to the definition of truth. As discussed in Chapter 4, different academic disciplines emphasise various interpretations of the objective and the positivist definition of truth. Analysing the concept of misinformation from a historical perspective could be even more problematic. Disinformation has been used as propaganda for centuries, but if the criterion of truthfulness is used to study the mechanism of spreading information, it may turn out that the Church and the monarch's religious propaganda did not involve misinformation. In St. Augustine's philosophy, God is the ultimate source of truth, and the satisfaction of one's epistemic needs should be seen as a means to an end: the divine truth. In this sense, propaganda to gather support to fight against followers of other religions (e.g. during the Crusades) or the lies spread by the Inquisition were, in fact, means to satisfy the pursuit of God's laws and are disinformation only in light of the current positivist definition of truth.

Ultimately, the spread of fake news could be seen partly as a manifestation of the natural need of public members to explore their environment in search of novelty. Additionally, fake news can be said to be a manifestation or a response to other problems and needs, such as loneliness or narcissism, which particularly affects younger people and leads them to spread unique and provocative content on social media (see Chapter 6). From a psychological standpoint, it seems more fruitful to address the causes of fake news sharing instead of relying on algorithms that are supposed to detect misinformation. Table 7.1

TABLE 7.1 The Main Characteristics of the Dominant Terms Referring to Untruthful Content

	Typical context	*Disciplinary focus*	*Sender intentions*	*Impact on recipient*	*Audience needs*	*Sender needs*	*Applicability to four models of PR*
Misinformation	*warfare*	*Single discipline*	—	—	—	—	*publicity*
Disinformation	*warfare, politics, PR*	*Single discipline*	*Yes*	—	—	—	*publicity, persuasion*
Malinformation	*public communication, PR*	*Interdisciplinary*	*Yes*	*Yes*	—	—	*publicity persuasion asymmetrical*
Conspiracy theories	*psychology, politics*	*Interdisciplinary: psychology and politics*	—	*Yes*	*Yes*	*Yes*	*persuasion, asymmetrical*
Fake news	*journalism, PR, psychology, politics*	*Transdisciplinary: media, public relations, psychology, politics*	—	*Yes*	*Yes*	*Yes*	*publicity persuasion asymmetrical symmetrical*

summarises the characteristics of misinformation, disinformation, malinformation, and fake news and their relevance for different models of PR.

The example of The War of the Worlds I used earlier is illustrative for another reason: it demonstrates that the phenomenon of fake news may be difficult to explain using a single-discipline approach. It's neither solely the psychological needs of audience members nor just the divisive tendencies observed in public members. When examining the media landscape and audiences as a unified system, an interdisciplinary approach should be employed to comprehend the micro-, meso-, and macro-level aspects of the problem.

Fake News Sharing as an Adaptation: An Interdisciplinary Explanation

At first glance, fake news is simply another distinct category of misleading content. In the commonly shared view of fake news, its static (versus dynamic) characteristics are sufficient to distinguish it from misinformation, disinformation, and malinformation. However, this only occurs when one adopts a mechanistic and static view rooted in early 20th-century transmission metaphors of communication. Could the integration of psychological and PR perspectives shed some light on the phenomenon, allowing for a better understanding and more effective solutions? Using situated social cognition and audience perspectives together appears to be effective.

Mischel (1968) suggested that the main shortcoming of traditional psychological concepts was their failure to account for the adaptive capacity of the human mind. Since humans as a species have been able to survive by sensing and rapidly adapting to even subtle changes in their environment (context), the mind, as the organ responsible for this adaptation, cannot be adequately described in static terms. According to the situated social cognition approach, the adaptive nature of using different content categories to describe positive and negative behaviour of ingroup versus outgroup members serves a purpose and is only meaningful if it fulfils communicative goals (Smith & Semin, 2007). In Mischel's concept of human personality, a situated person is a constructor of meanings that are skilfully extracted from the context of different situations, thanks to their knowledge of culture, similar genetic code, and individual learning history (Mischel & Shoda, 2010). In agreement with Mischel's views, an interdisciplinary explanation of the phenomenon of fake news sharing is proposed here.

The evidence discussed thus far allows for the following interpretation of the contemporary members of publics, who operate in a news and technology-reliant communication landscape, which is a contributing factor to the proliferation of fake news. High levels of fake news circulation and the propensity to share it by contemporary members of publics could be explained as (1) a joint by-product of the individual needs of audience members to seek novel information, (2) newsworthy content produced in abundance by media and content creators often with the intention to format information as novel and divisive, (3) which is subsequently received by members of publics and interpreted as issues causing divisions. Divisive and untruthful content is shared without conscious consideration of its facticity, as it is primarily motivated to satisfy the need to belong to groups formed around issues (which result in the formation of publics). Accordingly, the following interdisciplinary definition of fake news sharing could be offered:

> Fake news sharing is a psychological, dynamic process: a result of a transaction between knowledge-, novelty- and identity-seeking members of publics, politicians using communication for divisive purposes, media trying to frame information as newsworthy and organisations trying to build reputation. As a result, a process emerges that co-creates meaning and satisfies the epistemic needs of stakeholders: members of publics, journalists and opinion leaders, thereby strengthening ingroup cohesiveness by creating divisions and polarization.

This evidence behind the proposed dynamic, psychological explanation of sharing fake news, which captures influences of different individual, group-level, and societal processes, is summarised in Figure 7.1

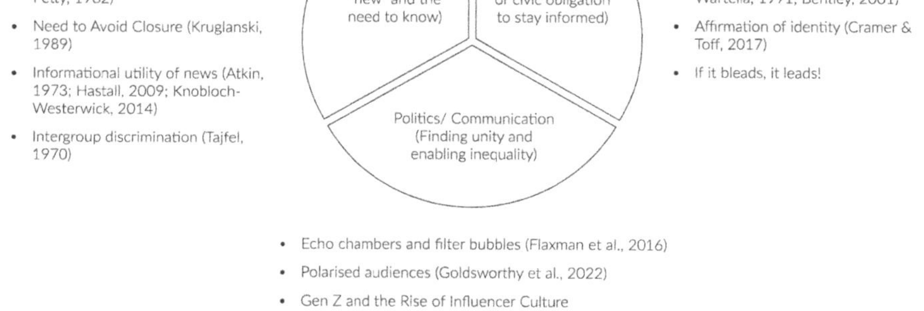

FIGURE 7.1 An interdisciplinary model of spreading fake news.

Content as the Facilitator of Building Relationships and Enabler of Inequality

Lasswell could be seen as ahead of his time in defining the role of content in terms of contemporary psychological concepts such as ingroup identification or outgroup hostility:

> The science of communication may be on the way to providing men with one of the forms of knowledge about themselves—about their ways of acting in concert, without which there can be no dependable basis for congenial relationships. Human beings are now cut off from one another by barriers that prevent sympathetic understanding.
>
> *(Lasswell, 1946, p. 74)*

For Lasswell, content was a necessary element in relationship building that would be based on sympathetic understanding, which was difficult to achieve when a multitude of 'symbols, fact and interpretations' existed in the communication sphere (Lasswell, 1946, p. 74). Over centuries, politicians and military leaders must have captured well the relationship-forming function of content and used propaganda to weaken relationships by waging misinformation wars. Three of the best-known Russian propaganda techniques have had exactly that goal: to sow confusion. It seems that the goal of those techniques was to disrupt relationships and provoke divisions. More recently, although content had been meant to be king, it has dangerously become a dictator. In some instances, it has become a goal rather than being an instrument for facilitating relationships. Everyone creates content (and seems to be pressured to do so) in fear that not creating it would lead to a 'digital disappearance'. In this context, digital peacocks thrive and find new, unique ways of producing content that is distinctive and divisive at the same time.

From the perspective of psychology, content has several unique properties – powers. Quantitatively, it can overwhelm and exhaust when too much of it is received. It can also create different quantitative expectations and prohibit audience members from analysing large chunks of information before judgement is reached. Qualitatively, the characteristics of content are equally interesting: it can divide or unite members of groups when it signals group membership. It can also satisfy the need for self-esteem and help individuals regain power and control over their environment. Situated social cognition researchers are convinced that it is a mistake to treat the content and context in which a person finds themselves as noise and a confounding factor in the study of basic cognitive processes (Smith & Semin, 2007). It is precisely the context and content that determine the adaptive nature of cognitive processes. Consequently, for example, situated social cognition does not see intelligence as independent thought processes but as their effective interaction with objects in the external world (Caporael, 1997). Information processing does not happen 'for its own sake' – it is pragmatic and directed towards action. The influence of context on the human mind is based on, among other things, imposing linguistic patterns, logical reasoning, and social coexistence (Bruner, 1991). Combined with the psychological evidence presented so far, it seems that relationships of members of publics could be better understood and facilitated, when the individual level of psychological analyses is employed. That would require a prescriptive approach, which is the focus of Chapter 8.

References

Aïmeur, E., Amri, S., & Brassard, G. (2023). Fake news, disinformation and misinformation in social media: A review. *Social Network Analysis and Mining*, *13*(1), 30. DOI: 10.1007/s13278-023-01028-5

Allcott, H., & Gentzkow, M. (2017). Social media and fake news in the 2016 election. *Journal of Economic Perspectives*, *31*(2), 236. https://doi.org/10.1257/JEP.31.2.211

Anderson, J. R. (1983). A spreading activation theory of memory. *Journal of Verbal Learning and Verbal Behavior*, *22*(3), 261–295. https://doi.org/10.1016/S0022-5371(83)90201-3

Anderson, J. R., Bothell, D., Byrne, M. D., Douglass, S., Lebiere, C., & Qin, Y. (2004). An integrated theory of the mind. *Psychological Review*, *111*(4), 1036–1060. https://doi.org/10.1037/0033-295X.111.4.1036

Anderson, N. H. (1981). *Foundations of Information Integration Theory*. New York Academic Press.

Arcuri, L., Maass, A., & Portelli, G. (1993). Linguistic intergroup bias and implicit attributions. *British Journal of Social Psychology*, *32*(3). https://doi.org/10.1111/j.2044-8309.1993.tb01001.x

Atkin, C. K. (1973). Instrumental utilities and information seeking. In P. Clarke (Ed.), *New Models for Communication Research* (Vol. 2, pp. 205–242). Beverly Hills, CA: Sage.

Bagnall, R. (2024, June 19). *The Future of AI with Dame Wendy Hall*. LinkedIn Post. https://www.linkedin.com/pulse/future-ai-dame-wendy-hall-richard-bagnall-hxwke/

Bakan, D. (1966). *The Duality of Human Existence: An Essay on Psychology and Religion*. Rand Mcnally. https://psycnet.apa.org/record/1967-02200-000

Bales, R. F., & Slater, P. E. (1955). Role differentiation in small decision-making groups. In Talcott Parsons, R. F. Bales, & James Olds (Eds.), *Family: Socialization and Interaction Process* (pp. 259–306). Routledge. https://doi.org/10.4324/9781315824307

Ball, J. (2017). *Post-Truth: How Bullshit Conquered the World*. Biteback Publishing Ltd.

Barnhurst, K. G., & Wartella, E. (1991). Newspapers and citizenship: Young adults' subjective experience of newspapers. *Critical Studies in Media Communication*, *8*(2), 195–209. https://doi.org/10.1080/15295039109366791

Bem, S. L. (2011). Bem sex role inventory. *PsycTESTS Dataset*. https://doi.org/10.1037/T00748-000

Bennett, L. W., & Livingston, S. (Eds.) (2020). *The Disinformation Age*. Cambridge University Press.

Bentley, C. (2001). No newspaper is no fun–even five decades later. *Newspaper Research Journal*, 22(4), 2–15. https://doi.org/10.1177/073953290102200402

Berelson, B. (1949). Events as an influence upon public opinion. *Journalism Quarterly, 26*(2), 145–148. https://doi.org/10.1177/107769904902600202
Berlyne, D. E. (1954). A theory of human curiosity. *British Journal of Psychology, 45*, 180–191.
Birnbaum, M. H. (1972). Morality judgments: Tests of an averaging model. *Journal of Experimental Psychology, 93*(1), 35–42. https://doi.org/10.1037/H0032589
Booth, R., & Milmo, D. (2025). Chinese AI chatbot DeepSeek censors itself in real-time, users report. *The Guardian*. https://www.theguardian.com/technology/2025/jan/28/chinese-ai-chatbot-deepseek-censors-itself-in-realtime-users-report
Brockhaus, J., Buhmann, A., & Zerfass, A. (2023). Digitalization in corporate communications: Understanding the emergence and consequences of CommTech and digital infrastructure. *Corporate Communications: An International Journal*, 28(2), 274–292. https://doi.org/10.1108/CCIJ-03-2022-0035
Brody, D. C., & Meier, D. M. (2021). Mathematical models for fake news. In D. C. Brody, L. P. Hughston, & A. Macrina (Eds.), *Financial Informatics: An Information-Based Approach to Asset Pricing* (pp. 405–423). World Scientific Publishing Company.
Bruner, J. (1991). The narrative construction of reality. *Critical Inquiry, 18*(1), 1–21.
Burnstein, E., & Vinokur, A. (1977). Persuasive argumentation and social comparison as determinants of attitude polarization. *Journal of Experimental Social Psychology, 13*(4), 315–332. https://doi.org/10.1016/0022-1031(77)90002-6
Cacioppo, J. T., & Petty, R. E. (1982). The need for cognition. *Journal of Personality and Social Psychology, 42*(1), 116–131. https://doi.org/10.1037/0022-3514.42.1.116
Caporael, L. R. (1997). The evolution of truly social cognition: the core configurations model. *Personality and Social Psychology Review, 1*(4), 276–298. https://doi.org/10.1207/S15327957PSPR0104_1
Cardoso-Leite, P., Buchard, A., Tissieres, I., Mussack, D., & Bavelier, D. (2021). Media use, attention, mental health and academic performance among 8 to 12 year old children. *PloS One, 16*(11). https://doi.org/10.1371
Carmi, E., Yates, S. J., Lockley, E., & Pawluczuk, A. (2020). Data citizenship: Rethinking data literacy in the age of disinformation, misinformation, and malinformation. *Internet Policy Review, 9*(2). https://doi.org/10.14763/2020.2.1481
Chaiken, S. (1980). Heuristic versus systematic information processing and the use of source versus message cues in persuasion. *Journal of Personality and Social Psychology, 39*(5), 752–766. https://doi.org/10.1037/0022-3514.39.5.752
Chaiken, S., & Trope, Y. (Eds.). (1999). *Dual-process Theories in Social Psychology*. The Guilford Press.
Chartered Institute of Public Relations. (2024). State of the Profession. https://cipr.co.uk/common/Uploaded%20files/Policy/State%20of%20Prof/CIPR_State_of_the_Profession_2024.pdf
Chen, S., Duckworth, K., & Chaiken, S. (1999). Motivated Heuristic and systematic processing. *Psychological Inquiry, 10*(1). https://doi.org/10.1207/s15327965pli1001_6
Chmiel, M. (2018). Fake News, My News, Real News: Source credibility crisis and the rise of PR professionals as indirect gatekeepers. In D. Verčič, A. Tkalac Verčič, & K. Sriramesh (Eds.), *A World in Crisis: The Role of Public Relations. Book of Abstracts of the the 25th BledCom Conference*. University of Ljubljana.
Clark, H. H., & Carlson, T. B. (1982). Hearers and speech acts. *Language, 58*(2), 332–373.
D'Ancona, M. (2017). *Post-Truth: The New War on Truth and How to Fight Back*. Ebury Publishing.
DeHovitz, R. E. (2014). The 1901 St Louis Incident: The first modern medical disaster. *Pediatrics, 133*(6), 964–965. https://doi.org/10.1542/PEDS.2013-2817
Dixon, S. J. (2025). Online usage per minute 2024. *Statista*. https://www.statista.com/statistics/195140/new-user-generated-content-uploaded-by-users-per-minute/

Douglas, K. M., Uscinski, J. E., Sutton, R. M., Cichocka, A., Nefes, T., Ang, C. S., & Deravi, F. (2019). Understanding conspiracy theories. *Political Psychology*, *40*(S1), 3–35. https://doi.org/10.1111/POPS.12568

Ecker, U. K. H., Lewandowsky, S., Cook, J., Schmid, P., Fazio, L. K., Brashier, N., Kendeou, P., Vraga, E. K., & Amazeen, M. A. (2022). The psychological drivers of misinformation belief and its resistance to correction. *Nature Reviews Psychology*, *1*(1), 13–29. https://doi.org/10.1038/s44159-021-00006-y

Eisend, M., & Küster, F. (2011). The effectiveness of publicity versus advertising: A meta-analytic investigation of its moderators. *Journal of the Academy of Marketing Science*, *39*(6), 906–921. https://doi.org/10.1007/s11747-010-0224-3

Fairlamb, S., & Cinnirella, M. (2021). To be or not to be tolerant? A Terror Management perspective exploring the ideological dilemma of tolerance and prejudice. *British Journal of Social Psychology*, *60*(2), 360–382. https://doi.org/10.1111/bjso.12407

Feuerriegel, S., Hartmann, J., Janiesch, C., & Zschech, P. (2024). Generative AI. *Business and Information Systems Engineering*, *66*(1), 111–126. https://doi.org/10.1007/s12599-023-00834-7

Fiedler, K., Semin, G. R., & Finkenauer, C. (1993). The battle of words between gender groups a language-based approach to intergroup processes. *Human Communication Research*, *19*(3). https://doi.org/10.1111/j.1468-2958.1993.tb00308.x

Fiske, S. T. (1980). Attention and weight in person perception: The impact of negative and extreme behavior. *Journal of Personality and Social Psychology*, *38*(6), 889–906. https://doi.org/10.1037/0022-3514.38.6.889

Fiske, S. T., & Taylor, S. E. (2020a). *Social Cognition: From Brains to Culture* (4th ed.). SAGE Publications.

Fiske, S. T., & Taylor, S. E. (2020b). Social Cognition evolves: Illustrations from our work on Intergroup Bias and on Healthy Adaptation. *Psicothema*, *32*(3), 291–297.

Flaxman, S., Goel, S., & Rao, J. M. (2016). Filter bubbles, echo chambers, and online news consumption. *Public Opinion Quarterly*, *80*(Specialissue1), 298–320. https://doi.org/10.1093/poq/nfw006

Fuller, S. (2018). *Post-Truth*. Anthem Press. https://doi.org/10.2307/J.CTVGD30V

Getchell, K., Dubinsky, J., & Lentz, P. (2023). A critique of transmission communication models in introductory management and organizational behavior textbooks. *Journal of Management Education*, *47*(5), 477–504. https://doi.org/10.1177/10525629231182156

Goldsworthy, A., Osborne, L., & Chesterfield, A. (2022). *Poles Apart: Why People Turn Against Each Other, and How to Bring Them Together*. Random House Business.

Gregory, A. (2022). Artificial intelligence, big data and all change. *Research Handbook on Strategic Communication*, 209–220. https://doi.org/10.4337/9781800379893.00021

Grimm, J. (2020a). The history of fake news. In J. Grimm (Ed.), *Fake News! Misinformation in the Media* (pp. 9–11). Louisiana State University Press.

Grimm, J. (2020b). The impact and future of fake news. In J. Grimm (Ed.), *Fake News! Misinformation in the Media* (pp. 65–72). Louisiana State University Press.

Hallahan, K. (1999). Content class as a contextual cue in the cognitive processing of publicity versus advertising. *International Journal of Phytoremediation*, *21*(1). https://doi.org/10.1207/s1532754xjprr1104_02

Hallahan, K. (2000). Enhancing motivation, ability, and opportunity to process public relations messages. *Public Relations Review*, *26*(4), 463–480. https://doi.org/10.1016/S0363-8111(00)00059-X

Hastall, M. R. (2009). Informational utility as determinant of media choices. In T. Hartmann (Ed.), *Media Choice: A Theoretical and Empirical Review* (pp. 149–166). Routledge.

Hebb, D. O. (1955). Drives and the C. N. S. (conceptual nervous system). *Psychological Review*, *62*(4), 243–254. https://doi.org/10.1037/h0041823
Higgins, E. (1996). Knowledge activation: Accessibility, applicability, and salience. In E. T. Higgins & A. W. Kruglanski (Eds.), *Social Psychology: Handbook of Basic Principles* (pp. 133–168). The Guilford Press. https://psycnet.apa.org/record/1996-98402-005
Hofstede, G. (1980). Culture and Organizations. *International Studies of Management & Organization*, *10*(4), 15–41. https://doi.org/10.1080/00208825.1980.11656300
Hunt, E., & Agnoli, F. (1991). The Whorfian hypothesis: A cognitive psychology perspective. *Psychological Review*, *98*(3). https://doi.org/10.1037//0033-295x.98.3.377
James, W. (1890). *The Principles of Psychology, Vol I*. Henry Holt and Co. https://doi.org/10.1037/10538-000
Janis, I. L. (1972). *Victims of Groupthink: A Psychological Study of Foreign-policy Decisions and Fiascoes*. Houghton Mifflin. https://psycnet.apa.org/record/1975-29417-000
Jo, S. (2004). Effect of content type on impact: Editorial vs. advertising. *Public Relations Review*, *30*(4), 503–512. https://doi.org/10.1016/j.pubrev.2004.08.003
Jones, E. E., & Nisbett, R. E. (1972). The actor and the observer: Divergent perceptions of the causes of behavior. In E. E. Jones, D. E. Kanouse, H. H. Kelley, R. E. Nisbett, S. Valins, & B. Weiner (Eds.), *Attribution. Perceiving the Causes of Behavior* (pp. 79–94). General Learning Press.
Kagan, J. (1972). Motives and development. *Journal of Personality and Social Psychology*, 22(1), 51–66. https://doi.org/10.1037/h0032356
Knobloch-Westerwick, S. (2014). *Choice and Preference in Media Use*. Routledge. https://doi.org/10.4324/9781315771359
Kovach, B. (2007). *The Elements of Journalism: What Newspeople Should Know And the Public Should Expect*. Three Rivers Pr.
Krone, K. J., Jablin, F. M., & Putnam, L. (1987). Communication theory and organizational communication: Multiple perspectives. In F. Jablin, L. Putnam, K. Roberts, & L. Porter (Eds.), *The Handbook of Organizational Communication: An Interdisciplinary Perspective* (pp. 18–40). Sage.
Kruglanski, A. W. (1989). *Lay Epistemics and Human Knowledge: Cognitive and Motivational Bases*. Plenum Press.
Kruglanski, A. W. (1996). Motivated social cognition: Principles of the interface. In E. T. Higgins & A. W. Kruglanski (Eds.), *Social Psychology: Handbook of Basic Principles* (pp. 493–520). The Guilford Press. https://psycnet.apa.org/record/1996-98402-017
Kunda, Z. (1990). The case for motivated reasoning. *Psychological Bulletin*, *108*(3), 480–498. https://doi.org/10.1037/0033-2909.108.3.480
Lasswell, H. D. (1946). Describing the contents of communication. In B. L. Smith, H. D. Lasswell, & R. D. Casey (Eds.), *Propaganda, Communication, and Public Opinion* (pp. 74–94). Princeton University Press.
Maass, A., & Arcuri, L. (1992). The role of language in the persistence of stereotypes. In G. R. Semin & K. Fiedler (Eds.), *Langauge, Interaction and Social Cognition* (pp. 129–143). Sage Publications.
Maass, A., Ceccarelli, R., & Rudin, S. (1996). Linguistic intergroup bias: Evidence for in-group-protective motivation. *Journal of Personality and Social Psychology*, *71*(3), 512–526. https://doi.org/10.1037/0022-3514.71.3.512
Maass, A., Salvi, D., Arcuri, L., & Semin, G. (1989). Language use in intergroup contexts: The linguistic intergroup bias. *Journal of Personality and Social Psychology*, *57*(6). https://doi.org/10.1037/0022-3514.57.6.981
Macnamara, J. (2020). *Beyond Post-communication: Challenging Disinformation, Deception, and Manipulation*. Peter Lang.

Maslow, A. H. (1943). A theory of human motivation. *Psychological Review*, *50*(4), 370–396. https://doi.org/10.1037/h0054346
Mischel, W. (1968). *Personality and assessment*. John Wiley & Sons Inc. https://psycnet.apa.org/record/2003-00025-000
Mischel, W., & Shoda, Y. (2010). The situated person. In B. Mesquita, L. F. Barrett, & E. R. Smith (Eds.), *The Mind in Context* (pp. 149–173). The Guilford Press.
Newell, A. (1990). *Unified Theories of Cognition*. Harvard University Press. https://psycnet.apa.org/record/1990-98981-000
Newell, A. (1992). Précis of Unified theories of cognition. *Behavioral and Brain Sciences*, *15*(3), 425–437. https://doi.org/10.1017/S0140525X00069478
O'Connor, C., & Weatherall, J. O. (2018). The Misinformation Age. *In The Misinformation Age*. https://doi.org/10.2307/j.ctv8jp0hk
O'Shaughnessy, N. (2020). From disinformation to fake news: Forwards into the past. In P. Baines, N. O'Shaughnessy, N. Snow (Eds.) *The Sage handbook of propaganda* (pp. 55–70). SAGE Publications Ltd. https://doi.org/10.4135/9781526477170.n5
Petty, R. E., & Cacioppo, J. T. (1986). Communication and persuasion. In *Communication and Persuasion*. Springer New York. https://doi.org/10.1007/978-1-4612-4964-1
Pohl, G. M. (2009). Public relations adding to businesses' bottom line. *Journal of Promotion Management*, *14*(3–4). https://doi.org/10.1080/10496490802620966
Pooley, J. D., & Socolow, M. J. (2013). Critical communication history| checking up on the invasion from mars: Hadley cantril, paul lazarsfeld, and the making of a misremembered classic. *International Journal of Communication*, *7*, 1920–1948. https://ijoc.org/index.php/ijoc/article/view/2117
Ra, C. K., Cho, J., Stone, M. D., De La Cerda, J., Goldenson, N. I., Moroney, E., Tung, I., Lee, S. S., & Leventhal, A. M. (2018). Association of digital media use with subsequent symptoms of attention-deficit/hyperactivity disorder among adolescents. *JAMA*, *320*(3), 255–263. https://doi.org/10.1001/JAMA.2018.8931
Radio Listeners in Panic, Taking War Drama as Fact. (1938, October 31). New York Times.
Reisner, A. (2025, March 20). The unbelievable scale of AI's pirated-books problem. *The Atlantic*. https://www.theatlantic.com/technology/archive/2025/03/libgen-meta-openai/682093/
Rommetveit, R. (1974). *On Message Structure: A Framework for the Study of Language and Communication*. John Wiley & Sons.
Rosengren, S. (2008). Publicity vs. advertising in a cluttered environment: Effects on attention and brand identification. *Journal of Current Issues and Research in Advertising*, *30*(2). https://doi.org/10.1080/10641734.2008.10505245
Ross, M., & Sicoly, F. (1979). Egocentric biases in availability and attribution. *Journal of Personality and Social Psychology*, *37*(3), 322–336. https://doi.org/10.1037/0022-3514.37.3.322
Simpson, D. D., & Ostrom, T. M. (1976). Contrast effects in impression formation. *Journal of Personality and Social Psychology*, *34*(4), 625–629. https://doi.org/10.1037/0022-3514.34.4.625
Skowronski, J. J., & Carlston, D. E. (1987). Social judgment and social memory: The role of cue diagnosticity in negativity, positivity, and extremity biases. *Journal of Personality and Social Psychology*, *52*(4), 689–699. https://doi.org/10.1037/0022-3514.52.4.689
Smith, E. R., & Semin, G. R. (2007). Situated social cognition. *Current Directions in Psychological Science*, *16*(3). https://doi.org/10.1111/j.1467-8721.2007.00490.x
Snyder, M. L., Stephan, W. G., & Rosenfield, D. (1976). Egotism and attribution. *Journal of Personality and Social Psychology*, *33*(4), 435–441. https://doi.org/10.1037/0022-3514.33.4.435
Sommerfeldt, E. J., & Yang, A. (2018). Notes on a dialogue: Twenty years of digital dialogic communication research in public relations. *Journal of Public Relations Research*, *30*(3), 59–64. https://doi.org/10.1080/1062726X.2018.1498248

Stasser, G., & Titus, W. (1985). Pooling of unshared information in group decision making. Biased information sampling during discussion. *Journal of Personality and Social Psychology*, *48*(6), 1467–1478. https://doi.org/10.1037/0022-3514.48.6.1467

Statista. (2025). Number of TikTok accounts removed from the platform from 3rd quarter 2020 to 1st quarter 2025. https://www.statista.com/statistics/1308893/tiktok-accounts-removed-by-reason/

Steiner, I. D. (1972). *Group Process and Productivity*. NY Academic Press.

Tajfel, H. (1970). Experiments in intergroup discrimination. *Scientific American*, *223*, 96–102.

The war of the worlds script - Orson Welles & the Mercury Theratre on the Air. (n.d.). Retrieved April 4, 2025, from https://jeff560.tripod.com/script.html

Thompson, G. (2020). Post-truth public relations. Routledge. https://doi.org/10.4324/9780429429125

Tkalac Verčič, A., Verčič, D., & Laco, K. (2008). Comparing advertising and editorials: An experimental study in TV and print. *Public Relations Review*, *34*(4). https://doi.org/10.1016/j.pubrev.2008.08.002

Tversky, A., & Kahneman, D. (1973). Availability: A heuristic for judging frequency and probability. *Cognitive Psychology*, *5*(2), 207–232. https://doi.org/10.1016/0010-0285(73)90033-9

Twenge, J. M., & Campbell, W. K. (2018). Associations between screen time and lower psychological well-being among children and adolescents: Evidence from a population-based study. *Preventive Medicine Reports*, *12*, 271–283. https://doi.org/10.1016/J.PMEDR.2018.10.003

Verčič, D., Selaković, M., Hung-Baesecke, F., Cheng, Y., Tkalac Verčič, A., Ljepava, N., & Stavreva, S. (2025). Ethical standards and guidelines for the use of artificial intelligence in public relations. https://www.dlib.si/details/URN:NBN:SI:DOC-DZGEHGBN

WE Communications. (2024). How Technology Is Changing Communicators' Relationship to Work. https://www.wecommunications.com/insights/energized-by-ai-how-technology-is-changing-communicators-relationship-to-work

Wojciszke, B. (1994). Multiple meanings of behavior: Construing actions in terms of competence or morality. *Journal of Personality and Social Psychology*, *67*(2), 222–232. https://doi.org/10.1037/0022-3514.67.2.222

Wojciszke, B., Brycz, H., & Borkenau, P. (1993). Effects of information content and evaluative extremity on positivity and negativity biases. *Journal of Personality and Social Psychology*, *64*(3), 327–335. https://doi.org/10.1037/0022-3514.64.3.327

Zerfass, A., Hagelstein, J., & Tench, R. (2020). Artificial intelligence in communication management: A cross-national study on adoption and knowledge, impact, challenges and risks. *Journal of Communication Management*, *24*(4). https://doi.org/10.1108/JCOM-10-2019-0137

Zickuhr, K. (2010). Generations 2010. https://www.pewresearch.org/internet/wp-content/uploads/sites/9/2010/12/PI_2010.12.16_Generations-and-Tech10_FINAL.pdf

8

THE FUTURE

Transdisciplinarity of Public Relations

Issues-Abundant Society

In Chapter 7, I presented a transdisciplinary perspective on fake news sharing. I suggested that the excessive production of content, which has been made even simpler with the use of artificial intelligence, poses risks for both PR audiences and practitioners. However, the role of PR has not yet been explicitly addressed, and the new responsibilities for practitioners require a more precise formulation. The following section provides a summary of the argument developed thus far and emphasises the need for micro-level analyses in public relations scholarship.

Brotherton's analysis (Brotherton, 2020) offers a valuable introduction to the phenomenon of falling for fake news, beginning with an examination of human cognitive architecture and its inherent biases. In addition to the mental set-up of members of publics, Brotherton identifies changes in the news landscape, such as the emergence of ambient news (i.e. news being omnipresent (Hermida, 2010)) and the limited information processing capacity of audience members, as factors contributing to the high fake news circulation. Brotherton's recommendations for combating fake news include the cultivation of critical thinking, media literacy, and scepticism – about the information we receive, as well as about our ability to understand it. This advice is valuable but only considers the audience's responsibilities. In this regard, a crucial question emerges that necessitates a comprehensive transdisciplinary understanding of the phenomenon of fake news sharing: Why do people collect information, develop knowledge, and then utilise it to categorise and make divisions?

DOI: 10.4324/9781003610403-8

First, the contemporary news environment can be looked at as an abundance of issues rather than an abundance of news. The change is not subtle. News is characterised as novel information presented as journalistic content. Dictionaries define news as reports of current events (e.g. Oxford English Dictionary, 2023). Communication research further supports the definition with several qualities: truth, importance, being interesting, and currentness (Carey, 1989). These definitions focus on the characteristics of the stimuli and suggest that reporting on current events will not always attract the attention of audiences. It seems that newsworthiness is not simply about reporting on what is recent. While these characteristics may be useful in the context of journalism or media studies, the psychological needs of audiences are not adequately addressed here. The question of why people seek information and form quick judgements should not be reduced to purely cognitive phenomena that portray humans only as explorers of their environment. The evolution of the concept of rationality in psychological science suggests one explanation. The change in psychology has been observed in understanding humans from imperfect logicians, who are bounded by limited mental resources, to appreciating the adaptive nature of cognitive biases is important here. Humans have survived and adapted not despite biases and heuristics they use when making judgements, but because of them. Decision-making algorithms have helped identify content worth pursuing and focus on aspects of communication that enhance understanding of the surrounding reality. One of the key functions of information processing involves deciding how the information (or the 'news') will help satisfy other needs that are shared with other similar individuals, such as one's group.

The context of contemporary PR practice has become increasingly complex. The first layer of complexity is related to psychology and, more specifically, how individuals interact with information and other people. Members of audiences faced with the abundance of information, which they perceive as issues, after having processed information qualitatively, become members of publics. This mechanism can be explained first by the need for information and secondly by the need to choose a group to which one belongs. In simple terms, members of publics develop their sense of belonging as they make judgements about social issues, which helps shape their attitudes – these are mental constructs that include feelings, thoughts, and intentions. Attitudes are a concept closely related to opinions, which can be understood as the external and explicit manifestations of attitudes.

The next layer of complexity is a psychological-technological one. Social media algorithms require users to convey complex topics concisely, which involves minimising the number of characters used. This task can become a burden because the task of 'summarising' and making trade-offs on complex topics – often leads to losing nuance. This results in audience members maintaining a state of heightened arousal, conditioning them to seek news and rewarding them with dopamine. Physiological evidence also suggests that this state is accompanied by a heightened level of cortisol, making it even more difficult to focus on single tasks for a prolonged period of time. Previously reported theories about how our body and mind work together suggest that when we are more alert, we can better recall information from our working memory, but we do this by processing smaller pieces of information more quickly. This occurs at the cost of more thorough elaboration, as it restricts access to long-term memory resources. Such judgements are inherently superficial and based on limited information. This situation can lead to subjective feelings of discomfort due to the need for greater certainty. Consequently, audience members resort to heuristic, low-elaboration evidence, relying on cues from other influential individuals or groups; earlier in life, these could be family members, peer groups, or symbolic groups they think they belong to. Political party leaders, party manifestos, values, and viewpoints that align with the subjectively perceived national character or national interest shape political attitudes.

The description of a society divided by various issues, where multiple publics exist, cannot be fully understood by examining it from just one perspective or using only one field of study. For example, psychological processes that govern how arousal impacts the retrieval of information from memory and leads to concentration on shorter versus longer portions of data, ultimately contributing to the formation of relevant attitudes, provide only one initial insight into the process of creating an issue-based society. Correspondingly, the identification of issues and the choice of a communication action based solely on the level of involvement do not appear to be sufficient to understand or predict how macro-level phenomena can entwine with lower-level phenomena. Members of publics do not only compare themselves to groups they belong to but also against the class, race, or gender they feel they represent or are a part of. Correspondingly, the class aspect and habitus – in isolation – should not be sufficient to understand the drive for novelty (news seeking) and socio-cognitive character of reliance on scarce information and resorting to normative social influence when confronted with conditions of limited information and pressures to form judgements quickly. One of the realisations that should be entertained is that we have arrived at a society which, in totality, is an all-issue public. Within each group of people, community, and nation, there is at least one topic that causes insurmountable divisions.

Recent examinations of an individual's current condition and position in society support the idea that micro, mezzo, and macro levels of analysis are necessary to understand this complex environment. For example, in *The Ideological Brain*, Zmigrod (2025) attempts to summarise a large body of biological, psychological, and political evidence to explain the causes and impact of mental rigidity and intolerance for ambiguity that members of publics exhibit in the social sphere. His cognitive-emotional concept of the nest involves 'the surrounding social context that envelopes the individual' (Zmigrod, 2025, p. 223) and represents what is known and where we feel safe. The metaphor is interesting as it demonstrates the role of context and content in shaping open-minded versus rigid approaches to others. The nest is meant to be shared with others. However, if the context of upbringing is characterised by inequality and competition for resources, the individual may turn to extreme ideology to protect their group. In particular, loneliness and feelings of rejection could prompt the individual to take radical action, develop prejudice, and turn against anyone and anything that is not consistent with one's own beliefs (Zmigrod, 2025). Individual conditions and characteristics have their social and societal consequences, and only when topical problems such as fake news are examined through the lens of several disciplines can we get closer to understanding them. But this requires overcoming barriers and turf wars.

Taken together, the psychological investigation into members of audiences and members of the public implies that a dual focus is necessary to consider both quantitative effects (related to audiences) and qualitative phenomena (related to members of publics). From a psychological perspective, a member of publics could be understood as an outcome of the interaction of (1) individual-level epistemic needs to explore the environment, (2) categorise information in a meaningful way, (3) compare the acquired information to its usability, (4) strivings to build a definition of self and (5) define the self as a member of various groups formed around issues and (6) act about these issues to satisfy corresponding individual and group motives.

PR as an Interdisciplinary Field and the Role of Psychology

It seems that in the second half of the 20th century, the two sister disciplines – psychology and sociology – looked at each other with some suspicion underpinned by endangered identities, but equally in a spirit of competitiveness. The identity threat that the disciplines could have experienced may be explained by the lack of awareness of the progress in how each respectively organised their methods of inquiry and answered ontological questions regarding human nature. While both seem to welcome experimentation as a means of understanding causal mechanisms and appreciate the theory-building potential of the quantitative method, a somewhat scattered history of sociological social psychology did not allow it to take into account the nature of psychological explanations of social learning and the origins of behaviour. Significant progress could be achieved by moving beyond the early 20th-century definitions of psychology that either proposed to explain human behaviour as conditioning (which disallowed the influence of internal mental processes on human action) or saw most behaviour as driven by repressed childhood memories. While psychology relies on experimentation, it does so to build a formal explanation of behaviour which occurs in context: of the language, other people, groups, society, and politics. Competitive tensions between sociological and psychological inquiries could be easily avoided by, for example, revisiting the micro-sociological approach as proposed by Michaels and Green (1978). This could benefit the practice of Public Relations.

Paisley (1972) argued that 'the capacity to explain phenomena at one level with concepts from a lower or higher level is a particular virtue of focal variable fields' (p. 6). In other words, it is not only permissible but also expected to be able to use concepts (theory, models, methods) from lower and higher-level fields in PR. While current PR scholarship occasionally draws on psychology, these intellectual excursions are sporadic, incidental, and incomplete. In line with the argument presented in Chapter 5, PR can be seen as a specialised field of knowledge and academic discipline that draws from other fields, such as psychology, sociology, cultural studies, and communication. The cubic diagram presented in Chapter 5, based on the original idea found in Dozier and Lauzen (2000), demonstrates that the boundaries of the discipline of PR exist only de facto, as the vertical and horizontal lines separating it from other fields exist only for definitional purposes. Public Relations, as a complex focal variable field, can slice through lower-level, specialised fields (e.g. anthropology, sociology, and psychology) to seek theoretical explanations and methods of inquiry that form a shared repertoire of research questions. The multilevel type of responses produced by such vertical investigations is expected to build a multifaceted understanding of relevant phenomena. At the same time, fundamental focal fields, such as communication, can be a source of theoretical integrative solutions to complex phenomena, for example, building relationships in general. As explained by Botan and Hazelton, 'we should be able to apply communication theory to explain and predict public relations practice and use public relations practice as a site for the development of communication theory' (Botan & Hazelton, 1989, p. xiii). Moving to a different area of the cubic diagram, the character of any complex field – PR is one of them – seems to be different from fundamental fields because it involves an area of specialism. It requires not only a theory that would be valid across all related phenomena but also provides practical evidence for dealing with a narrow set of tasks (e.g. how to build a relationship between a large organisation in a democratic country and a group of activist publics).

The psychology of PR, I propose here, does not involve competition between disciplines but appreciates their additive and complementary functions. Also, it seems intuitively attractive to retain Bernays's position that a good practice of PR requires a good grasp of several disciplines. In that sense, a new perspective should not create tensions between existing paradigms. Instead, it offers a more comprehensive understanding of PR phenomena and answers questions from a micro-level, intra- and interindividual level of analysis. The benefits of the applied psychological perspective in PR involve the methodological advantage of the ability to test models and mechanisms of behaviour. It also comes with an understanding of quantitative methods and internal validity, which is required when a theory involving basic mental processes is pursued (and has implications for the choice of sampling techniques). The philosophy of research that underpins psychological methods places a strong emphasis on the cumulative nature of knowledge and welcomes replications of studies that provide insights into the complex, often indirect nature of relationships between different mental processes. Finally, the psychological view of human behaviour looks at it as a dynamic outcome of internal and external processes: socialisation, normative and informational social influences. Applied psychology deals with contextualised settings (Howitt, 1991), and the narrow context of investigation materialises in the practice of PR, a complex focal field.

The complexity inherent in the practice of PR requires close collaboration from practitioners and scholars. One group of factors that could account for the gap between the practice and the theory of PR is related to the nature of research that PR scholarship is after, and the focus on searching for new theories. The search for novelties characterises the significant change in the scientific production process and can be considered a shift 'from an imperative to preserve the truth to an interest in the novelty of an invention' (Stichweh, 2015). Qualitative research is a natural ally of novelty. Its unit of measurement is words, and identifying new perspectives and meanings is naturally easier when conducting interviews or analyses of media content. Therefore, building models and causal connections between phenomena could appear less glamorous and novel. The experience with the search for novelty in psychology could serve as a valuable lesson for PR. Academic psychology used to ask questions: 'How is it new?' or 'How does it alter our understanding of human behaviour?' even 20 or 30 years ago, and it led some scientists to be in a state of frenzy to identify breakthroughs. In the aftermath of the replicability crisis that affected psychology, valuing the cumulative nature of psychological evidence appears to be playing a positive role in the discipline's development. The realisation that not only new and innovative ideas deserve publication in peer-reviewed journals but also replication research, which leads to the willingness to repeat previously tested designs in different contexts and circumstances with different populations, appears to be a much-needed necessity.

Nicolescu (2014) offers the following definitions:

Multidisciplinarity concerns itself with studying a research topic in not just one discipline only, but in several at the same time. Any topic in question will ultimately be enriched by incorporating the perspectives of several disciplines. Multidisciplinarity brings a plus to the discipline in question, but this 'plus' is always in the exclusive service of the home discipline. In other words, the multidisciplinary approach overflows disciplinary boundaries while its goal remains limited to the framework of disciplinary research.

Interdisciplinarity has a different goal than multidisciplinarity. It concerns the transfer of methods from one discipline to another. Like multidisciplinarity, interdisciplinarity overflows the disciplines, but its goal still remains within the framework of disciplinary research. Interdisciplinarity even has the capacity of generating new disciplines, like quantum cosmology and chaos theory.

(Nicolescu, 2014, p. 187)

To introduce transdisciplinarity, one should first establish if disciplinarity exists in public relations, as 'there is no transdisciplinarity without disciplinarity' (Nicolescu, 2014, p. 187). Looking at Nicolescu's definitions, it is quite clear that public relations is an interdisciplinary field. Topics such as opinions, attitudes, relationships, or, recently, wellbeing are studied in PR by means of the transfer of theory and methods from other fields. This integrative approach started with Bernays, who used concepts from several disciplines, among them psychology, to enrich his practice (probably as much as to build his reputation for using psychology to attract clients). Although concepts like attitudes, information processing, or knowledge activation were occasionally imported into PR, the goal of investigations has remained unchanged. The nature of interdisciplinary investigations in PR has historically focused on mezzo-level analyses, but this scope has changed, and macro-level processes have gained considerable attention (Edwards, 2020; Edwards & Ihlen, 2023; Ihlen & Verhoeven, 2012). This cannot be said about the position of psychology in PR. Theoretical developments of psychological concepts that had been previously used to build PR theories did not result in updating PR ideas that those psychological concepts constituted. However, as discussed in Chapter 3, the character of those inspirations was somewhat scattered.

Note that not all interdisciplinary borrowings have contributed positively to the advancement of PR. The reliance on the old vanity measures (today: AVE) that newsagents introduced to inform artists and the nouveau riche if they were a subject of conversations should not be used as a measure of the relationship between the organisation and its publics. AVE makes sense if one is obsessed with headlines, but from that perspective, using AVE transforms PR into a cheaper form of advertising or paid journalism. AVE has its obvious downsides (a lack of appreciation for content and a lack of examination against measurable objectives of PR programmes), but it also defies the definition of PR. At best, one could view AVE as a measure of relationships between PR communicators and journalists. Additionally, while AVE may indirectly indicate audience awareness of topics raised by PR communicators, it does not serve as a direct measure of that awareness. Ultimately, PR, which primarily relies on content creation, faces the risk of losing its distinct identity and being overshadowed by AI tools.

Public Relations could be seen as a practical field that values diversity of backgrounds and different ways into the profession (St. John III et al., 2014). In this sense, multidisciplinarity has practical value for PR, and the context of higher education in PR is inclusive in this regard. Again, this approach comes with several caveats, as former practitioners, who are often invited to teach topics with considerable relevance for PR, for example, media relations and advertising, and who might be experts in their respective fields, often lack basic theoretical preparation to teach the theory of PR. The case of Ewen, the author of *PR: A Social History of Spin* (Ewen, 1996), is particularly illuminating. When Ewen was tasked with teaching a PR course in 1993, he lacked experience and preparation for the subject and began by reading the writings of Edward Bernays. Then, he invited a reporter from New York Newsday to one of his classes and staged a publicity stunt. He told students that the reporter would join the class, 'fully expecting that she'd be inconspicuously observing a routine class session in process' (Ewen, 1996, p. 23). He subsequently discussed with the students what everyone should wear and how to act to achieve a dramatic and slightly mischievous effect. The session resulted in a story published in New York Newsday that made references to the mesmerism of PR and 'power other than reason'. This case is disconcerting for two reasons. First, due to Ewen's teaching, a distorted image of PR has continued to populate the public imagination. Secondly, his students were taught about the image of public relations rather than public relations itself. The responsibility for the quality of university training is a significant one and could be one of the barriers to the profession engaging in closer dialogue with academics. One of the first signals of academic expertise is the quality and level of preparedness of university graduates. As much as PR should not be taught as a practice of manipulating audiences and mesmerising the public, the psychology of PR should not mean 'powers other than reason'.

If my current argument is based on psychological theories from the 1960s and 1970s, the central focus of the proposed psychology of public relations would likely be on how audience members process information and the role of PR in this process, specifically facilitating information exchange and knowledge building. However, at least two important developments have been observed in psychology in the past 50 years: (1) today, content is seen as influencing the quality of judgements and the contents of attitudes, and (2) the adaptive nature of cognitive-motivational processes has been noticed. That means that we should see members of publics as communicators in context, whereby content is exchanged purposefully. Its function is not only to build socially sensitive knowledge. The act of communicating serves several not directly observable processes: self-validation, confirmation or expression of group membership, building attachment, and avoiding loneliness. Intuitively, these processes have one distinctive element in common: building relationships. The CIPR's definition of public relations, which states that PR involves building relationships based on mutual understanding, again reminds us of the object of PR: relationships. Today, although some authors continue to contest the ethical nature of PR influences on journalists (Bauer & Bucchi, 2008; Davies, 2008; McChesney, 2013) and journalists rarely acknowledge that their work is influenced by PR practitioners (DeLorme & Fedler, 2003) it has been recognised that there is a synergetic relationship between the two professions (Bentele & Nothhaft, 2008; Currah, 2009; Evans, 2010; Macnamara, 2014). For instance, in one study commissioned by the Joseph Rowntree Foundation and conducted by researchers from Cardiff University's School of Journalism, Media and Cultural Studies, a significant proportion of the content in four UK quality daily newspapers was found to consist of 60% wire copy or PR material.

Furthermore, an additional 20% of the content contained elements of these materials, while only 12% was attributed solely to reporters. The landscape of content production is largely a co-creative one, with many different stakeholders, including marketers, PR communicators, journalists, and politicians, contributing to it, albeit with varying goals. The benefits of including a psychological perspective in the practice of PR seem attractive and could help develop a stronger stance against equating the professional activity of PR with the production of content as its main goal.

In Chapter 3, I explained that, in my view, attempts to incorporate psychology into public relations scholarship constitute psychology in PR rather than the psychology of PR. Then, I discussed how methods and theories of psychology apply to topical goals of PR practice, hoping to demonstrate the need for a consistent line of psychological thinking and inquiry. I did not, however, explain what the psychology of public relations would entail. The following paragraph addresses my concerns and summarises them in the format of a question checklist. Practitioners and scholars interested in understanding PR phenomena in their full complexity are invited to explore the micro-level of analysis as it interacts with processes observed at higher levels. The following questions should be asked:

1 What is/could be the micro-individual level explanation of the observed phenomenon?
2 Is the proposed explanation sound from the perspective of current psychology?
3 What is the process/model that explains the behaviour(s) of audience members that are part of the phenomenon?
4 What are the individual-level mental processes involved in the mechanism?
5 Has the proposed mechanism behind the behaviour of audience members been tested experimentally?

6 What is the psychological theory that fits the proposed explanation in terms of the goals of PR practice?
7 Has the psychological theory that is said to explain the phenomenon evolved since its introduction? Are you using the most recent version of it?
8 In the proposed model that explains the phenomenon, do concepts from higher levels exist that could overlap or compete with the psychological explanation? What tests/analyses need to be conducted to establish which of the concepts fits the model better?
9 How does psychology support/fit with higher-level explanations (sociology, anthropology, critical studies)?
10 Do higher-level disciplines offer competitive or overlapping explanations of the observed phenomenon?

To effectively prepare future practitioners for better integration of psychology into the practice of public relations, the pedagogy of higher education curricula must also change. As previously discussed, for example, in the UK in 2023, among more than 400 modules delivered in existing public relations undergraduate programmes, only a few contained explicit mention of psychology in their names. Not only is a more significant change necessary, but it also seems essential to introduce at least one module that comprehensively covers the modern science of psychology. The suggested contents of a psychological module for public relations purposes would include the following topics:

1 Memory, attention, information processing, and knowledge activation principles.
2 Social cognition, situated social cognition, and embodiment.
3 Attitude formation, change, and measurement. Theories of persuasion. Hot and cold cognition. Automatic cognition.
4 Emotions, morality, and relationships.
5 Decision-making and biases.
6 Stereotypes, group formation, and group identity. Discrimination.
7 Leadership and management.
8 The psychology of media, advertising, and celebrity.
9 The Self, Social Media, and Fake News.

Each of the topics must be supplied by an introduction to relevant psychological methods, with a particular focus on the quantitative methodology, the use of statistics, and experimentation.

Transdisciplinarity of Public Relations

Nothhaft and Zerfass (2023) argue that it is pointless to construct a precise definition of public relations as a subject of study and research because PR did not emerge as an intellectually coherent project in the first place. They also suggest that differences between communication disciplines might be better understood as habits of thought rather than logical distinctions. Indeed, PR is an interdisciplinary field of scholarly investigations with roots in different disciplines (Ihlen & van Ruler, 2007). However, the practice of PR is transdisciplinary. Transdisciplinarity is defined as 'integrating of perspectives from academic and other stakeholders and/or communities of practice' (Simon & Vienni-Baptista, 2025), and this approach suggests that not only should academics be involved in theoretical projects and, correspondingly, in practical ventures, academics should also play their part. The goal of transdisciplinarity is not to advance a particular field of study or rigorously follow a single theoretical tradition but to understand the present world (Nicolescu, 2014). This concept fits the context of PR very nicely. Ultimately, the primary concern of a PR practitioner should not be solving a task by applying findings from a specific discipline but instead identifying the best available solution.

Co-production of knowledge seems to be the right approach for the challenges PR practitioners deal with on an everyday basis: artificial intelligence, climate change, fake news, DEI (or a lack of support of it), social media and its impact on news reception and polarisation of audiences, blurring the lines between business and politics – to name just a few. These phenomena arise at the intersection of politics, science, technology, and culture, and PR scholarship has devoted considerable attention to them recently (e.g. Gregory, 2022; Hejlová et al., 2025; Pompper, 2021; Rosie Jahng et al., 2020; Topić & Lodoforos, 2021).

At the same time, 'the dominant discourses of economics, sociology and political science lack vocabularies to make sense of the untidy, uneven processes through which the production of science and technology becomes entangled with social norms and hierarchies' (Jasanoff, 2004, p. 2). To achieve the necessary balance, not only interdisciplinarity, understood as a dialogue between disciplines, but also transdisciplinarity, which involves the involvement of different stakeholders to address the goals of PR practice, seems required. As argued eloquently by Simon, 'transdisciplinary co-produced research emphasizes inclusiveness and iterative, deliberative negotiation as the mechanism for building shared understandings as a precondition for making progress jointly' (Simon et al., 2018, p. 482).

The first stakeholder that should be involved in addressing PR goals is the audience. As argued previously, audience members should be investigated qualitatively and quantitatively to understand the mechanisms of their behaviour and the contents of their attitudes – this aspect emphasises the need for primary research in every PR programme. Secondly, practical projects should be informed by the presence of scholars, as well as theoretical investigations should involve collaborations between academia and practitioners. Although a few positive examples exist, collaborations between academia and industry typically occur at an unbalanced level of seniority, expertise, or power. Experienced managers are invited to give presentations to students and explain the intricacies of everyday PR practice, or select scholars may be invited to attend practitioner gatherings. For example, during conferences or symposia, scholars are invited to present highlights of their research that are related to the practice of the discipline. These occurrences should continue to happen, but additional opportunities for thought exchange, which provide a sense of partnership, could be considered. For example, a mingling of early-career scholars and junior practitioners should serve as an opportunity to identify emerging challenges and brainstorm solutions or ideas. But perhaps more importantly, these thought exchanges can inform instant modifications to PR curricula (from employer to academia direction) and revitalise the interest in applying valid theoretical concepts to pressing practical issues (from scholarship to practice direction). In my view, the transdisciplinarity of PR should also involve close partnerships between universities, businesses, and professional educators that would inform the identification of missing skill sets and the development of relevant elements of curricula to address employers' needs.

The next requirement for achieving transdisciplinarity in PR is associated with the concept of the unity of knowledge (Nicolescu, 2014) and the 'one science' goal envisaged by Bertrand Russel. When pursuing PR goals, all three levels of analysis should be involved, and the integration of theoretical perspectives should involve careful examination of the terminologies used. Theoretical constructs should be integrated by preserving their definitions, context, mechanisms, and applications. For example, when integrating psychological knowledge, psychological terms should be defined using their scientific, rather than popular, definitions. Additionally, the meaning of psychological concepts related to mental processes should not be altered during integration with mezzo-level PR theories. This is important because fundamental mental processes do not change their character when a specialised field of PR makes use of them. After all, attitudes, information processing, or knowledge activation mechanisms do not change formally when an individual is involved in forming a judgment about an issue relevant to PR. When a psychological mechanism is proposed to explain a PR phenomenon, one should be used fully and consistently with the original theory. Any irregularities should be investigated with an appreciation for contextual factors rather than by asserting that context does or does not exist (see the discussion on internal versus external validity in Chapter 4).

Accordingly, names and labels proposed by theory should be preserved for clarity and to maintain the potential for feeding evidence from subsequent psychological investigations. In summary, micro-level phenomena remain unchanged when we observe their influence on other levels. Changing names impedes progress and prevents other disciplines from observing how phenomena are applied. Lessons learnt by Byford and Tileagă (2014) can also be helpful here. Their project involved an interdisciplinary use of history and psychology. Byford and Tileagă (2014) noted that for 'borrowing' to be effective, any analysis should be transformative rather than confirmatory, and researchers should be aware of the limitations of the disciplines involved. In parallel to Theaker's (2013) argument about the apparent convergence of disciplines, the object of each of the disciplines should be realised first, its goals identified, then areas of overlap discussed, and only then – the lines between disciplines removed.

A related consideration is about the timeliness of integration. The transdisciplinary integration of psychological theory in PR has a better potential for finding meaningful connections when the constructs being integrated are based on recent versus older studies. The cumulative body of knowledge in psychology often provides a rationale for revisiting older constructs or developing them in new directions. While delving into past developments in psychological science can be a satisfying and enriching activity on its own, discovering connections between PR questions and the answers the science of psychology has provided recently allows us to avoid being misled. Newer theories are expected to provide more comprehensive and accurate explanations.

One of the obstacles to bringing practitioners and academics together to work on business problems that are underpinned by societal phenomena is the lack of a common frame of reference, which involves a shared lexicon and measurement methods. Communities of practitioners often use terms differently from academics. Among practitioners, confusion can, for example, exist between sustainability and CSR (Bansal & DesJardine, 2015), and other practitioners are tired of the concept of sustainability (Nelson, 2025). It appears that the concept of transdisciplinarity would necessitate the existence of a shared framework of reference. This can be achieved by using the United Nations Sustainable Development Goals framework (UN SDG, UN Department of Economic and Social Affairs, 2015). The UN SDGs, a multistakeholder agenda adopted on the global level, open up the possibility of PR programmes to increase their impact at the societal level by informing political decisions and monitoring progress using national-level statistics.

Responsibility for Building Dialogue Relationships in the Practice of PR

The post-truth condition (D'Ancona, 2017) has changed the practice of PR, opening a new post-classical era, where emotions and stunts become the appreciated and effective means of communication with publics (Thompson, 2020). Instead of being a facilitator of relationships and connections (Lasswell, 1946), the instrument – content – has now become the goal. Concurrently, ethical issues have been raised in the context of declining standards in journalism (Iggers, 2018), particularly as content workers have replaced many journalists. Recently, due to the growing popularity of generative artificial intelligence tools, fears of being replaced by AI among journalists and PR professionals have become increasingly common. Content, which was supposed to become a king, has evolved into an autocratic dictator.

Dozier and Lauzen (2000) use the term 'irreconcilable differences in the context of powerless publics' to describe situations in which audiences demand mutually beneficial relationships with an organisation. However, its behaviours are unacceptable to an activist public. It happens when powerless publics 'are affected by the behavior of a focal organization but lack sufficient resources to demand mutually beneficial relationships with that organization' (Dozier & Lauzen, 2000, p. 12). From a micro psychological perspective, if groupings of individuals operate in a state of permanent issue overload, they may not be able to identify the source of communication and distinguish one organisation from another. In my view, the current communication condition is characterised by a unified response from members of publics, who are overloaded with the quantity of information, divided by its quality and choose to regain their power and control over their epistemic environment by sharing distinctive but also divisive content.

The biased nature of 'handling' knowledge by members of publics and tactical responses to abundant and divisive information seems to have become a weapon of individuals who experience powerlessness. In the struggle to regain power, sharing knowledge can be used as a tactic, which can lead to endangering relationships between organisations and their publics. Although this is only a working hypothesis, evidence related to personal relationships seems to support it. One of the key aspects of relationships, both intimate and in the public sphere, involves sharing knowledge. Research on building relational confidence in remote teams (Keppler & Leonardi, 2023) suggests that exchanging knowledge requires confidence and is a function of perceived proximity to other colleagues. Sharing knowledge is also closely related to trust and requires strong connections (Han et al., 2020). Trust fosters an atmosphere of cooperation (Kacperska & Łukasiewicz, 2020). Thus, trust appears to be one of the core components of relationships, which enables the sharing of knowledge in a two-way manner. Without trust, not only will organisations be unable to communicate their messages effectively, but they will also be unable to listen to their publics. In the context of an increasingly lonely society and a generation Z grappling with the challenges of relationship-building, the role of PR practitioners in addressing these issues may soon become a compelling concern.

The psychological perspective presented here follows the conclusions reached by Krone et al. (1987) that neither mechanistic, psychological, interpretive-symbolic, nor system-interaction models of organisational communication should be considered superior. Using Kruglanski's searchlight metaphor

(1989) presented earlier in this volume, the psychology of PR offers a view of a previously unavailable set of Lego blocks (information) that explain the mechanisms of Public Relations communication's reception and processing by individuals (members of audience and members of publics), as well as its influence on judgement formation, attitude change and aspects of the relationships they build of often divided publics. Reversing the rhetorical emphasis of the definition of organisational advocates who 'use symbolic exchange to come to agreements about cultural structures, events and actions' (Toth, 1992, p.6) we may benefit from the psychological argument advanced in this book. Focusing on members of publics and their process of forming contextually relevant social knowledge, we gain access to their needs, attitudes, as well as the reasons for divisions and search for inequality (Fiske & Taylor, 2020). The purpose of the psychology of PR is to investigate the object of public relations and formulate practical advice about the process of building relationships between publics and organisations, political parties, the government, or the state. The full appreciation of the responsibility for such relationships is possible only when psychological needs and processes responsible for the judgement formation of audiences are considered. The responsibility for building relationships does not exclusively fall on businesses; however, communication and PR professionals working for any stakeholder should realise the consequences of managing the production of content responsibly and have the objective of fostering relationships at heart.

According to some scholars, PR should acknowledge its role in society and contribute to it positively (Edwards, 2012, 2020; Ihlen & Verhoeven, 2012). However, when organisations actively tackle social issues in their promotional campaigns (e.g. DEI, gender stereotypes), the scholarship looks at such activities as Marketing Public Relations (MPR, Harris, 1993), Integrated Marketing Communications (Schultz et al., 1993) or brand activism (Du Toit, 2016; Kotler & Sarkar, 2021). This can be an obstacle to fully appreciating the contribution of PR in the organisational and societal context. As discussed in Chapter 4, PR is often involved in the development of external-facing communication campaigns, for example, by gathering evidence about attitudes towards topical issues. Ultimately, promotional communication co-created by PR and marketing departments has an impact on the perception of social phenomena, such as typical gender roles in society (Chmiel, 2024).

Molleda and Moreno (2006) and Sriramesh and Verčič (2002) argued that the cultural context of the society influences how PR practitioners carry out their tasks. The political context of the current practice of PR in Western societies can be seen through the lens of frequent experiments with what democracy means and entails. Democracies have been infused with populism to satisfy the need for representation of multiple, often conflicted publics that can be found within each society. The 'wrangle in the marketplace' (Heath,

1992) has become increasingly heated and emotionally driven. The economic context has been evolving towards competition, decoupling, and deglobalisation (Witt et al., 2023). Today, the characteristics of the members of publics constitute the most important context for the practice of PR. By incorporating a psychological perspective into PR, we can move closer to a 'paradigm of public relations that features it as being capable of adding value to the full functioning of society' (Heath, 2006, p. 95). Following the findings of the project with Thompson (Chmiel & Thompson, 2024) and our recognition of the due diligence that should be required from professional PR communicators, I argue that PR, understood as a profession that seeks to build and maintain relationships between the organisation and its publics, needs to reconsider its communications priorities. First, the outcomes of PR that consider the effects on the individual level on both ends of the relationship should be taken into account. The idea that each party in a relationship should be considered equal and their interests must be considered for a symmetrical relationship to occur is not new in Public Relations. Previously, Kent and Taylor (2002) borrowed the concept of dialogue from Martin Buber to recognise that individuals are not merely meant to achieve desired (organisational) goals. The concept of dialogic public relations encompasses five key characteristics: mutuality, propinquity, empathy, risk, and commitment (Kent & Taylor, 2002).

In the practice of Public Relations, the dialogic approach to PR would require professionals and scholars to become responsible for the epistemic pollution (Lamy & Beyneix, 2022) created by the industry of PR in a quantitative and qualitative sense. Quantitatively, I would encourage professionals to revisit the need for creating content that is merely a manifestation of the communicative capabilities of an organisation and does not serve any deeper goals. To put it simply, too much content creates an environment in which audience members are unable to function due to informational overload and may respond violently by mishandling content in the public sphere. With their resources depleted by low-quality and meaningless content, there is also not much space for engaging in more important cognitive activities. However, especially young audience members are not able to see that they often operate in a state similar to addiction, which requires them to be constantly glued to their phones. The onus of limiting the production of content falls on the communicators, who can limit the epistemic pollution they participate in creating.

The second aspect of the epistemic responsibility of PR communicators is qualitative. Content that is interesting and distinctive will most typically lead to some form of division. For PR communicators, this means inspecting the communication they produce to ensure it is not divisive and that their communication policies do not involve creating vulnerable or lonely audiences. Empathetic appreciation of the experience of members of publics who feel not listened to by organisations that do not respond to emails, restrict communication on social media, or do not respond to comments, is among the practices that are the easiest to eliminate. The wellbeing and needs of members of publics should be looked at with proper attention, also from a longer, temporal perspective. As explained by Kent and Taylor (2002), 'dialogic communication is relational. It involves an understanding of the past and the present, as well as an eye toward future relationships' (Kent & Taylor, 2002, p. 26). Consequently, now equipped with the repertoire of psychological methods to study the effects of PR programmes, the responsibility for unintended consequences should be assumed.

Finally, mutuality and empathy in a dialogic relationship require considering the outcomes of PR activities on those who perform them. The toll that communicators pay for communicating and engaging in meaningful relationships has been somewhat paved over. From a psychological perspective, the wellbeing of professionals should also be considered as a function of the relationships that they build with their publics, and not only as an outcome of their workload, the leadership style of their managers, or their work arrangements. In a recent paper, I looked at the work environment of PR professionals in the UK and the US to understand the impact of flexible work schemes and office space allocation policies on their wellbeing (Chmiel, 2025). PR communicators can also be affected by loneliness, and these findings should not be surprising, as one would not expect the profession of PR to have developed immunity against conditions that affect many members of society. On the contrary, PR communicators, who use communication as a tool and build professional relationships, can also suffer from loneliness when working from home and are unable to communicate face-to-face with their peers. The last element of due diligence for PR communicators is the responsibility for their own physical and mental health. Scientific psychology can help in that area, too.

References

Bansal, T., & DesJardine, M. (2015, February). *Don't Confuse Sustainability with CSR*. Ivey Business Journal. https://iveybusinessjournal.com/dont-confuse-sustainability-with-csr/

Bauer, M. W., & Bucchi, M. (Eds.) (2008). *Journalism, Science and Society*. Routledge. https://doi.org/10.4324/9780203942314

Bentele, G., & Nothhaft, H. (2008). The intereffication model: Theoretical discussions and empirical research. In *Public Relations Research: European and International Perspectives and Innovations* (pp. 33–47). VS Verlag für Sozialwissenschaften.

Botan, C. H., & Hazelton, V. (1989). *Public Relations Theory*. Lawrence Erlbaum Associates.

Brotherton, R. (2020). *Bad News: Why We Fall for Fake News*. Bloomsbury Publishing Plc.

Byford, J., & Tileagă, C. (2014). Social psychology, history, and the study of the Holocaust: The perils of interdisciplinary "borrowing". *Peace and Conflict*, *20*(4). https://doi.org/10.1037/pac0000054

Carey, J. W. (1989). *Communication As Culture. Essays on Media and Society*. Unwin Hyman.
Chmiel, M. (2024). Societal impact of Brand Public Relations on gender equality: Evidence for a mediation-type mechanism. *Corporate Communications: An International Journal 29*(6), 796–817. https://doi.org/10.1108/CCIJ-04-2024-0059
Chmiel, M. (2025). Loneliness, office space arrangement and mental well-being of Gen Z PR professionals. Falling into the trap of an agile office? Journal of Communication Management, *29*(3), 379–400. https://doi.org/10.1108/JCOM-03-2024-0046
Chmiel, M., & Thompson, G. (2024). Gen Zs seeking companionship. Loneliness, individual and collective narcissism as predictors of sharing fake news. In D. Verčič, A. Tkalac Verčič, & K. Sriramesh (Eds.), *Public Relations and Human Well-being: Book of Abstracts of the 31st International Public Relations Research Symposium BledCom* (pp. 52–53). University of Ljubljana.
Currah, A. (2009). *What's Happening to Our News*. Reuters Institute for the Study of Journalism, Department of Politics and International Relations, University of Oxford (RISJ).
D'Ancona, M. (2017). *Post-Truth: The New War on Truth and How to Fight Back*. Ebury publishing.
Davies, N. (2008). *Flat Earth News: An Award-winning Reporter Exposes Falsehood, Distortion and Propaganda in the Global Media*. Chatto & Windus.
DeLorme, D. E., & Fedler, F. (2003). Journalists' hostility toward public relations: An historical analysis. *Public Relations Review*, *29*(2), 99–124. https://doi.org/10.1016/S0363-8111(03)00019-5
Dozier, D. M., & Lauzen, M. M. (2000). Liberating the intellectual domain from the practice: Public relations, activism, and the role of the scholar. *Journal of Public Relations Research*, *12*(1), 3–22.
Du Toit, C. (2016). *Brand Activism, Inc.: The Rise of Corporate Influence*. Ubmm Holdings LLC.
Edwards, L. (2012). Defining the 'object' of public relations research: A new starting point. *Public Relations Inquiry*, *1*(1), 7–30. https://doi.org/10.1177/2046147x11422149
Edwards, L. (2020). *Understanding public relations: Theory, culture and society*. SAGE Publications Ltd.
Edwards, L., & Ihlen, Ø. (2023). Social theory in public relations: Insights and directions. In C. Botan, & E. Sommerfeldt (Eds.), *Public relations theory III* (pp. 213–227). Routledge https://doi.org/10.4324/9781003141396-15
Evans, T. (2010). We are all in PR now. *British Journalism Review*, *21*(2), 31–36. https://doi.org/10.1177/0956474810374531
Ewen, S. (1996). *Pr!: A Social History Of Spin*. Basic Books.
Fiske, S. T., & Taylor, S. E. (2020). Social Cognition evolves: Illustrations from our work on Intergroup Bias and on Healthy Adaptation. *Psicothema*, *32*(3), 291–297.
Gregory, A. (2022). Artifical intelligence, big data and all change. In J. Falkheimer & M. Heide (Eds.), *Research Handbook on Strategic Communication* (pp. 209–220). Edward Elgar.
Han, S. H., Yoon, S. W., & Chae, C. (2020). Building social capital and learning relationships through knowledge sharing: A social network approach of management students' cases. *Journal of Knowledge Management*, *24*(4), 921–939. https://doi.org/10.1108
Harris, T. L. (1993). *The Marketer's Guide to Public Relations: How Today's Top Companies are Using the New PR to Gain a Competitive Edge*. Wiley.
Heath, R. L. (1992). The wrangle in the marketplace: A rhetorical perspective of public relations. In R. L. Heath & E. L. Toth (Eds.), *Rhetorical and Critical Approaches to Public Relations II* (pp. 17–36). Routledge. https://doi.org/10.4324/9781315045474

Heath, R. L. (2006). Onward into more fog: Thoughts on public relations' research directions. *International Journal of Phytoremediation*, *21*(1), 93–114. https://doi.org/10.1207/s1532754xjprr1802_2

Hejlová, D., Koudelková, P., Moravcová, H., Romenti, S., & Valentini, C. (Eds.). (2025). *Responsibility in Strategic Communication: Truth or Trap? - Advances in Public Relations and Communication Management*. Emerald Group Publishing.

Hermida, A. (2010). Twittering the news. The emergence of ambient journalism. *Journalism Practice*, *4*(3), 297–308. https://doi.org/10.1080/17512781003640703

Howitt, D. (1991). *Concerning Psychology: Psychology Applied to Social Issues.*. Open University Press.

Iggers, J. (2018). Good news, bad news: Journalism ethics and the public interest. In *Good News, Bad News: Journalism Ethics and the Public Interest*. Taylor and Francis. https://doi.org/10.4324/9780429500145

Ihlen, Ø., & van Ruler, B. (2007). How public relations works: Theoretical roots and public relations perspectives. *Public Relations Review*, *33*(3), 243–248. https://doi.org/10.1016/j.pubrev.2007.05.001

Ihlen, Ø., & Verhoeven, P. (2012). A public relations identity for the 2010s. *Public Relations Inquiry*, *1*(2), 159–176. https://doi.org/10.1177/2046147x11435083

Jasanoff, S. (2004). The idiom of co-production. In S. Jasanoff (Ed.), *States of Knowledge: The Co-Production of Science and the Social Order* (pp. 1–12). Routledge Taylor & Francis Group. https://doi.org/10.4324/9780203413845

Kacperska, E., & Łukasiewicz, K. (2020). The importance of trust in knowledge sharing and the efficiency of doing business on the example of tourism. *Information*, *11*(6), 311. https://doi.org/10.3390/INFO11060311

Kent, M. L., & Taylor, M. (2002). Toward a dialogic theory of public relations. *Public Relations Review*, *28*, 21–37.

Keppler, S. M., & Leonardi, P. M. (2023). Building relational confidence in remote and hybrid work arrangements: novel ways to use digital technologies to foster knowledge sharing. *Journal of Computer-Mediated Communication*, *28*(4). https://doi.org/10.1093/JCMC/ZMAD020

Kotler, P., & Sarkar, C. (2021). *Brand Activism: From Purpose to Action*. Idea Bite Press.

Krone, K. J., Jablin, F. M., & Putnam, L. (1987). Communication theory and organizational communication: Multiple perspectives. In F. Jablin, L. Putnam, K. Roberts, & L. Porter (Eds.), *The Handbook of Organizational Communication: An Interdisciplinary Perspective* (pp. 18–40). Sage.

Kruglanski, A. W. (1989). Lay epistemics and human knowledge: Cognitive and motivational bases. In *Lay Epistemics and Human Knowledge*. Springer US. https://doi.org/10.1007/978-1-4899-0924-4

Lamy, E., & Beyneix, I. (2022, March 22). *Fighting Epistemic Pollution (Fake News, Business BS) with Extended Corporate Social Responsibility*. LSE Business Review. https://blogs.lse.ac.uk/businessreview/2022/03/07/fighting-epistemic-pollution-fake-news-business-bs-with-extended-corporate-social-responsibility/

Lasswell, H. D. (1946). Describing the contents of communication. In B. L. Smith, H. D. Lasswell, & R. D. Casey (Eds.), *Propaganda, Communication, and Public Opinion* (pp. 74–94). Princeton University Press.

Macnamara, J. (2014). *Journalism and PR: Unpacking 'Spin', Stereotypes, and Media Myths*. Peter Lang Publishing Inc.

McChesney, R. Waterman. (2013). *Digital Disconnect: How Capitalism Is Turning the Internet Against Democracy*. New Press.

Michaels, J. W., & Green, D. S. (1978). Behavioral sociology: Emergent forms and issues. *The American Sociologist*, *13*(1), 23–29.

Molleda, J. C., & Moreno, Á. (2006). Transitional socioeconomic and political environments of public relations in Mexico. *Public Relations Review*, *32*(2), 104–109. https://doi.org/10.1016/J.PUBREV.2006.02.002

Nelson, S. (2025, April 11). *Juliet Kinsman is Over the Word 'Sustainability.'* Influence. https://influenceonline.co.uk//2025/04/11/juliet-kinsman-is-over-the-word-sustainability
Nicolescu, B. (2014). Methodology of transdisciplinarity. *World Futures*, *70*(3–4). https://doi.org/10.1080/02604027.2014.934631
Nothhaft, H., & Zerfass, A. (2023). Public relations in a Postdisciplinary World: on the impossibility of establishing a constitutive PR theory within the tribal struggles of applied communication disciplines. In C. Botan, & E. Sommerfeldt (Eds.), *Public Relations Theory III* (pp. 247–265). Routledge.
Oxford English Dictionary. (2023). News. In *Oxford English Dictionary*. Oxford University Press. https://doi.org/10.1093/OED/3469979534
Paisley, W. (1972). *Communication Research as a Behavioral Discipline*. Stanford University, Institute for Communication Research.
Pompper, D. (2021). *Public Relations for Social Responsibility: Affirming DEI Commitment with Action (Communicating Responsible Diversity, Equity, and Inclusion): Pompper, Donnalyn: Amazon.co.uk: Books* (D. Pompper, Ed.). Emerald Publishing Limited.
Rosie Jahng, M., Lee, H., & Rochadiat, A. (2020). Public relations practitioners' management of fake news: Exploring key elements and acts of information authentication. *Public Relations Review*, *46*(2), 101907. https://doi.org/10.1016/J.PUBREV.2020.101907
Schultz, D., Lauterborn, R., & Tannenbaum, S. (1993). *Integrated Marketing Communications*. NTC Business Books.
Simon, D., Palmer, H., Riise, J., Smit, W., & Valencia, S. (2018). The challenges of transdisciplinary knowledge production: from unilocal to comparative research. *Environment and Urbanization*, *30*(2), 481–500. https://doi.org/10.1177/0956247818787177
Simon, D., & Vienni-Baptista, B. (2025, April 15). Transforming Society ~ Reimagining collaborations and methodologies for global societal challenges. https://www.transformingsociety.co.uk/2025/04/30/reimagining-collaborations-and-methodologies-for-global-societal-challenges/
Sriramesh, K., & Verčič, D. (2002). International public relations: A framework for future research. *Journal of Communication Management*, *6*(2), 103–117. https://doi.org/10.1108/13632540210806973
St. John III, B., Lamme, M. O., & L'Etang, J. (2014). Pathways to public relations: Histories of practice and professio. In B. St. John III, M. O. Lamme, & J. L'Etang (Eds.), *Pathways to Public Relations*. Routledge. https://doi.org/10.4324/9780203074183
Stichweh, R. (2015). Scientific disciplines, history of. In *International Encyclopedia of the Social & Behavioral Sciences: Second Edition*. https://doi.org/10.1016/B978-0-08-097086-8.03048-8
Theaker, A. (2013). *The Public Relations Handbook*. Routledge. https://doi.org/10.4324/9780203804827
Thompson, G. (2020). Post-truth public relations. Routledge. https://doi.org/10.4324/9780429429125
Topić, M., & Lodoforos, G. (Eds.) (2021). *The sustainability debate: Policies, gender and the media Critical studies on corporate responsibility, governance and sustainability*, Volume *14*. Emerald Publishing Limited.
Toth, E. L. (1992). The case for pluralistic studies of public relations: Rhetorical, critical and excellence perspectives. In R. L. Heath & E. L. Toth (Eds.), *Rhetorical and Critical Approaches to Public Relations* (pp. 3–16). Routledge.

UN Department of Economic and Social Affairs. (2015). Transforming our world: The 2030 Agenda for sustainable development. https://sdgs.un.org/2030agenda
Witt, M. A., Lewin, A. Y., Li, P. P., & Gaur, A. (2023). Decoupling in international business: Evidence, drivers, impact, and implications for IB research. *Journal of World Business*, *58*(1). https://doi.org/10.1016/j.jwb.2022.101399
Zmigrod, L. (2025). *The Ideological Brain: A Radical Science of Susceptible Minds.* Viking.

INDEX

Pages in *italics* refer to figures and pages in **bold** refer to tables.

For Product Safety Concerns and Information please contact our EU
representative GPSR@taylorandfrancis.com
Taylor & Francis Verlag GmbH, Kaufingerstraße 24, 80331 München, Germany

www.ingramcontent.com/pod-product-compliance
Ingram Content Group UK Ltd.
Pitfield, Milton Keynes, MK11 3LW, UK
UKHW020003200926
475702UK00015B/2455
* 9 7 8 1 0 4 1 0 0 5 4 6 9 *